John D. Lee

Aggatha Ann Woolsey

George Prince

Sarah Bowman

James Havens Imlay

Ann Eliza Coward

John Hardison Redd

Elizabeth Hancock

Hosea Stout

Louisa Taylor

Allen Taylor

Sarah Lovisa Allred

William M. Allred

Reddick Allred

William Taylor

Elizabeth Patrick

Isaac Allred

Mary Calvert

Gathering in Harmony

GATHERING IN HARMONY

A Saga of Southern Utah Families,
Their Roots and Pioneering Heritage, and
the Tale of Antone Prince,
Sheriff of Washington County

by
Stephen L. Prince

THE ARTHUR H. CLARK COMPANY
Spokane, Washington
2004

copyright © 2004 Stephen L. Prince
ISBN 0-87062-327-3

Library of Congress Cataloging-in-Publication Data

Prince, Stephen L.
  Gathering in harmony : a saga of Southern Utah families, their roots
and pioneering heritage, and the tale of Antone Prince, sheriff of
Washington County / by Stephen L. Prince.
        p. cm.
Includes bibliographical references and index.
  ISBN 0-87062-327-3 (alk. paper)
  1. Prince family. 2. Prince, Antone, 1896-1977. 3. Mormons—United
States—Biography. 4. Church of Jesus Christ of Latter-day
Saints—History. I. Title.
BX8693.P75 2004
289.3'092'2792—dc22

                        2003024446

TABLE OF CONTENTS

ILLUSTRATIONS

For my family

PREFACE

SOUTHERN UTAH IS HEARTLAND for our family, and the larger-than-life hero who bestrode its red rock horizon was Antone Prince, my grandfather, for nearly nineteen years the sheriff of Washington County, Utah. From childhood, I was fascinated by accounts of his exploits as sheriff. One thing led to another and I found myself exploring in the generations beyond Antone, first genealogically and then in a serious effort to understand the lived experience of these ancestors, the shape of their world, the patterns of their memories, the values they honored. What I found was a family saga—a century of vivid intersections between an ordinary family and the extraordinary events that make up Mormon history and the settlement of the West.

This book originated in a challenge from my brother Greg almost a decade ago to write a biography of Antone Prince. I immediately brushed it off, but then later reconsidered it. Antone was one element in a family pattern that created the identity Greg and I inherited. How much of who we were had come from who our family was and where they had been? I did not write this family history as an egotistic exercise of reading myself back into the past. I wrote it as the soul-enlarging exercise of understanding a world shatteringly different from mine.

Gathering in Harmony begins with George and Sarah Prince, Antone's great-grandparents, in England. They followed the hope of wealth as sheep-raisers to South Africa, which was periodically racked by conflict with the native tribes. When they reached

Utah, they settled in the south, where their many children married with other Mormon settlers, producing dozens of Prince descendants, among them, three generations later, Antone.

Another branch of the family came into view in northeastern Missouri. Isaac Allred, William Taylor, and their families were settled on the Salt River when the missionaries found them in the early 1830s. They provided hospitality, shelter, and food for Zion's Camp, became willing congregations for formal and informal sermons, and dug graves for its cholera victims. Hosea Stout's diary provided an important window on the family, having married one of the Taylor daughters. New Jersey provided another branch, and so did Tennessee. John D. Lee writes appreciatively of John H. Redd as one of the most memorable of his many missionary converts. The Redd family were counted among Lee's few supporters after the 1857 tragedy at Mountain Meadows and appeared often in his diaries.

This network of kith and kin consisted of plain folks, the ordinary people who followed the more glamorous Mormon leaders. Collectively, their lives represent a cross-section of early Mormon history: emigrants, founding families, hunters, farmers, fighters when they had to be. I have written the book as a series of individual narratives illustrating a Mormon chronology from the earliest days of Mormonism in Missouri, Illinois, and Iowa to the trek across the plains and the settlement in Utah. I have tried to understand and recreate the forces that influenced these people in their journey and the way they themselves helped to shape events. The narrative recounts how New Harmony in Washington County became home, and concludes with the exploits of Antone B. Prince.

Although it is the story of a family, it is shaped as an account of Mormon and western American history as experienced by an extended family. My search for understanding led me into fascinating places. In addition to reading widely in published sources about a century of world and American history, I spent many rewarding hours in archives with primary sources. Among the most valuable were the following libraries: the Library and Archives of the Family and Church History Department, Church of Jesus Christ of Latter-day Saints, Salt Lake City; the Utah State Historical Society, also in Salt Lake City; the Harold B. Lee Library at Brigham Young University, Provo, Utah; the Dixie College Archives, St. George, Utah; the California State University library at Northridge; the UCLA Research Library; the Library of Congress; and the Huntington Library, San Marino, California, where I discovered "A Trip Across the Plains in the Year 1849," attributed to Martha Morgan, previously unknown to LDS literature. It was written by a non-Mormon member of the 1849 Allen Taylor Company and is now the only known daily journal of the company.

Earlier versions of some chapters appeared in *Mormon Historical Studies*, *Utah Historical Quarterly*, and the *Journal of Mormon History*. I appreciate their editors' encouragement and efforts to make the articles accessible for a broader audience.

I express appreciation first and foremost to my family: to my brother, Gregory A. Prince, for his constant prodding, suggestions, and help in the early editing of each chapter; to my wife, Meredith, for her patience and understanding; to my cousin, Robert Prince; to my parents, Clayton and Joy Prince, who spent many hours gathering information and who gave unwavering support; and to my brother John Prince. Lavina Fielding Anderson, William G. Hartley, and Douglas D. Alder gave critical reviews and encouragement. My research was made both more productive and more pleasant by the willing assistance of Ronald O. Barney and Steve Sorensen of LDS Church Archives; Gloria Werner and Claire Bellanti of the UCLA Library; and the staff of Huntington Library in San Marino, California. Drawing from *The Chicago Manual of Style* (14th edition), [*sic*] is used following a word misspelled or wrongly used in the original. I tried not to overuse the device. For errors of omission and commission, however, I alone remain responsible.

GEORGE AND SARAH BOWMAN PRINCE
They dreamed of Australia, but with their son Francis and
George's brother John went to South Africa in 1841.

Chapter I

INTO AFRICA

THERE ARE FEW EVENTS in one's life that are so indelibly etched in the memory that they can be recalled in detail many years later. When George Prince wrote his short autobiography in 1875, he had no trouble remembering the day—26 June 1841—that he and his family departed England for their long voyage to South Africa.[1]

Australia, not South Africa, was supposed to be their destination after they decided to leave England. Thousands of emigrants were granted free passage to Australia and New Zealand, financed by the sale of enormous quantities of almost uninhabited lands that were available for settlement: In 1841, nearly fifteen thousand English men and women emigrated to Australia and New Zealand (in addition to thirty thousand to America and twenty-four thousand to Canada).[2] In sharp contrast, only fifty-five individuals, including the Prince family, went to Port Elizabeth, South Africa.

The attractions of Australia were several. To begin with, the climate was almost the opposite of the cool, dreary weather of England, with most areas experiencing substantially more sunshine and warmer weather than could be found anywhere in the British Isles. And Australia was, after all, an entire continent, with plentiful land for the new settlers and therefore greater opportunities than could be had in England. Though the British

[1]George Prince, "Autobiography, 28 August 1875." George's autobiography consists of three handwritten pages that serve as a preface to "Life History."
[2]Sir George E. Cory, *The Rise of South Africa*, 4:391.

government stopped giving land to new settlers in 1831, land was cheap and did not exceed one pound an acre until after 1842. These factors alone were enough to persuade large numbers of English emigrants to leave their native land in favor of a new life down under. George Prince had originally been drawn to Australia, but he was a shepherd, and the burgeoning sheep industry in South Africa tugged harder.

A precious cargo had arrived in the Eastern Cape of South Africa in 1789, consisting of six sheep that had been bred in Holland from sheep presented to the ruling House of Orange by Spain. Sheep had long been in the Eastern Cape, but these sheep were different. Their coats were thicker and curlier, and the wool was especially fine. These were Spanish merinos, the best-known wool-bearing sheep in Europe.[3] The woolen mills of the Industrial Revolution, in full spate in England by the 1840s, created an important market, especially as the English belatedly realized that South Africa, only half as far as Australia, was a more practical source of wool. Thus, on that fair June day in 1841, twenty-five-year-old George, his twenty-two-year-old wife, Sarah Bowman Prince, their eleven-month-old son Francis, and George's eighteen-year-old brother John set off together on what they thought would be the greatest adventure of their lives—but which, as it turned out, was the prelude to one still greater.

The South African coastline is notable for its scarcity of good natural harbors, and Port Elizabeth, on the western edge of Algoa Bay, was the only port in the Eastern Cape. Given such a natural monopoly, shipping commerce was the town's lifeblood. But for the hopeful immigrant, fresh from England, the town was a huge disappointment. One immigrant who had landed at Port Elizabeth just a few months earlier wrote: "As we approached land, and saw the little town of Port Elizabeth before us, I certainly thought I had never beheld so miserable looking a place. . . . The first glance—nay the second and the third—by no means improved my previous impressions of the place."[4] Several years of growth

[3] *Illustrated History of South Africa: The Real Story*, 130.
[4] Alfred Cole, *The Cape and the Kafirs*, 60.

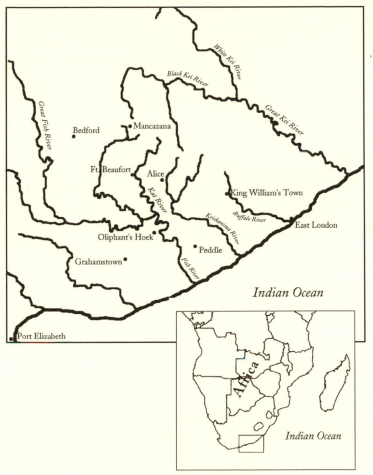

South Africa's Eastern Cape

apparently did not bring any improvement for other first impressions, as the Archdeacon Nathaniel James Merriman, arriving with his wife, Julia, eight years later in 1849, confided candidly in his diary: "A more dreary looking place than Port Elizabeth I hardly ever saw."[5]

[5]Nathaniel James Merriman, *The Cape Journals of Archdeacon N. J. Merriman*, 1848–1855, 18.

Fortunately, the Prince family did not linger in Port Elizabeth but set off by wagon for Grahamstown, about eighty miles to the east. The countryside improved rapidly after leaving the barren, treeless environs of Port Elizabeth. The trip to Grahamstown was long and probably quite hot, but the Merrimans, passing over the same countryside, responded appreciatively to the "charm of jolting along through woods filled with flowering mimosa and cactus and aloes of various kinds, and many other strange and beautiful shrubs."[6]

Grahamstown, founded as a garrison village in 1809, had scarcely a dozen houses in 1820, when the first British settlers received their land grants. However, by 1841 it had grown into a thriving town and was, by all descriptions, immensely more attractive than Port Elizabeth. It was the center of all activity in the region, and it was there that nearly all of the new immigrants first traveled before either settling down or moving on. The new settlers had been so carefully matched with the work that awaited them that there was no call upon them to act as pioneers or be pressed by adversity to cut out a new career for themselves.

Apparently the Princes stayed for three or four years in Grahamstown, where their first daughter, Mary Ann, was born in June 1843. By the time their next child, Richard, was born in May 1846, they had moved to Oliphant's Hoek, an area about forty miles northeast of Grahamstown on the Kat River which would become their home for several years to come.[7] As the name

---

[6]Ibid., 19.

[7]Mary Ann Prince was born in Grahamstown on 3 June 1843, while six more children were born at Oliphant's Hoek, an Afrikaans term that means "Elephant's Bend" or "Corner", referring to the landform shaped by the Fish River. The family thus consisted of Francis (born 31 July 1840 at Sterford, Cambridge, England; he was named for the couple's first son, born in 1838, who died at eleven months), Mary Ann, Richard (born 26 May 1846), William (born 23 October 1848), and Sophia (born 15 November 1850). They were followed by George (born 26 January 1854, exact location unknown, South Africa); Susanna (born 14 November 1855 at Mancazana, South Africa); Sarah Ann (born 16 May 1858, exact place not known, South Africa); and Lucy Naomi (born 29 December 1861 at Kaysville, Utah). There also was a *District of Oliphant's Hoek* southwest of Grahamstown on Algoa Bay; the name of the main settlement of the district was changed in 1856 in honor of the first baptismal name of Queen Victoria and thus appears on subsequent maps as *Alexandria*. William Prince said he was born on the Kat River, which is part of the northeastern Oliphant's Hoek. Cecil Prince Reid, "Biography of William Prince," typescript, n.d., Library, Daughters of Utah Pioneers Museum, Salt Lake City, Utah.

would imply, Oliphant's Hoek was once filled with great herds of elephants. However, many years before the Prince family settled there, ivory had "tempted many an adventurous spirit to enter upon the perilous but exciting life of a hunter. Thousands of these animals were slain."[8] Though a few elephants and lions reportedly still inhabited the deepest recesses of the area, these magnificent animals were rarely seen. Springbok, a species of African antelope, was also once plentiful but had since virtually disappeared from the area, much to the delight of farmers in the area. The largest mammal to be seen regularly was the baboon that, despite its often savage and ugly disposition, posed no great danger to the settlers.

Here the Prince family settled down to raise children and sheep. It is possible that they moved onto land that already had been cultivated and which included a home and outbuildings. Beginning in 1836, the Dutch settlers in the area, resistant to British rule, launched their Great Trek northward into the interior of the Eastern Cape and Orange Free State, vacating land and property in the process.[9]

The subtropical climate was considered very healthful, with hot summers and mild, dry winters. With no heavy industry in the entire country, the skies were much brighter and more beautiful than those in England. Nighttime could also be spectacular, leading Alfred Cole, an Englishman who had immigrated to the Eastern Cape a few months before the Prince family, to rhapsodize:

> And now for a glorious night in the magnificent climate of South Africa! Can anything be more beautiful, more enchanting? The sky is of that deep, dark blue, which we never see in northern climates: the moon is shining as she can only shine in such a sky; the stars . . . beautifully bright and distinct; perfect stillness rests on everything around.[10]

---

[8]Thomas Baines, *Journal of Residence in Africa, 1842–1849*, II:32.

[9]The Cape Colony is the area originally settled by the Dutch and enlarged through the successive Frontier Wars. By 1798, the conquered territory had reached the Fish River as its far eastern boundary and, by 1850, the Great Kei River. The Eastern Cape was bordered by the Indian Ocean.

[10]Alfred Cole, *The Cape and the Kafir*, 136–137.

The Merrimans found this region delightful in their 1849 travels:

> After our return from Mancazana, we took a journey to Bathurst together and subsequently to Oliphant's Hoek. This latter ride afforded us great pleasure. The novel sight to us in this land of large forest trees, the novel smell of a moist atmosphere with a most luxurious vegetation of ferns and other plants under the boughs of the huge forests and the constant charm of birds around us singing their evening song, though not in the most musical notes, seemed to transport us back to England in a way that I have not before experienced in the Colony.[11]

Ironically, this English-seeming landscape of the Eastern Cape was overwhelmingly populated by the Dutch, whose Dutch East India Company had established a colony at Table Bay, site of the future Cape Town, in 1652; their trekboers (pioneers) had moved into this area in the 1750s and 1760s. For the next twenty years, they dispossessed and pressed into servitude the Khoikhoi (known to the Europeans as Hottentots), but treated the Xhosa (whom they called Kaffirs) with healthy respect, mainly due to the fact that they were greatly outnumbered. In 1781, they ordered the Xhosa to move east of the Fish River, to leave them in undisturbed possession of the territory, and then assassinated the resistant Xhosa leaders during a parley. This was the first of nine Frontier Wars (1780–1878), each one of which ended with the Xhosa being driven further east.

The British had acquired Cape Town and the rest of South Africa in 1796; they restored it briefly to Holland in 1801, but took it back the next year.[12] It had been part of the British Empire ever since. An annual reminder was the celebration of Queen Victoria's birthday on 24 May, but as Merriman noted critically, the conquered Boers were not necessarily enthusiastic. "There was not much spare loyalty in this part of the Colony," he observed. "The military demonstration of Parade, Band and feu-de-joie [fireworks] seemed to excite no great attention from the civilians."[13]

---

[11]Merriman, op.cit., 60.
[12]Leonard Thompson, *A History of South Africa*, 32–83, passim.
[13]Ibid., 50.

In 1846, approximately the time the Prince family moved to Oliphant's Hoek, a sudden conflict blew up after a decade of peace. The War of the Axe, as it was known, began when a young Xhosa helped himself to an axe in a store near Fort Beaufort, apparently without any intention of paying for it. He was apprehended and transported with three other prisoners under the guard of four armed Khoikhoi policemen to Grahamstown to stand trial. Along the way, forty Xhosa warriors attacked the party. The Khoikhoi to whom the accused Xhosa was handcuffed was stabbed to death. One of the rescue party then hacked off the manacled hand of the dead Khoikhoi, and the young Xhosa made his escape, apparently still wearing the handcuff. The British demanded the return of the escapee, but the Xhosa chief steadfastly refused and attacked the British column sent to compel his obedience. Thousands of warriors crossed the Fish River to attack the European settlements in the Eastern Cape.

In their own conflicts, the Xhosa did not kill women and children; however, in the War of the Axe, they also targeted British boys, who might grow up to become soldiers. According to a fragment of family history, Sarah Prince hid five-year-old Francis under a pile of dirty laundry, although it is not clear when or for how long she employed this ruse.

Under ordinary circumstances, Thomas Baines reported in his journal in 1848, the Xhosa were not a blood-thirsty people but possessed many traits of "honor and good faith." However, in war they utilized practices that were meant to terrorize the enemy, such as one described by Alfred Cole:

> The culprit is rubbed all over with grease, he is then taken to an anthill, against which he is placed and secured to the ground; the anthill is then broken, and the ants left to crawl over him and eat his flesh from his bones, which they do in time most effectually. I doubt whether the Inquisition ever invented a torture so horrible and lingering as this must be.[14]

As had been the case in previous frontier wars, the British troops concentrated on destroying the dwelling, cattle, crops, and

---

[14]Cole, op.cit., 191–192.

grain reserves of the Xhosa who, facing mass starvation, sued for peace after one year of fighting. After the war was over, wheat was cultivated in the fertile land of Oliphant's Hoek on an even larger scale than before. It was once thought to be the finest wheat in the world; but for nearly thirty years, farmers had to contend with "rust," a fungus that would usually attack sporadically, but this time seemed to ravage the entire crop. The English settlers, generally unwilling to learn from the Dutch who had been at the Cape for generations longer than had they, were unprepared to grow anything other than wheat and other grains which were also attacked by rust. Thomas Baines noted ruefully: "It became a proverb that an Englishman could not succeed till he had thrice ruined himself."[15] Merriman, who observed the devastation wreaked by this widespread fungus agreed: "Had they commenced sowing pumpkins and indian corn instead of wheat much misery would have been saved, but it takes an Englishman a long time to learn anything that is un-English."[16]

The next crisis was, again, a military one. In December 1850 the British Governor, Sir Harry Smith, who had distinguished himself in India (1845–46) during the war with the Sikhs, sent troops to evict the Xhosa from Kat River, deeming the land was too good for non-whites.[17] Highhandedly the British troops deposed and humiliated a senior Xhosa chief, igniting the Eighth Frontier War, which lasted for three years and claimed far more lives on all sides—British, Xhosa and Khoi—than any previous conflict.

This time, some of the Dutch and the Khoikhoi took the field with the Xhosa against the British. At the outset, the Xhosa took the offensive, forcing many colonists to abandon their farms. Although there is no published record of the exact location of the attacks, it is reasonable to assume that Oliphant's Hoek suffered several attacks, since it was located on the boundary of the colony.[18] Richard Prince, five years old at the time of the 1851 war, later told his family tales of this experience:

---

[15]Baines, op.cit., 33.
[16]Merriman, op.cit., 82.
[17]*Illustrated History of South Africa*, 134.

[Richard] was stationed on a hill overlooking the valley. It was his duty to watch for the Negroes. When he saw them approaching, he notified the people. They gathered in a block house for safety, which had port holes in [it]. The men shot through these portholes [*sic*] at the Negroes. When the battle was over, hundreds of Negroes were laying around dead. They buried them in trenches. John [Prince], a brother of George, was killed in the last battle.[19]

Ultimately the British went back to their tried and true strategy of systematically destroying Xhosa food supplies and soon, faced again with possible starvation, the native people were forced to surrender. Life slowly returned to normal following the cessation of hostilities. By 1853 there were five children in the Prince family and Sarah was expecting a sixth child the following January.

One evening George had a dream (he would later call it a manifestation) that was so real that he felt compelled to share it with Sarah. Two men appeared dressed in black broadcloth suits and high hats, and George had the impression that what they told him was true.[20] He knew neither who these men were nor what message they were carrying. Neither did he know that their message was a result of an event which took place in a far distant land more than two decades earlier, nor that the men in the dream weren't yet in South Africa.

---

[18]These events further confirm that the Prince family lived at Oliphant's Hoek at the Kat and Fish rivers, not in the district of Oliphant's Hoek further south. The Eighth Frontier War started at the eastern boundary of the Cape Colony, which at that time was the Kat River, while there is no evidence that the conflict extended southward as far as Oliphant's Hoek District.

[19]"Biography of Richard Prince, Pioneer;" Juanita Williams Davis Kossen, "Life of George Prince."

[20]Kate B. Carter, comp., *Treasures of Pioneer History*, 6:270. The story seemed to grow with time, and his daughter Sophie Schurtz wrote a narrative for the Daughters of the Utah Pioneers which said: "One evening at the end of a hard day's travel as he was making his rounds to see that everything was all right for the night, someone called him by the name of 'George.' He turned and beheld a personage clothed in a long white robe, who told him that the Gospel had been restored and would be brought to him by two men, warning him to heed their teachings and accept them. He was told that he would know the men immediately upon seeing them. The gathering of Israel was also explained to him and urging that it should be done speedily lest part of his family be left behind. When he returned home he related the incident to his wife." However, the story he always related to his grandchildren was the far less glamorous one of a dream in which he merely saw two men; this seems more likely to be what actually happened.

It would take more than two years for the dream to be fulfilled, and what he would experience in future years as a result of it would make the dream perhaps the most important event of his life. Yet had he been told at the time how much it would change the direction of his life, he probably wouldn't have believed it.

Chapter II

Salt River Saints

TO THE FAMILIES that began arriving in 1819, the Salt River Valley of northeast Missouri must have appeared similar to the Bluegrass region of Kentucky that they had recently left. The uplands were a mixture of large expanses of prairie grass and islands of hardwood forests, while nearer to the river and its tributaries the prairie gave way to dense stands of timber. Game was bountiful, and the timber provided ample building material. Land was plentiful and inexpensive compared to the rising prices back in Kentucky.[1] And to sweeten the deal, Missouri was about to become the twenty-fourth state of the young nation.

Missouri was originally a part of a vast area of land known as Louisiana that was added to the United States in the Louisiana Purchase of 1803. Between 1804 and 1820 the region, much larger than the future state of Missouri, was governed as a territory. Missouri requested statehood in 1818, but a provision in the U.S. House of Representatives to exclude slavery in the new state postponed statehood and precipitated a serious crisis between the North and the South, as southerners fought to extend the domain of slavery.

People were awakened to the gravity of the issue, in the words of the now elder statesman Thomas Jefferson, "as though a fire bell had rung in the night."[2] At issue was the fact that at the time there were equal numbers of slave and free states, and northerners, in particular, were not anxious to upset the balance, for they

---

[1]Michael J. O'Brien, *Grassland, Forest, and Historical Settlement*, xvii.
[2]John A. Garraty, *The American Nation to 1877*, 253.

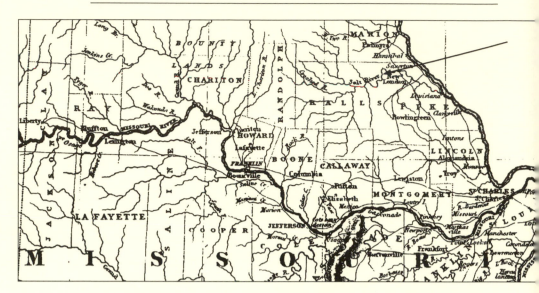

From *Map of the State of Missouri*, published by Hinton & Simkin & Marshall, London, 1 September 1831, showing the location of the Salt River.

feared that a southern majority in Congress would attempt to force slavery on the entire country. In compromise it was decided that all future states north of 36°30', which coincided with the southern borders of Kentucky and Virginia, would be free, while those south of the line would be slave states, with the notable exception of Missouri, which was north of the line but would still be a slave state. To balance the numbers, the free state of Maine was created at about the same time. The decision to make Missouri a slave state was critical not only for future immigration patterns but also for the welfare of a certain group of people which later tried to make Missouri its home.

Designated as a slave state, Missouri was automatically an extension of the South, and the vast majority of the new settlers came from the adjacent southern states of Kentucky and Tennessee. Due to a prior influx of settlers in these states, land had become relatively scarce. In Kentucky, for example, the population in 1775 was approximately 150; by 1820 the combined population of Tennessee and Kentucky was nearly a million.[3] In addition, the soil was depleted from years of overproduction, driving many farmers to new, more fertile land. Prospects of abundant, fertile land, available at low cost, was the major attraction of the new state of Missouri.

When it was first offered for sale by the federal government in 1818, land in the Salt River valley sold for less than two dollars an acre; to put this in the context of the time, one acre cost the same as a pocket bible, and twenty-five acres of good land could be purchased for the price of one horse.[4] The availability of good land at such prices was enough to begin a migration from Tennessee and Kentucky to Missouri. The area was sparsely populated at the time, and the influx of new settlers seemed like a flood to one newspaper reporter:

> The motion of the Tennessee and Kentucky caravans of movers, flowing through our town [St. Charles] with their men servants and maid servants, their flocks and their herds, remind the citizens of the patriarchal ages. As in the days of our father Abraham, some turn to the Boons [Boone's] Lick, some to the Salt River—lands of promise.[5]

Contrary to such descriptions, however, initial movement into the Salt River Valley was very slow. In the first twelve years that it was offered to the public, for example, only about 11 percent of the available land had been sold.[6] One of those who did purchase land during this period, in 1829, was a gentleman from Bedford County, Tennessee, named James Allred. He was joined by his brother-in-law John Anderson Ivie, by his brothers Isaac and John in about 1830, and still later by his brother William. In November 1831, William Taylor, of Bowling Green, Kentucky, followed two brothers-in-law, Ludson Green Patrick and Levi Turner, to Missouri and bought eighty acres of prime land in the

---

[3]O'Brien, op. cit., 72.   [4]Ibid., 73.
[5]*Missouri Gazette and Public Advertiser*, 9 June, 1819.
[6]O'Brien, op. cit., 157.

Salt River Valley near the Allred settlement.[7] The Taylor and Allred families, though brought together by fate, would become bound by faith and intermarriage.

The area was still very much the frontier, and living conditions were substandard compared to more "civilized" areas to the east. Parley P. Pratt, who traveled through the region in the early 1830s, wrote:

> We passed down the south side of the Missouri river, among a thin settlement of people—mostly ignorant but extremely hospitable. Some families were entirely dressed in skins, without any other clothing; including ladies young and old. Buildings were generally without glass windows, and the door open in winter for a light.[8]

Such living conditions would be trying under normal conditions, but the first winter was particularly difficult for the family of Isaac Allred:

> The snow fell in November about two feet deep and stayed on the ground all winter, and towards spring there came a thaw and then a freeze, [making] a crust on the snow that we could walk on. . . . I frosted my feet so that I could not be out much for a long while, and my two younger brothers, Reddick and Reddin, twins, had no shoes. . . .[9]

Traffic to and through the Salt River Valley steadily increased. In the first four years of the new decade, nearly three times as many parcels of land were sold as in the preceding twelve years. In addition, the state road, a "great highway from east to west"[10] which traversed Missouri from the Mississippi River in the east to Independence on the western edge of the state, was situated adjacent to the properties of the Allred, Ivie, and Taylor families.

In the summer of 1831, two gentlemen from Ohio entered the valley on their way to join about two-dozen of their compatriots in a religious conference in western Missouri. Arriving at Salt

---

[7] Pleasant Green Taylor, "Record of Pleasant Green Taylor; Reddick N. Allred, "The Diary of Reddick N. Allred;" Wayne J. Lewis, "Mormon Land Ownership as a Factor in Evaluating the Extent of Mormon Settlements and Influence in Missouri 1831–1841," 46.

[8] Parley P. Pratt, *The Autobiography of Parley P. Pratt*, 58.

[9] William Moore Allred, "Autobiography."

[10] Allred, op cit.

River on 4 August, one of the men, John Murdock, became ill and was forced to spend the next week in bed at the home of William Ivie, the son of John Anderson Ivie and nephew of Isaac Allred. Remaining with his ailing companion at the Ivie home was Hyrum Smith, the older brother of Joseph Smith, the founder of a new faith whose members were called "Mormonites" because of a book, published the previous year, called the *Book of Mormon*.

Subsequent to the book's publication, Joseph and Hyrum Smith, along with four other men, met in Fayette, New York, on 6 April 1830, to organize formally the new religion, which was named *The Church of Christ*.[11] The organization was the culmination of visions and visitations experienced by Joseph Smith over a period of about ten years that called him to restore the true Christian religion. For future members of the church, the most important event of this period was the visit of a heavenly messenger named Moroni to Joseph Smith during the night of 21 September 1823. A statue of the Angel Moroni, which would later crown numerous temples of the church, holds in one hand clasped plates symbolic of the *Book of Mormon*, the ancient religious record received by Smith that night. In his diary in 1832 Smith wrote of the angel:

> He revealed unto me that in the Town of Manchester, Ontario County, N[ew] Y[ork] there was plates of gold upon which there was engravings which was engraven by Maroni [Moroni] and his fathers, the servants of the living God in ancient days, deposited by the commandments of God and kept by the power thereof and that I should go and get them.[12]

Joseph Smith received possession of the plates in 1827 and "by the gift and power God" began to translate them. He made little progress, however, until Oliver Cowdery, an itinerant schoolteacher, arrived in Harmony, Pennsylvania, where Joseph was residing. Cowdery immediately began acting as scribe, recording

---

[11]To avoid confusion with several other congregations similarly named, the official name was changed in 1838 to *The Church of Jesus Christ of Latter-day Saints*, and its members have since frequently been referred to simply as "the Saints."

[12]*The Essential Joseph Smith*, 28.

the torrents of dictation that spilled forth from Joseph. The book that came from the plates is a chronicle of several peoples who lived in the Americas long before the arrival of Columbus. Far more than a mere narrative history, the book is replete with religious teachings that complement the Bible.

First published in early 1830, the *Book of Mormon* was central to the new religion, immediately setting the movement apart from other restorationist attempts. It provided a sweeping historical context for the New World, at once explaining the origin of the American Indians and relating the New World to a divine plan for humankind.

The new book taught that the American Indian was a remnant of the house of Israel, to whom great promises had been extended. Referring to these people as "Lamanites," a *Book of Mormon* prophet declared: "At some period of time they will be brought to believe in his [God's] word, and to know of the incorrectness of the traditions of their fathers; and many of them will be saved."[13] The first members of the church fully believed these promises and were moved to bring about their fulfillment. Thus, when Joseph Smith pronounced a revelation that they should "go unto the Lamanites and preach my gospel unto them,"[14] they were willing and ready to go, though they were not exactly sure where they were going: The destination was stated to be "the borders by the Lamanites,"[15] but at that time this could have meant virtually anywhere along the western frontier of the United States—a massive area, to be sure.

Nevertheless, within just a few weeks, the four missionaries who had been called to preach to the Indians set out on foot for the uncertain journey, only with necessary provisions and some copies of the *Book of Mormon*. Traveling through western New York into Ohio, they entered an area popularly known as the Western Reserve because in colonial times it was allotted to Connecticut as a "western reserve." One of the missionaries, Parley P. Pratt, was familiar with the area, having lived there previously,

---

[13] *Book of Mormon*, Alma 9:17.
[14] *Doctrine and Covenants*, 28:8. Hereafter known as *D&C*.   [15] *D&C*, 28:9.

and they ended up visiting a prominent preacher in Kirtland named Sidney Rigdon, under whom Pratt had studied. Rigdon read the *Book of Mormon* and shared the message with his congregation, and within three weeks of the missionaries' arrival, 127 persons were baptized.

It was in Ohio that the missionaries must have decided upon their destination. The Delaware Indians once inhabited the section of the Atlantic coast where the state of Delaware was formed. However, most of the Indians had left Delaware before the Revolution and subsequently inhabited a region along the Ohio River and north to Lake Erie. Indeed, the city of Kirtland was built upon land that once belonged to the Delawares. By the 1820s the Indians in the east found themselves under increasing pressure to surrender their lands and move westward beyond the Mississippi, and the Delawares, anticipating that they would be forced to move at some point, began relocating as early as 1828 to an area near the Kansas River just west of the Missouri border. The people of Kirtland undoubtedly knew of the Indian migration, and it was the new land of the Delawares, just beyond the fledgling town of Independence, Missouri, that became the destination of the missionaries.

Unfortunately, they arrived in mid-winter, and though William Anderson, the aged chief of the Delawares and son of a Scandinavian father and an Indian mother, listened patiently and sympathetically to their message, he informed the missionaries that it wasn't a good time to talk:

> We feel truly thankful to our white friends who have come so far, and been at such pains to tell us good news, and especially this new news concerning the Book of our forefathers; it makes us glad in here—[placing his hand on his heart].
>
> It is now winter, we are new settlers in this place; the snow is deep, our cattle and horses are dying, our wigwams are poor; we have much to do in the spring—to build houses, and fence and make farms; but we will build a council house, and meet together, and you shall read to us and teach us more concerning the Book of our fathers and the will of the Great Spirit.[16]

---

[16]Pratt, op. cit., 44.

But the missionaries could not wait until spring, for government Indian agents were in control of the area and the missionaries had not obtained the required permit to enter Indian lands and teach the gospel. The local Indian agent immediately informed them that they were in violation of the law and ordered them to desist until they secured permission from the Superintendent of Indian Affairs in St. Louis, General William Clark, of Lewis and Clark fame. A written request was made, but a favorable response was not received (it is unsure whether any response at all was ever sent) and so the missionaries settled for a time in Independence before beginning the return trek.

Although the "Lamanite mission" was unsuccessful in converting the Lamanites, it shaped the future of the church by "planting seeds" in two areas—Kirtland and Independence—which would become gathering sites for the church. While the missionaries were still in Independence, Joseph Smith announced at a conference in Fayette, New York, that members of the church were to move to Ohio;[17] in the middle of winter they began their relocation to Kirtland.

But Kirtland was not destined to be their land of promise. A gathering to a place of refuge called "Zion" was a dominant concept of the early church, and at a conference in Kirtland in June 1831—just four months after the move to Kirtland had commenced—Joseph Smith announced a revelation which directed him and other church leaders to go to Missouri, where the land of their inheritance would be revealed. In addition, twenty-six missionaries were called to travel in pairs to Missouri, preaching along the way.[18] The missionaries who had gone a few months earlier to teach the Lamanites were familiar with Independence, and it was probably no coincidence that a site near Independence was chosen as a meeting place.

Among those called to go to Missouri were John Murdock and Hyrum Smith, who were to make their journey by way of Detroit. This was by no means the most direct route that could

---

[17]*D&C*, 38:32.   [18]*D&C*, 52:3–8, 22–33; 56:5–7.

be taken to Missouri, but one could cross Lake Erie by steamboat rather quickly and without effort, and thus the entire journey of the missionaries, from Kirtland to Fairport and then to Detroit aboard the steamer *William Penn*, took but a single day. After arriving in Detroit on 15 June, they gradually made their way south, preaching all the way but evidently with no success. Murdock recorded in his journal:

> August 1st travelled 28 miles and crossed the Illinois River. 2nd, 30 miles to Mississippi River Louise-Ana [Louisiana] Ferry and got my feet wet by which I took a violent cold by which I suffered near unto death. 3rd, crossed the river into Missouri. Travelled 25 miles to New London, found it a very wicked place.... Thursday 4th, arrived at Salt River where we preached next day, but I was sick and I went to bed, and we continued there near one week and then I gave my watch in pay to Wm. Ivy [William Ivie] to carry me in a wagon to Charidon 70 miles.[19]

These early missionaries were preaching, with great zeal and enthusiasm, about the prophet of their new church and, perhaps more importantly at the time, about the *Book of Mormon*. It is easy to imagine how much of their conversation during their one-week stay at the home of William Ivie was directed toward the new book. But the Salt River residents were skeptical, as witnessed by Isaac Allred's son, Reddick:

> My parents were members of a school of Presbiterians [*sic*] and brought up their children to reverence a God and were very exemplary in their lives, so that when a new religion was introduced they naturally looked at it with suspicion, having been taught that Prophets and Apostles were no longer needed, so some cried false Prophet.[20]

In addition to the skepticism which Murdock and Smith encountered, there was another problem: Though they spent an entire week with the Ivie family, undoubtedly having many conversations regarding the new religion, the missionaries did not have a copy of the *Book of Mormon* with them! By coincidence, William McLellin, who lived a few miles upriver in the small

---

[19]John Murdock, "Journal." [20]Allred, op. cit., 5:298.

town of Paris, had met just a few days earlier with David Whitmer and Harvey Whitlock, two of the other missionaries who were on their way to Independence, and had purchased a copy of the book from them. Just three days after the departure of Murdock and Smith from the Ivie household, McLellin was traveling through the area and arrived at the Salt River settlement where he stopped for breakfast at the Ivie home, carrying with him a copy of the *Book of Mormon*:

> Augst 14 I rose early paid 50 cts and rode on 3 ms to a Mr Ivey's and fed my horse and took breakfast. Here two Elders had staid about a week (viz) Hiram Smith and John Moredock though they were gone. They had no book with them and when Mrs Ivy found that I had a book she said she must see it and when she saw it she said I must sell it to her which I did. . . .[21]

The *Book of Mormon*, as well as the new religious message, made an immediate and favorable impression on the Allred and Ivie families, but by now the missionaries were all on their way to the western boundary of the state and thus the full measure of the impact which they had on the Salt River families remained for the moment unrealized. In the meantime, Joseph Smith and the group traveling with him arrived in Independence well before any of the missionaries, each of whom had stopped along the way to preach the gospel. Joseph had no way of knowing exactly when the others would arrive and decided to hold the conference, the major objective of the trip, on August 4, though the majority of the missionaries were still in transit.

The return trip to Kirtland from Independence began on August 9—two days before John Murdock and Hyrum Smith were able to resume their trip *westward* from the Salt River. By chance, on 13 August Joseph Smith and his group encountered a few of the missionaries who were still on their journey, and he informed them that he had received a revelation on 20 July that Zion, the promised land and gathering place for the Saints, was to be built in Independence, Jackson County, Missouri.[22] This

[21]William E. McLellin, *The Journals of William E. McLellin, 1831–1836*, 32.
[22]*D&C*, 57:1,3; 62.

turned out to be very important for the Salt River families, for the majority of the Saints at the time lived in Kirtland, Ohio, and the quickest, most direct route from Kirtland to Independence went right through the Salt River Valley.

The gathering to Zion began almost immediately, and during the spring and summer of 1832, three to four hundred Saints arrived in Missouri to settle in Jackson County. Some went by way of St. Louis and up the Missouri River, but others went by way of Salt River, as Reddick Allred recorded that "Elders were passing every few months from Kirtland to Jackson County— the gathering place for the Saints. . . ." Isaac Allred opened his house to the Mormon elders for their meetings, and one of those who stopped in late summer of 1832, George Hinkle, baptized Isaac and James Allred and John Ivie as well as various members of their families. They became the first converts to Mormonism in eastern Missouri[23] and through them the Salt River branch of the church, also known as the Allred settlement, was formed.

These Salt River settlers were now part of the exciting new religious movement. What great fortune, they must have thought, to be living in the same state where the gathering would take place. The distance from east to west was not great and could be traversed in but a few days, and at least several members of the settlement were soon anxious to become a part of the gathering. But never, not in their wildest dreams, could they have imagined just how far they would have to travel before they found their place of peace.

---

[23]William Taylor's son Pleasant Green claimed that his father was the *first* convert to be baptized in Missouri, but William McLellin followed Hyrum Smith and John Murdock to Independence and met Hyrum on 19 August 1831; he was baptized by Hyrum the next day, about a year before any baptisms took place at Salt River. Additionally, it has been variously reported that William Taylor was baptized in 1832 or 1834; according to family and LDS Temple Index Bureau records, the 1834 date seems more likely to be accurate.

Chapter III

REDEMPTION OF ZION

THOSE WHO ACCOMPANIED Joseph Smith on his journey to Missouri in the summer of 1831, as well as the missionaries who were to meet him there, knew that somewhere in the state was the "land of their inheritance," their Zion. Their high expectations, however, were at first unfulfilled as they reached Independence and found a crude frontier village with little more than about a dozen log houses, three stores, a schoolhouse and a brick courthouse. This was the very edge of civilization in the United States and hardly the paradise they had anticipated.

Upon their arrival, Sidney Rigdon, who was probably the second most important leader in the church at the time, was very unimpressed and urged an immediate return to Ohio. Even Joseph Smith experienced mixed feelings:

> The meeting of our brethren, who had long awaited our arrival, was a glorious one, and moistened with many tears. It seemed good and pleasant for brethren to meet together in unity. But our reflections were many, coming as we had from a highly cultivated state of society in the east, and standing now upon the confines or western limits of the United States, and looking into the vast wilderness of those that sat in darkness; how natural it was to observe the degradation, leanness of intellect, ferocity, and jealousy of a people that were nearly a century behind the times, and to feel for those who roamed about without the benefit of civilization, refinement, or religion.[1]

Joseph became more visionary, however, as he climbed a hill near Independence and was able to partake of the magnificent

---

[1] Joseph Smith Jr., *History of the Church of Jesus Christ of Latter-day Saints*, 189.

vista. From there he could see that the site of the town was advantageous, on the edge of a great territory that extended across the plains all the way to the Rocky Mountains. And almost immediately there was a noticeable shift in attitude towards this new, "promised" land:

> The country is unlike the timbered states of the East. As far as the eye can reach the beautiful rolling prairies lie spread out like a sea of meadows; and are decorated with a growth of flowers so gorgeous and grand as to exceed description. . . . The forests are a mixture of oak, hickory, black walnut, elm, ash, cherry, honey locust, mulberry, coffee bean, hack berry, boxelder, and bass wood. . . . The shrubbery is beautiful. . . . The soil is rich and fertile. . . . The season is mild and delightful nearly three quarters of the year, and as the land of Zion, situated at about equal distances from the Atlantic and Pacific oceans . . . it bids fair—when the curse is taken from the land—to become one of the most blessed places on the globe.[2]

William Wines Phelps, one of those who traveled with Joseph Smith from Kirtland to Independence, was an experienced newspaper editor, writer, and printer; he gave a description of the area which was very similar with the notable exception of the climate:

> The weather is warmer than in York state, and when it grows cold at night with the wind from an easterly direction, depend upon a deluging rain before morning, and then it clears off hot enough to roast eggs.[3]

Phelps was called specifically to locate in Jackson as a printer, and within a year had fulfilled his calling by establishing and publishing a monthly paper for the church called the *Evening and Morning Star*. The influence exerted by this publication made him one of the most important individuals connected with the early growth and success of the community of Saints in Independence. But perhaps even more important to the immediate success of the endeavor was the Colesville branch.

The gathering to Independence had actually begun even before the revelation was given designating the town as the loca-

---

[2]Ibid., 197–198. This description is attributed mostly to Sidney Rigdon, who was commanded to "write a description of the land of Zion."

[3]William W. Phelps, 1831 letter to the *Ontario Phoenix*, Canandaigua, New York.

tion of the Saints' Zion. A group of about sixty Saints from Colesville, New York, which had been among the first to be organized into a branch of the church by Joseph Smith, moved en masse to Ohio where a revelation was given to Joseph that they should take their "journey into the regions westward, unto the land or Missouri, unto the borders of the Lamanites."[4] The Colesville branch thus constituted the third group—along with Joseph Smith's party and the missionaries—which was to meet at the western borders of Missouri. Their journey was not an easy one, as they carried their belongings and provisions in twenty-four wagons, but they still arrived at Independence in late July 1831—well before the arrival of most of the missionaries.

The Colesville branch settled as a group twelve miles west of Independence in an area that later would become a part of Kansas City. These sixty committed members provided a foundation for the gathering. Their leader, Newell Knight, wrote of their commitment:

> But our feelings can be better imagined than described, when we found ourselves upon the Western frontiers. The country itself presented a pleasant aspect with its rich forests bordering its beautiful streams, and its deep rolling prairies spreading far and wide, inviting the hand of industry to establish for itself homes upon its broad bosom. And this was the place where . . . Zion should be and our hearts went forth unto the Lord desiring the fulfillment, that we might know where to bestow our labors profitably.[5]

They were easterners and were not accustomed to a frontier life, but the Colesville Saints tackled the tasks before them with "cheerful hearts, and a determination to do [their] best."[6] They were also very stoic, for whereas Newell Knight stated simply, "We passed the winter in a tolerably comfortable manner," Parley P. Pratt was probably much more objective when he wrote: "The winter was cold, and for some time about ten families lived in one log cabin, which was open and unfinished, while the frozen ground served for a floor."[7]

---

[4] *D&C* 54:8.
[5] Newell Knight's Journal in George Q. Cannon, ed., *Scraps of Biography*, 71.
[6] Ibid.   [7] Ibid.; Pratt, op. cit., 56.

But the winter did not last forever, and with the spring thaw came an ever-increasing number of those who wanted to join the gathering. By the time Joseph Smith returned to Ohio in May 1832, after his second trip to Independence, the population of Saints in Jackson County approximated three hundred. Within the next year the number doubled, and the stream of people from the East, many of them poor, continued to grow despite efforts of church officials to prevent a mad rush to Zion.

And so the church, though still relatively small in total membership, had two centers—Kirtland and Independence—with nearly all the leadership in Ohio, but with the promise for the future in western Missouri. Kirtland was the home of Joseph Smith and most of the church hierarchy, but written notice of all of Smith's revelations, parts of the *Book of Mormon* and explanations of church doctrine were printed monthly in *The Evening and Morning Star* in Independence to allow the members there to be kept up to date.

In contrast, the leadership at Salt River, from the time of the first baptisms on 10 September 1832, could best be described as the blind leading the blind, as none of the early converts had much knowledge of the new religion. They believed in the *Book of Mormon* and in Joseph Smith as a prophet, but this was a rapidly expanding and evolving church, and the Salt River learned of new developments only as those going to and from Independence happened to travel through the area.

Nevertheless, news of the gathering most certainly reached the settlement at an early date. An editorial on 17 September 1831 in the *Missouri Intelligencer & Boon's Lick Advertiser* in nearby Columbia, in the whole extremely unflattering to the Mormons, noted the return trip of some of the missionaries to Kirtland:

> Some of the leaders of this sect, we are told, passed through this place . . . on their return to Ohio. We understand, that they have determined to migrate to Jackson County, on the extreme edge of this state; for which purpose they have purchased a sufficiency of land whereupon to locate the whole of the believers of Mormonism.[8]

---

[8]Quoted in William Mulder and A. Russell Mortensen, *Among the Mormons*, 71.

Armed with this knowledge, the new members at Salt River immediately focused on joining the Saints in western Missouri. Yet when Isaac Allred sold his land at Salt River in 1833 in preparation for going to Zion, he found that the gathering had been put on hold as the Saints were ignominiously expelled from Jackson County.[9]

No simple explanation for this expulsion is possible. Perhaps the Saints' biggest sin was to be "Yankees" who didn't believe in slavery, while the original settlers in Jackson County were southerners who did. William W. Phelps, in an 1831 letter to a New York newspaper, captured the essence of the vast chasm of mutual distrust separating fellow countrymen in Independence:

> The inhabitants [of Missouri] are emigrants from Tennessee, Kentucky, Virginia, and the Carolinas, etc., with customs, manners, modes of living and a climate entirely different from the northerners, and they hate yankees worse than snakes, because they have cheated them or speculated on their credulity, with so many Connecticut wooden clocks, and New England notions. The people are proverbially idle or lazy, and mostly ignorant; reckoning nobody equal to themselves in many respects, and as it is a slave holding state, Japheth will make Canaan serve him, while he dwells in the tents of Shem.[10]

The Saints were not attempting to subvert the institution of slavery, but an article in *The Evening and Morning Star* addressed to "Free People of Color" in July 1833, suggested otherwise. Phelps had written the article to caution the missionaries about proselytizing among slaves or former slaves, but by inviting free Negroes and mulattos to come to Jackson County, it was perceived as anti-slavery and precipitated a firestorm of criticism and persecution from the non-Mormon Missourians.

Even as Phelps had declared that the people in Independence were "idle or lazy, and mostly ignorant," citizens of Jackson County felt much the same about the Mormons. In a circular issued on 18 July 1833, it was stated that "Zion was made up of the very dregs of the society from which they came—lazy, idle, and

---

[9]William M. Allred, "Early History of William M. Allred."
[10]William W. Phelps, 1831 letter to the *Ontario Phoenix*.

vicious."[11] Even a Mormon sympathizer, Alexander Majors, who was convinced that the Mormons had been "good" citizens and perfectly law-abiding, recounted many years later his late teen-age impressions:

> They, of course, were clannish, traded together, worked together, and carried with them a melancholy look that one acquainted with them could tell a Mormon when he met him by the look upon his face almost as well as if he had been of a different color.[12]

Having very little in common with the old settlers, the Saints were indeed clannish, but that in itself was no great sin. However, as their numbers increased, so also the fear grew that they might soon take control of the county. "The day is not far distant . . . ," some warned, "when the sheriff, the justices, and the county judges will be Mormons, or persons wishing to court their favor from motives of interest and ambition."[13]

The non-Mormons misunderstood, perhaps even feared, other aspects of this new religion. The frontiersmen certainly feared and hated the Indians, and yet here was a church that proselytized among the Indians and declared their divine destiny. In addition, not only did the Saints claim to receive revelations, which was blasphemy to many outside of the church, but they also declared "openly that their God hath given them this country of land, and that sooner or later they must and will have the possession of our land for an inheritance."[14] This was true in a sense, but Phelps had published in *The Evening and Morning Star* in July 1833 that possession could not be taken without making "regular purchases of the same according to the laws of our nation." The intent from the beginning was to purchase land in order to have a secure gathering place, but the Mormons never anticipated that land ownership would become meaningless in a land of liberty.

Isolated hostile incidents against the Saints occurred in 1832, but by 1833, when the Mormon population of about twelve hundred comprised one-third of the population of Jackson County,

[11]Carrie Westlake Whitney, *Kansas City, Missouri, Its History and Its People, 1808–1898*, 80.
[12]Alexander Majors, *Seventy Years on the Frontier*, 45.
[13]*Western Monitor*, August 2, 1833.   [14]Whitney, op. cit., 81.

such attacks became more frequent. On 20 July, what began as an assembly of four or five hundred disgruntled citizens turned into a mob that destroyed the Mormon printing office and looted a general store and blacksmith shop. Just three days later another mob gathered, this time with guns, clubs, and whips, forced some Saints to admit that the *Book of Mormon* was a fraud, and declared their intention to destroy the Mormon dwellings and crops unless all the Saints left Jackson County. The helpless Mormons had no choice but to bow to the demands of their Christian enemies and agree that the leaders and their families would leave Jackson County before the first of January 1834, and that all of the Saints would be out by the following 1 April.

When the news of trouble in Independence reached Kirtland, Joseph Smith immediately counseled the Saints through revelation to remain quiet and peaceable, forgiving the trespasses of others.[15] The Mormon leaders in Independence decided to heed the advice of their Prophet and sought to resolve the conflict through legal means. When the anti-Mormons saw that the Saints were not leaving, but were preparing to bring legal action instead, they were enraged and the rout was on. After several armed skirmishes in which two non-Mormons were killed, Colonel Thomas Pitcher, with the connivance of Lieutenant Governor Lilburn Boggs, called out the local militia and demanded that the Mormons surrender their arms. News spread that the Saints had no weapons, and Missouri jackals rushed to attack almost every Mormon settlement in Jackson County, driving the inhabitants from their homes and destroying their property.

Few Missourians living elsewhere condoned the barbaric treatment of the Mormons in Jackson County. The Missouri press almost universally deplored the outrage and most newspapers in the state carried editorials condemning the action. The St. Louis *Free Press* said on 15 August:

> Had the individuals of this sect, or even the whole body of it committed legal offenses, the civil tribunals of our country could have

---

[15]*D&C* 98.

given sufficient redress, but to proceed against them as a religious body . . . must be considered *persecution* in the most odious sense of the word. . . .[16]

Probably no paper championed the Saints' cause in Jackson County with more zeal than the *Salt River Journal*. In an editorial that was reprinted in the politically powerful St. Louis *Missouri Republican* on 30 November 1833, the editor of the Salt River newspaper asked:

> Are the people of Jackson County determined to drive off the Mormons on account of their peculiar religious tenets? Were the worshippers of the moon to settle in this State, no one would have the right to molest them, on account of these tenets.[17]

But the public support in other parts of the state was of no help to the refugees of Jackson County. Frightened and helpless, more than a thousand Mormons, including half-clad women and children, were forced to suffer severely from the cold and rain as they hastily made their way across the Missouri River. Parley P. Pratt described the scene in his autobiography:

> Thursday, November 7th. the shore began to be lined on both sides of the ferry, with men, women, and children, goods, wagons, boxes, chests, provisions, etc., while the ferrymen were very busily employed in crossing them over. . . . Hundreds of people were seen in all directions. Some in tents, some in the open air around their fires while the rain descended in torrents. . . . The scene was indescribable, and, I am sure, would have melted the hearts of any people on the earth, except our blind oppressors, and a blind and ignorant community.[18]

While some of the Saints had already begun an aimless journey to a new county, the majority were still huddled on a riverbank, trying to protect themselves from the biting cold while hopefully awaiting word of what to do from their Prophet. Suddenly cries arose in the camp to look towards the heavens. There were hundreds of meteors streaking across the sky; "what looked like stars commenced falling, all of them vanishing before they

---

[16]Quoted in Loy Otis Banks, *Missouri Historical Review*, XLIII (July 1949), 327.
[17]Ibid., 331.   [18]Pratt, op. cit., 82.

reached the ground, and it continued from a half to three-quarters of and hour, while everything was as bright as day."[19] It was one of the great meteor showers of the century, visible across the United States; but as the Jackson County Saints gazed at the skies, they sank to their knees in the snow, and "every heart was filled with joy at this majestic display of signs and wonders, showing the near approach of the coming of the Son of God."[20]

Word from Joseph Smith was not immediately forthcoming, and most of the Saints took refuge in Clay County, where the residents received them kindly, helped them to find shelter and furnished needed provisions. But, despite the hospitality of their new neighbors, living conditions were not good, and on 15 December 1833, W. W. Phelps wrote a despairing letter to the church leaders in Kirtland:

> The situation of the Saints, as scattered, is dubious, and affords a gloomy prospect. No regular order can be enforced; nor any usual discipline kept up.... I know it was right that we should be driven out of Zion, that the rebellious might be sent away—But, brethren, if the Lord will, I should like to know what the honest in heart shall do?[21]

It is curious that even after so much persecution, the Saints accepted at least some of the responsibility for their fate in Jackson County because of their disobedience. Joseph Smith himself evidently felt somewhat the same way, as he suggested in a letter to Vienna Jacques in September 1833, immediately after learning of the outbreak of atrocities in Jackson County:

> I am not at all astonished at what has happened to you, neither to what has happened to Zion ... it is vain to warn and give precepts, for all men are naturally disposed to walk in their own paths as they are pointed out by their own fingers, and are not willing to consider and walk in the path which is pointed out by another.... [22]

Joseph Smith ordered the Saints in Missouri to keep title to their land in Jackson County, so as to remain as near to Zion as possible, and to appeal to President Andrew Jackson for federal

---

[19]Judge Joseph Thorp, *Early Days in the West*, 76.
[20]Pratt, op. cit., 83.   [21]*Times and Seasons*, 6:12.
[22]Fawn M. Brodie, *No Man Knows My History*, 133.

aid against their oppressors, but offered no immediate assistance. However, the Saints in Missouri had already communicated with Governor Daniel Dunklin regarding the Jackson County situation and he received a response from the governor through his attorney general, Robert W. Wells, which made the initial offer of military assistance:

> From conversation I have had with the Governor, I believe I am warranted in saying to you, and through you to the Mormons, that if they desire to be replaced in possession of their property, that is, their houses in Jackson county, an adequate force will be sent forthwith to effect that object.... The militia have been ordered to hold themselves in readiness. If the Mormons will organize themselves into regular companies, or a regular company of militia, either volunteers or otherwise, they will, I have no doubt, be supplied with public arms.[23]

Armed with this news, Parley P. Pratt and Lyman Wight traveled to Kirtland in February 1834, where they made an eloquent appeal to the Ohio Saints to go to the aid of their distressed brothers. Smith was impressed and announced to members of the "high council" in Kirtland that he was going to Zion to help redeem it. The high council supported him unanimously in this decision.

A revelation received that same day directed that messengers should be sent out in all direction to gather food, clothing, and money as well as to recruit members to assist their brethren in Missouri.[24] The endeavor became known as "Zion's Camp." Despite pleas from the Prophet, few in the East volunteered for the camp, though recruitment efforts in Kirtland met with more success. Hyrum Smith and Lyman Wight were sent northwest from Kirtland to seek out more recruits while Joseph's company traveled in a more westerly direction. The designated meeting place of the two parties was Salt River, specifically at the farm of James Allred. The "Allred settlement," as the Salt River branch of the church was commonly called, was not only directly on the route from Kirtland to Jackson County, but the relatively large population of church members there offered a safe haven where

---

[23]*History of the Church*, 1:446–47.   [24]*D&C* 103.

the marching Saints could rest for a few days before continuing their long journey.

On 4 May, armed with "old muskets, rifles, pistols, rusty swords, and butcher knifes," an army of more than eighty volunteers began the one-thousand-mile march.[25] With Joseph Smith as the commander-in-chief, the army of Israel continued its long trek west, frequently marching thirty-five miles a day despite blistered feet, oppressive heat, heavy rains, high humidity, hunger, and thirst. The difficult conditions were very trying on the group, and quarreling and contention within the camp became vexing problems. Some of the malcontents blamed Joseph Smith for their discomfort, and many of the leaders began looking on Joseph, who had never claimed perfection, as a prophet who had human failings. After all, he had been told in a revelation in 1830: "And in temporal labors thou shalt not have strength, for this is not thy calling."[26] Only in spiritual matters, at least during this long march, would his decisions remain unquestioned.

After more than one month on the road, Zion's Camp finally arrived at Salt River on Saturday, 7 June, and camped on the property of James Allred, the brother of Isaac, "in a piece of woods by a spring of water and prepared for the Sabbath."[27] The settlement expected their arrival, having already prepared a place to hold meetings. Shortly after the expedition crossed the Mississippi River, the *Salt River Journal* reported that members of the party "were, with few exceptions, well provided with firearms and accoutrement of war." While not holding a high opinion of the Saints themselves, the newspaper nevertheless seemed to support their cause:

> We regard the Mormons as a set of deluded and deceived fanatics, yet they have their rights and privileges. . . . In their case we believe the arm of the law is neutralized and their hope of protection will be in their ability to resist brute force. The only cause of regret is that the citizens of Jackson County have so far forgotten the principles of duty.[28]

---

[25] *Painesville Telegraph*, May 8, 1834.   [26] *D&C* 24:9

[27] Heber C. Kimball, "Extracts from his Journal," *Times and Seasons*, 6:788–89.

[28] *Salt River Journal*, reprinted in *Missouri Intelligencer*, June 21, 1834.

On Sunday morning meetings were held on the Allred property, at which Joseph Smith and others spoke.[29] William Taylor, who was a neighbor of the Allreds, attended the meeting and reportedly was converted immediately; he and his wife Elizabeth, along with some members of their family, subsequently were baptized.[30] Later that afternoon, Hyrum Smith and Lyman Wight, who had parted from the main company in Ohio to go to Michigan, rejoined Zion's Camp, bringing with them some new recruits. The addition of these new volunteers swelled the number in the camp to nearly two hundred—mostly men, but also at least ten women and eight children.

During their stay of five days at Salt River, members of the expedition relaxed and reorganized. Weapons were repaired in a shop in the Allred settlement by two members of the camp who were skilled gunsmiths. The bivouacked Saints were not certain what they would encounter once they reached Jackson County, but while at Salt River they took part in military exercise by drilling, inspecting firelocks, practicing the use of swords, and taking part in sham battles. By this time Zion's Camp had been further strengthened as James Allred and ten others of the Salt River branch joined the camp, "which now numbered two hundred and five men, all armed and equipped as the law directs."[31] Included among these new members were: Robert McCord, a son-in-law of William Taylor; Isaac Allred, son of James who was the first to cement bonds between the Taylor and Allred families by marrying William Taylor's daughter, Julia Ann, in 1832 (though a nephew of Isaac Allred, to avoid confusion he was known frequently as Isaac Allred Jr.); Martin Allred, another son of James; Andrew Whitlock, a son-in-law of James Allred; and Edward, James R., John A. and William S. Ivie.

After their sojourn at Salt River, Zion's Camp resumed the march to western Missouri. Heber Kimball recorded the following regarding their departure:

---

[29]Pleasant Green Taylor, in his autobiography, named also Parley Pratt and his brother Orson as speakers.

[30]Temple Index Bureau records and *Autobiography of Joseph Allen Taylor.*

[31]*History of the Church,* 2:88 footnotes.

June 12th we left Salt River and traveled about fourteen miles, encamping that night on the prairie. The inhabitants of Salt River manifested a great respect for us, and many of them accompanied us some distance on our journey.[32]

One family which may have accompanied the expedition all the way to Clay County was that of Allen Taylor, the second son of William Taylor, who at the age of nineteen, in September 1833, had married fifteen-year-old Sarah Lovisa Allred, daughter of the elder Isaac Allred. Allen was baptized along with his parents while Zion's Camp was in Missouri (most likely at Salt River), and the first child of Allen and Sarah Lovisa was born in Clay County on 27 June, indicating that they had traveled to western Missouri at exactly the same time as Zion's Camp did. In their religious fervor they named the child Isaac Moroni Taylor, after Sarah's father, Isaac Allred, as well as the heavenly messenger, Moroni, whose appearances to Joseph Smith laid the foundation for the translation and publication of the *Book of Mormon*.

The same day that Zion's Camp left the Allred settlement, Joseph Smith dispatched Orson Hyde and Parley Pratt to Jefferson City, as George A. Smith remembered, "to accept His Excellency's [the governor's] proposal to reinstate the Saints on their lands in Jackson County and leave them there to defend themselves."[33] Three days later Hyde and Pratt returned to the camp with the news that the governor "refused to fulfill his promise of reinstating the brethren on their lands in Jackson County."[34] The governor's refusal insured that Zion's Camp would not march into Jackson County, which was originally its principal objective. Nevertheless, the camp trudged onward with the lessened objective of trying to reach some sort of compromise with the hostile residents of Jackson County.

News of the coming of "The Army of Zion" preceded them into every settlement. As they marched across Missouri, carrying a white flag upon which the word "peace" had been inscribed (which, in combination with the weapons they were bearing, sent a mixed message to all who saw the army pass by), armed

---

[32]*Times and Seasons*, 6:1088.   [33]George Albert Smith, "History."   [34]Ibid.

militias from several counties were forming to meet and defeat the Mormons, who they thought were coming to do battle. Within a week the Saints arrived in Clay County and set up camp between two branches of the Fishing River.

Across the Missouri River, at Williams Ferry, a mob had gathered and threatened to destroy the Mormons. But suddenly a violent storm moved through the area:

> In a short time it commenced thundering and the clouds arose.... The lightning flashed and thunder roared one continual sound and flash so connected one could hardly hear any interval between the flash and the peal of thunder....[35]

The storm was so intense that Zion's Camp had to abandon their tents and take refuge in an old Baptist meetinghouse. A flash flood inundated the lowlands and made crossing the river impossible. The storm also made the aggressors' ammunition useless and the frustrated mob was forced to call off the attack.

Three days later, after being advised by sheriff Cornelius Gillium that to enter Jackson County with arms would be an act of insurrection, Joseph Smith received a revelation, known among the Mormons as the "Fishing River Revelation," which commanded the Saints "to wait a little season for the redemption of Zion."[36] On the evening of the following day, Asiatic cholera broke out in the camp. Of the sixty-eight members of the camp who eventually contracted the disease, fourteen died, including William Taylor's son-in-law of just one month, Robert McCord.

Under these circumstances, Smith had no choice but to disband Zion's Camp, and he soon returned to Kirtland. Stopping once again at Salt River, he preached and "told the Saints that they could not get possession of their lands but to gather up to Clay County."[37] The expedition had failed to accomplish its objective and also was marred by dissension and apostasy among its ranks, as some wondered openly how a mission commanded by God could possibly falter. But on the positive side, bonds were created between those who remained faithful, which shaped the

[35] Levi Hancock, Autobiography, 55.   [36] *D&C* 105:13
[37] Reddick Allred, op. cit., 5:299.

core of church leadership. Indeed, when the Quorum of the Twelve Apostles and the First Quorum of Seventy were formed in February 1835, nine of the original Apostles and all seven presidents of the Seventy's quorum, as well as all sixty-three other members of that quorum had served in the army of Israel that marched to western Missouri in 1834.

Unfortunately, Zion's Camp also left a residue of ill will. Many Missourians, who otherwise had been friendly to the Mormons, were antagonized by the intrusion of a large force of armed men from outside the state. There had been no armed conflict, yet the expedition was perceived by many as an attempt to utilize military force to gain possession of land upon which the religious community of Zion would be built. Though the next several years were relatively peaceful for members of the church, the legacy of Zion's Camp ultimately would come back to haunt the Mormons in Missouri.

Chapter IV

OUT OF MISSOURI

WHEN THE PROPHET SPOKE, the faithful listened. On the return trip from western Missouri after Zion's Camp was dismissed, Joseph Smith encouraged the Saints at Salt River to pull up their stakes and move to Clay County. They may have moved immediately to the western part of the state had it not been the middle of the growing season, still a few months before crops could be harvested. William Taylor and Isaac Allred also faced another obstacle which delayed their move: Their wives, Elizabeth Taylor and Mary Allred, were pregnant, and both families decided to remain at Salt River until after the birth of the children in late January 1835.

Isaac Allred, having sold his land two years prior when he originally considered going to Jackson County, was able to move his family when spring arrived and settled along the Fishing River in Clay County, near his son-in-law and daughter, Allen and Sarah Lovisa Taylor. Taylor's father William, on the other hand, had gradually extended his land holdings from the original 80 acres in 1831 to a total of 160 acres and was not able to sell his property until October 1835. After that he finally moved his family to western Missouri, where he purchased 160 acres of land in 1836, also along the Fishing River but in Ray County.

The citizens of Clay and adjacent counties received the Saints in a friendly manner and furnished a base from which the latter could work to get back their lands in Jackson County. Many of the Mormons settled on prairie lands that pioneers from Kentucky and Tennessee had passed up to establish homes along the wooded creeks. Judge John Thorp, who had provided shelter for some Mormon families in 1834, recalled many years later: "The Mormons, in the main, were industrious, good workers, and gave general satisfaction to their employers, and could live on less than any people I ever knew."[1] Colonel Alexander Doniphan also remembered the Mormons in Clay County as a "peaceable, sober, industrious, and law-abiding people."[2]

Despite the generally favorable treatment they were given in Clay County, the Saints' intention was to return to Jackson County, whose residents were still opposed to them. Some hostility to the Mormons also existed in Clay County from the first, especially on the part of a few Protestant preachers. Among the most vociferous of these was a Baptist minister named Riley, who preached that the Mormons "must either clear out or be cleared out."[3] The influence of such people grew as the Mormons' temporary residence in Clay County took on an air of permanency. When the number of Saints increased to such an extent that they threatened to gain political control, the Gentiles, as non-Mormons were called by the Mormons, became extremely uneasy.

Realizing these concerns, Bishop Edward Partridge and William W. Phelps took two exploratory expeditions in the spring of 1836, hoping to find potential sites for Mormon settlements in northern Missouri, a region commonly referred to as the "Far West." Most of this territory was prairie, covered by tall grass, with timber only along the streams and rivers. Partridge and Phelps found an uninhabited region in northern Ray County along Shoal Creek, and although they feared that there was not enough timber available to support a large population, began purchasing land in the area.

Shortly thereafter, isolated hostilities broke out in Clay County, including a mob attack on a Mormon settlement near

[1]Thorp, *Early Days in the West*, 76.
[2]*Kansas City Journal*, 5 June 1881.
[3]Joseph Smith, *History of the Church*, vol. 2, p. 97.

the Fishing River, in which many were harassed and one man
was nearly whipped to death.[4] On 29 June 1836, friendly leading
citizens at Liberty held a public meeting to review the situation
with the intent of preventing a war from erupting. The committee report noted "their rapid emigration" and "their large land
purchases," as well as some of the same complaints against the
Mormons that had been voiced in Jackson County.[5] The Saints
were charged with no crimes, but once again were judged to be
non-slaveholding easterners, opposed to slavery and keeping a
"constant communication with the Indian tribes on our frontier,
with declaring, even from the pulpit, that the Indians are a part
of God's chosen people and are destined by heaven to inherit this
land, in common with themselves."[6] But in stark contrast with
the Jackson County experience, the resolutions passed at the
meeting merely asked the Mormons to leave the county, even
offering them financial help to resettle.

When the resolutions were brought to the attention of the
Mormon leaders, the Saints held a mass meeting at which they
denied any intention to incite the slaves or to invite Indians to
join with them in taking over the land. Nevertheless, confident
that they would soon begin moving to Shoal Creek, church leaders agreed to stop immigration and instructed the Saints to prepare to vacate Clay County by summer's end.

Heeding their leader's counsel, Mormon families streamed
northward and slightly east into unsettled parts of northern Ray
County during August. Along Shoal Creek, leaders platted and
started building a town named Far West, which was intended to
be the main Mormon settlement. An estimated three thousand
Saints moved to the region, including Isaac Allred and Allen
Taylor, who on 30 August 1836, purchased side-by-side 80- and
40-acre plots on Long Creek in Grant Township, about eight
miles from Far West. William Taylor had purchased 120 acres in
southern Ray County just a few weeks before the Saints began

---

[4]Drusilla Hendricks, "Historical Sketch." 10.
[5]Joseph Smith, *History of the Church*, vol. 2, p. 57.
[6]*History of the Church*, 2:448–450.

their move to the north and was unable to move his family until he sold his 160 acres in Ray County in June 1837, after which he bought an 80-acre parcel in Grant Township adjacent to the land owned by his son Allen.[7] Also settling in Grant Township in 1837 were Isaac Allred's brothers James and William.

The Saints were anxious to have a place to call their own, and Colonel Alexander W. Doniphan, a friend of the Saints who was elected to the Missouri House of Representatives in the fall of 1836, sponsored a Mormon petition for the creation of a new county out of the northern area of Ray County. The area was sparsely settled, and to the politicians the formation of an exclusively Mormon county was considered an excellent solution to the "Mormon problem." Two new counties were quickly formed, named Caldwell and Daviess after two famous Indian fighters from Kentucky, and there was a general understanding that Caldwell County, the location of Far West as well as the area on Long Creek where the Allreds and Taylors had settled, would be primarily for the Saints.

Mormons streamed into Caldwell County from nearby counties and the East. By 1838 the population reached approximately five thousand, all but about one hundred being Mormons. They were able to produce beautiful crops on the prairies which southern pioneers regarded as "fit only for Indians and Mormons." Far West, the county seat, seemed to rise almost magically above the high rolling prairie and already was the home of some three thousand Saints.

While Caldwell County continued to grow, the leadership of the church for the greater part remained in Kirtland, but that was about to change. Joseph Smith and some of the elders in Kirtland, caught up along with others in a speculative craze that swept the country, borrowed money from banks in Ohio and New York with which to buy land that seemed destined to continue to appreciate in value. In November 1836, they organized the Kirtland Safety Society Bank Company, with Sydney Rigdon as president and Joseph Smith as cashier. When the Ohio legislature

---

[7]Caldwell County Recorders Office.

refused to grant the bank a charter, the Mormon promoters changed the name of the institution to the Kirtland Safety Society Anti-Banking Company, and officers began to issue notes, many of which were used to pay off debts owed by the Mormons.

Within a month neither merchants nor other banks would touch the notes, which became virtually worthless. Since the Anti-Banking Company was operating illegally without a charter, Smith was arrested and fined one thousand dollars and court costs. Numerous suits were filed against him by creditors involving claims of more than thirty thousand dollars. Right or wrong, Joseph Smith took the blame in the eyes of many Mormons as well as Gentiles.

In this dark period of economic distress many members of the church apostatized. Despite efforts to quell the unrest, the deplorable condition of the church at Kirtland failed to improve, and finally in January 1838 Joseph Smith and Sydney Rigdon fled to Missouri. The trip to Missouri, in the middle of a cold winter, was extremely difficult. Along the way the Prophet resorted to cutting and sawing wood but was still unable to earn enough to meet his needs. But upon reaching Far West, Smith and Rigdon were joyfully received by the Saints, many of whom regarded the difficulties in Kirtland as God's way of bringing the Prophet among them to stay.[8]

Smith's arrival was followed by the movement of hundreds of Saints from the East, particularly many of the faithful who had remained in Kirtland. But desirable locations in Caldwell County were taken up, and so the new immigrants spread into surrounding counties, particularly Daviess. Pursuant to a revelation given on 26 April 1838, which commanded the gathering of the Saints at Far West and the establishment of stakes in the region round about, Smith, Rigdon and others went up the Grand River to seek a site for a stake in Daviess County.[9] Of the journey Smith later wrote:

---

[8]James B. Allen and Glen M. Leonard, *The Story of the Latter-day Saints*, 10–115.

[9]*D&C* 115. Using the analogy of a great tent upheld by cords fastened securely to stakes, a Mormon stake was set apart as an area of church population and strength which would sustain and uphold the restored Zion.

In the afternoon I went up the river about half a mile to Wight's Ferry, accompanied by President Rigdon, and my Clerk, George W. Robinson, for the purpose of selecting and laying claim to a city plat near said ferry in Daviess County . . . which the brethren called "Spring Hill," but by the mouth of the Lord it was named Adam-ondi-Ahman, because, said He, it is the place where Adam shall come to visit his people, or the Ancient of Days shall sit, as spoken of by Daniel the Prophet.[10]

After a stake of the church was organized at Adam-ondi-Ahmen (shortened by the Saints to 'Diahman) on 28 June, the settlement grew so rapidly that it threatened to overtake Far West. All was not well, however, at Far West. Some of the dissenters from Kirtland had preceded the prophet. Oliver Cowdery, David and John Whitmer, and Lyman Johnson had found refuge some twenty-five miles from Far West in the home of William McLellin, who had left the church in 1836 for reasons of his own. In February 1838, the presidency of the church in Missouri—David Whitmer, W. W. Phelps, and John Whitmer— were tried by a general church council and released, mostly because they had sold their land in Jackson County contrary to church policy and the "law of God." Two months later Oliver Cowdery and David Whitmer, two of the three witnesses to the *Book of Mormon*, were excommunicated, as were four of the twelve apostles within the next few months.

Sidney Rigdon was particularly incensed to find the dissenters still living among the faithful as he drove into Far West in early April. Rigdon gradually escalated the rhetoric until he directed a thinly-veiled threat to the dissenters in a sermon, warning: "If the salt have lost [its] savour, wherewith shall it be salted? It is thenceforth good for nothing, but to be cast out, and to be trodden under foot of men."[11] Soon afterward a document signed by eighty-four citizens, many of them members of a recently organized secret society known as the "Danites," ordered Oliver Cowdery, David and John Whitmer, W. W. Phelps, and Lyman

---

[10]*History of the Church*, 3:35.
[11]Brigham H. Roberts, *Comprehensive History of the Church of Jesus Christ of Latter-day Saints*, 1:438.

Johnson, the leading dissenters, to leave the county or face "a more fatal calamity." The dissenters took the warning very seriously and left Far West almost immediately.

Emboldened by their strong-arm success in squelching dissension, the Danites, led by Sampson Avard, redirected their focus to the defense of the church against mobs. A speech on July 4 by Sidney Rigdon further incited the Danites as well as other members of the church. Rigdon, a fiery orator, delivered a declaration of independence for the Saints from any further mob violence or illegal activity and issued a warning to the enemies of the church:

> We take God and all the holy angels to witness this day, that we warn all men in the name of Jesus Christ, to come on us no more forever; for from this hour, we will bear it no more, our rights shall no more be trampled upon with impunity. The man or the set of men, who attempts it, does it at the expense of their lives. And that mob that comes on us to disturb us, it shall be between us and them a war of extermination, for we will follow them, till the last drop of their blood is spilled, or else they will have to exterminate us: for we will carry the seat of war to their own houses, and their own families, and one party or the other shall be utterly destroyed.[12]

With Joseph Smith's permission, the Liberty press published the speech, and newspapers throughout Missouri took note of it and published angry editorials in rebuttal. Missourians also became resentful that Mormons had moved into Daviess County, believing that it was understood that they would confine themselves to Caldwell County. Tensions grew and finally erupted during an election on 6 August in Gallatin, Daviess County. Isaac Allred's son Reddick gave a concise account of the conflict:

> The few ranchers in Caldwell and Davies [sic] counties raised false reports about the lawlessness of the Mormons and at an election in Galiton [sic], Davis [sic] County they forbade any Mormon to vote and surrounded the polls to prevent it, but a fight ensued and the Mormons cleared the way and voted. This was enough to wake up the whole of Jackson, Clay, Ray and Carlton Counties into a howling mob, and they began to make raids upon outside settlements.[13]

---

[12]Crawley, "Two Rare Missouri Documents," *BYU Studies*, 527.
[13]Reddick Allred, op. cit., 5:300.

Increasing hostilities, both actual and threatened, made it advisable for the Saints to organize into military bodies for self-defense. Acting upon advice from General Alexander Doniphan, brigadier general for northern Missouri, the Saints formed two such units, one at Far West, and the other at Adam-ondi-Ahman. Lyman Wight, resident of 'Diahman, and George M. Hinkle, resident of Far West and the man who baptized the Allred family at Salt River, were selected to serve as commanding officers of the newly organized units.[14] Many who belonged to these legitimate units were also members of the Danite clan, although little, if any, effort was made to distinguish between one's activities in either group, each of which was organized into companies of tens and fifties.[15]

On 9 September, it was learned that guns and ammunition were being transported to the mob in Daviess County to fight the Mormons. Captain William Allred, brother of Isaac, took his company of ten to intercept the wagons as they left Richmond, a distance of about twenty miles from Far West. When all were mounted, Joseph Smith said to Captain Allred: "I want you to ride as fast as your horses can carry you, and you will get those arms."[16] On the side of the road near Richmond, Allred's company discovered a broken down, unattended carriage:

> On nearing it, we saw that it was empty. . . . We soon discovered a trail in the high grass where something heavy had been dragged from near the carriage. We followed this trail a short distance and found a wooden box, containing seventy-four United States yaugers. . . . The prediction of the prophet was fulfilled, and the long-range guns, which were the best then known, were in our hands.[17]

Three prisoners were taken by Captain Allred to Far West and charged with attempting to smuggle arms to a mob. Judge Austin King ruled that the prisoners were being held illegally and should be released, but the arrest and imprisonment of the wagon crew created such excitement that Judge King advised

[14]*History of the Church*, 3:161–163.   [15]Ibid., 3:181–182.
[16]Daniel Tyler, *Scraps of Biography*, 33.   [17]Ibid., 34.

General David Atchison of the Missouri state militia "to send two hundred or more men, and dispel the forces in Daviess County and all the assembled armed forces in Caldwell. . . ."[18] Four companies of mounted riflemen from Clay County under the command of General Doniphan marched to Far West, where Doniphan demanded that the prisoners and the arms taken when the supply wagon was intercepted be turned over to him. The Mormons complied fully, except for those guns that had been sent to their brethren in Daviess County to aid in their defense.

A semblance of peace had hardly been established in Daviess County when trouble broke out in Carroll County. During the summer of 1838, George Hinkle and John Murdock, two of the missionaries who had been instrumental in the conversion and baptism of the Salt River Saints, had purchased a large number of lots at DeWitt, "a very beautiful place with broad acres of rich soil covered with grass and plenty of timber nearby, pleasantly located on the bank of the Missouri River, which at that place was about a half a mile wide."[19] Here they planned to develop a Mormon colony to serve as a port on the Missouri River for persons and supplies going to and from Far West. Older inhabitants became alarmed when they learned of the purchases, feeling that the Mormons had violated their agreement to confine themselves to Caldwell County, and demanded that the Saints leave DeWitt.

On the very day that General Atchison discharged the militia in Daviess County, Carroll County anti-Mormons marched upon DeWitt and threatened to kill every Mormon who remained in the town after 1 October. George Hinkle defiantly declared that the Saints would defend their rights to remain in DeWitt. As the non-Mormon forces continued to increase, the Saints also received reinforcements and began building barricades. William Moore Allred, a son of Isaac, who "was in most all of the campaigns and witnessed many troubles and unjust treatments of the Saints," later wrote:

---

[18]*History of the Church*, 3:75.   [19]Zadoc Judd, "Autobiography."

> In 1838 I went with a company to assist a settlement that was besieged by the mob in the town of DeWitt on the Missouri River in Carroll County. We arrived there in the night and decided to go and attack the mob right then. They were camped only a little way from the town. When we got to his picket guard, he fired on us and raised the rest of the camp. They commenced shooting toward us but the bullets went over our heads. . . . There were none of us hit. George H. Hinkle, the man who baptized me, was our commander. He said he found there was a deep gully between us and their camp and only a narrow bridge to cross. He ordered us to retreat which we did in good order. Finally we made a treaty with them and agreed to leave the place.[20]

The Saints at DeWitt had been experiencing systematic starvation and grievous privations. Though forced to defend themselves, many believed it wrong to fight, and it "almost rocked their faith in the Gospel" to take up arms and try to kill their brethren.[21] Church leaders appealed to the governor for assistance, but their pleas were ignored and the tired, hungry Mormons were forced to abandon DeWitt on 11 October.

Even as the refugees from DeWitt began to arrive in Far West, attacks against Mormons in Daviess County began anew. Joseph Smith and Sidney Rigdon rallied the Mormons in Far West and called on them to fight in defense of their brethren. A company was sent to Daviess County on 16 October, but a severe snowstorm temporarily prevented any skirmishes. William Moore Allred, a member of the company recalled: "When I awoke in the morning as I lay on the ground there was about 6 inches of snow on me. The hunger and misery I encountered cannot be described."[22] When lighter snow began to fall, the Mormons prepared for battle. Now they were on the offensive, scattering the Gentiles like chaff before the wind. They attacked and seized Gallatin and Millport and, venting frustration fostered by years of persecution, burned cabins, carried off supplies, and rounded up livestock.

Mormon depredations in Daviess County outraged local citi-

[20]Allred, William M., op. cit.   [21]Judd, op. cit.
[22]William Allred, op. cit.

zens and angry mobs began to retaliate immediately. Rumors spread among the Gentiles that the Mormons intended to lay waste to the entire northwestern part of the state. With the war intensifying, Joseph Smith realized that the outside settlements could not protect themselves and dispatched Allen Taylor, among others, to notify these Saints to move into Far West for their safety. When Allen's father William Taylor moved his family into town, they found that they, like many other refugees, had to live in the streets:

> So many of the Saints had gathered here to escape mob violence that shelter could not be obtained. They arrived at night and made their beds upon the ground. The snow fell during the night to the depth of ten inches, covering beds, clothings, shoes, stockings as they lay spread upon the ground.[23]

Two days after many of the Saints from the smaller settlements had moved into Far West, a battle took place that was a turning point in the "Mormon War." Sixteen-year-old Reddick Allred, while returning with his father's ox team from Daviess County, was eating supper at Isaac Morley's house in Far West when his father arrived and informed him that a mob was attacking families on Log Creek, just a few miles from their home.

> He told me to go home, (8 miles) that night so we could move out the next day. . . . I got home at one o'clock [A.M.] all right and found all well. As I drove across the Public Square in Far West. . . . I saw Apostle David Patton [sic] on his horse rallying his men to go out to defend the exposed Saints.[24]

David W. Patten, a member of the Council of the Twelve Apostles and a Danite leader who was called "Captain Fear Not" by the Mormons, had been dispatched to rescue three Mormon prisoners who had been taken illegally by Missouri Militia from their home in Caldwell County. Just before dawn on 25 October, Patten located the militia camp on Crooked River and the Mormons attacked with guns and corn knives. Isaac Allred was able

---

[23]Taylor, "Record of Pleasant Green Taylor."
[24]Reddick Allred, op. cit., 5:301.

to hear the gunfire though it was five miles distant.[25] The Mormons won the battle and the prisoners were rescued, but Captain Patten was mortally wounded.

The Saints not only lost a brave and popular leader in the death of Patten, but the exaggerated reports of the "massacre," in which only one militia member had been killed, brought the power of the state government to bear on the Mormons. Governor Lilburn Boggs, who had been unresponsive to any of the numerous Mormon pleas for protection from Gentile mobs, suddenly took aggressive action when the Mormons no longer appeared to be on the defensive.

Rumors circulated that fourteen thousand Mormons were armed and might have allies among the Indians beyond the Platte. On 27 October, the same day that David Patten was laid to rest at Far West, Governor Boggs responded to the rumors and reports of the "massacre" at Crooked River by issuing his infamous "extermination order" to General John B. Clark, saying:

> I have received ... information of the most appalling character, which changes the whole face of things, and places the Mormons in the attitude of open and avowed defiance of the laws, and of having made open war upon the people of this state. Your orders are, therefore, to hasten your operations. ... The Mormons must be treated as enemies and must be exterminated or driven from the state, if necessary for the public peace—their outrages are beyond all description.[26]

Three days later, on 30 October, a force of two hundred militiamen from Livingston County, under the command of Colonel William O. Jennings, did their best to carry out the governor's order. Haun's Mill was a small settlement about sixteen miles due east of Far West on the north bank of Shoal Creek. Jacob Haun built the mill between 1835 and 1836 after moving there from Green Bay, Wisconsin, and by 1838 about thirty families of Saints had settled there. Joseph Smith repeatedly warned the Haun's Mill Saints to move into Far West for safety, but they

---

[25]Ibid.
[26]Letter from Lilburn Boggs to General Clark, 27 October 1838, in *Document containing the Correspondence in relation to Mormon disturbances*, 61.

chose to remain at the village, trusting in the Lord and in a recently signed treaty with militia leaders to protect them.

The Mormons at Haun's Mill were enjoying a beautiful autumn afternoon, with a gentle breeze rustling through the corn and stirring the colored leaves of the trees, when suddenly, at about four o'clock, the Livingston militia burst out of the timber to the north of the mill. A few seconds later the air was filled with screams intermingled with gunshots as the troops rode in and the Mormons scattered. Though men and women fled to a blacksmith shop or into the woods, the mob fired mercilessly. After every male in the settlement had been killed, wounded, or driven into the woods, the place was thoroughly looted. Ten-year-old Sardius Smith was found hiding in the blacksmith shop and was killed by a militiaman, who justified his act by saying: "Nits will make lice, and if he had lived he would have become a Mormon."[27] Seventeen Mormons, including two children and an old man who was hacked to death, were murdered and eleven were severely wounded.

At the same time the Haun's Mill massacre was taking place, about three thousand militiamen—"the whole army," in the eyes of William Moore Allred—under the command of General Samuel Lucas, encamped on Goose Creek, about a mile from Far West, in preparation of storming the town the next morning. Allred was with a company of about fifty men on a scouting party when they encountered the army. The troops came so close that he expected to be fired upon, but the troops returned to their camp.[28]

Allred was on guard duty the next morning and watched Charles Rich, carrying a white flag, and a small company of Mormons ride out of Far West to meet with army officers. After a short meeting, Rich turned and was walking away when Captain Bogart of the militia shot at him.[29] Although no one was injured, the Mormons perceived this as the kind of treatment they could expect from the Missouri troops.

[27]Roberts., op. cit., 1:482.   [28]William Allred, op. cit.   [29]Ibid.

Joseph Smith heard late at night of the massacre at Haun's Mill and was receiving reports from his scouts that the state militia outnumbered his own by at least five to one, and was growing hourly in strength. He could visualize another massacre of his people and, according to George Hinkle, Smith secretly sent emissaries to try to arrange for a conference with General Lucas.[30] Whether or not they were actually sent by Smith, Colonel Hinkle and John Corrill did meet with General Lucas the next morning and agreed to the following terms of surrender: The Mormon leaders were to surrender for trial and punishment; Mormon property was to be confiscated to pay for damages; the balance of the Saints were to leave the state; and they were to give up their arms.

Colonel Hinkle told Joseph Smith, Lyman Wight, Parley P. Pratt, and George W. Robinson that militia officers wanted to talk to them. They consented but were shocked and surprised when Hinkle turned them over to General Lucas as prisoners. Hyrum Smith and Amasa Lyman were taken prisoner the next day. Hinkle claimed that he considered this the only way to end the war, but to the Mormons it was treachery and they considered him a traitor.

The capture of the Mormon leaders set off the mob in wild celebration. "I shall never forget the night that Joseph and Hyrum went into the camp of the mob," wrote William Moore Allred, "such yelling and screaming and swearing. I have never heard such vile profanities."[31] Zadoc Judd, a Canadian convert who was among the refugees from DeWitt camping in the streets of Far West, recalled that the yell of the mob "far exceeded any human noise that ever I heard, both for loudness and terror. It was plainly heard all over the town of Far West and was continued loud and long, ferocious, for nearly one half hour."[32]

A court-martial quickly was held and the prisoners were sentenced to be shot the following morning. General Lucas ordered General Doniphan to carry out the order, but Doniphan was incensed with the injustice of the affair and replied:

---

[30]Letter of George M. Hinkle to W. W. Phelps, 14 August 1844, as quoted in Pearl Wilcox, *The Latter Day Saints on the Missouri Frontier*, 346–349.
[31]Ibid.   [32]Judd, op. cit.

It is cold-blooded murder. I will not obey your order. My brigade shall march for Liberty tomorrow morning at eight o'clock and if you execute those men, I will hold you responsible before an earthly tribunal, so help me God.[33]

General Lucas, fearing the consequences should Doniphan carry out his threat, neither executed the prisoners nor called Doniphan to account for insubordination.

With their leaders in custody, the Mormon men in Far West were required to assemble and to hand over their weapons to the militia. They were then advised "not to gather together, and not organize with bishops and presidents any more but live in a scattered condition like the other people."[34] One by one the men came forward, surrendered their weapons, and signed a treaty stipulating that their property should be sold to defray the expense of war. It was only after being told that they had until the next spring to leave the state that they were permitted to return to their homes.

The homes to which they returned, however, were in many cases not what they had left, with crops destroyed and household items burned. William Taylor and his family found that "about seven thousand of this mob had camped at or near this place, turning their horses into the cornfield."[35] Taylor's neighbor Isaac Allred had only one team of horses that had not been killed. Feather beds were torn to pieces and food had been stolen.[36] Many whose homes had been destroyed, such as the Ira Judd family of DeWitt, were forced to seek shelter elsewhere:

My uncle went with Allen Taylor who lived about eight miles from Far West. He had previously raised a good crop of corn, which he generously shared with my uncle. His house was small—a one room log cabin, but we were welcome and were quite comfortable considering what we had been.[37]

A few dozen men who feared retribution from the militia, particularly those who had taken part in the Battle of Crooked

---

[33]*History of the Church*, 3:190–191.   [34]William Allred, op. cit.

[35]Taylor, op. cit.   [36]William Allred, op. cit.

[37]Judd, op. cit. For many years Zadoc lived with his uncle, Ira Judd, rather than with his own family.

River, did not return home at all, but rather fled into Iowa and Illinois. William Moore Allred, realizing that "the mob were still hunting for those that had taken an active part in the campaign," left the area to spend "a month or two" with his brother John near Quincy, Illinois, "until the excitement died away."[38] Others, such as Captain William Allred, Martin C. Allred (son of James), and Andrew Whitlock (son-in-law of James Allred) were arrested and taken to Richmond, along with Joseph Smith and the other previously captured leaders, to stand trial before Judge Austin King. After two weeks' imprisonment, Judge King, who ruled that nothing could be proven against them, discharged William and Martin Allred and Andrew Whitlock, along with twenty others. Four days later, on 28 November, the remaining prisoners at Richmond were released or given bail, with the exception of Joseph and Hyrum Smith, Sidney Rigdon, Lyman Wight, Caleb Baldwin, and Alexander McRae, who were sent to jail in Liberty, Clay County, to stand trial for treason and murder.[39]

With Joseph Smith and his counselors in jail, the mantle of leadership fell upon Brigham Young as the senior member of the Council of the Twelve Apostles. Young had maintained a low profile during the autumn conflicts, but as the new leader he had become the "most wanted" Mormon and was forced to maintain a disguise in order to escape arrest. Meanwhile, the Mormons in Caldwell and Daviess counties were suffering grievously at the hands of their enemies. In December they appealed to the General Assembly to rescind the expulsion order of the governor, to restore their lands, and to appropriate funds to pay for the damages they had sustained, but by late January 1839, it became apparent to Mormon leaders that the Missouri legislature would not act in their behalf.

---

[38]William Allred, op. cit.

[39]*History of the Church*, 3:209, 211–212. Of the fifty-three who were arrested, all but four—Captain William Allred, Andrew Whitlock, Daniel Garn, and Sidney Turner—were affiliated with the Danites to some degree, according to sworn testimony (some of which, such as in the case of Sampson Avard, was less than truthful). According to the testimony of both George Hinkle and Sampson Avard, Martin C. Allred and William Moore Allred were Danites. See D. Michael Quinn, *The Mormon Hierarchy: Origins of Power*, 480–485.

With the last flicker of hope gone, the harassed and defenseless Mormons began to move eastward in the dead of winter. Allen Taylor's wife, Sarah Lovisa, had just given birth to a son, William Riley Taylor, on 5 February, but even the burden of a newborn child could not delay the exodus. Many of the Saints were poor or destitute, and more than two hundred men, including William Taylor and his eldest son John, signed a covenant at the request of Brigham Young to "assist one another, to the utmost of our abilities," in removing from Missouri.[40] Those with land to sell found they could get but a fraction of its worth or, as in the case of William Taylor, virtually nothing at all.

The Taylors left their home on 8 February 1839, receiving only a neck yoke worth about $2.50 in compensation for their land, and began yet another journey in search of their Zion. Along the way, an elderly couple named Singleton lost their only horse, and William Taylor lived up to the covenant which he had signed by taking one of his best horses and hitching it to the old man's wagon, telling him simply to "go in peace." Weather conditions were often "very bad, having snow, rain, mud, etc. to contend with."

The harsh conditions took their final toll on William Taylor, who was weakened by exposure to the elements and later contracted typhoid. A short time before his death he gathered his fourteen children to his bedside and "counseled them to rally around the priesthood and the main body of the Church," and secured a promise from his unmarried children that they would not marry outside of the church.[41] And then, on 9 September 1839, along the road between Warsaw and Lima, Illinois, William Taylor died and was buried on the land of Colonel Levi Williams, who threatened to dig up Taylor's body and give it to the hogs. To protect her husband's grave, Elizabeth Patrick Taylor called upon her boys to gather pools of lye and make a fence around it.[42] William Taylor had not found his Zion, but at least, at long last, he could rest in peace.

---

[40]*History of the Church*, 3:251–254. William and Martin C. Allred were also signatories. Only a partial list of those who subscribed to the covenant was preserved.
[41]Taylor, op. cit.   [42]Ibid.

Chapter V

KINGDOM ON
THE MISSISSIPPI

HAVING BEEN DRIVEN from their gathering places in Missouri—first Jackson County and then Far West—the wandering Saints must have wondered if there really was safety in numbers. Though they questioned the wisdom of another mass gathering, the immediate focus was on finding a place of refuge. Backtracking to the east seemed to be the only option, for to the west was Indian country, which was not open for settlement, to the north was Iowa with plenty of land but little timber, and going south meant traveling through hostile communities in Clay and Jackson counties.

Thus in the winter of 1839 the Saints went eastward, traveling two main routes that converged near Palmyra, just a few miles north of the former Taylor and Allred settlements at Salt River. From there most headed to Marion City on the Mississippi River to be ferried across to Quincy, Illinois.

The citizens of Quincy treated the Mormons, most of whom were too exhausted and impoverished to travel any further, not only with sympathy but also with respect. The town's Democratic Association was particularly instrumental in assisting the homeless exiles, organizing a reception committee that helped provide food, housing, and temporary employment. Furthermore, the citizens adopted resolutions that condemned the Missouri mobs and government officials. Soon, Governor Thomas

Carlin, himself a citizen of Quincy, and others were encouraging the Saints to locate in Illinois.

In the following weeks thousands of Saints arrived at the western bank of the Mississippi across from Quincy, but only about twelve families could cross each day since just one ferry-boat was in operation.[1] The crossing was complicated by a spring thaw that filled the river with ice floes, but when a cold spell set in, the river froze over and scores of families hurried to cross the ice. Before long there were nearly three times as many refugees as residents of Quincy, and many of the destitute Saints were forced to endure a meager existence, supporting each other as much as possible since the overwhelmed citizens of Quincy could no longer provide care for all. Typical was the experience of Drusilla Hendricks, whose husband, James, was incapacitated by a wound he suffered in the Battle of Crooked River. Within two weeks of their arrival in Quincy they were on the threshold of starvation, as Drusilla recorded:

> I went to work and washed everything and cleaned the house thoroughly as I said to myself, "If I die I will die clean." Along in the afternoon Brother Rubin [Reuben] Allred came. He lived fifteen miles away. He went to the bed where my husband lay and asked him if we had any prospects for bread at all and received the answer that we had none. He asked me for a sack and then went to his wagon and brought in a sack of meal and he also made me a present of a washboard saying, "You had to leave everything and I felt you were out of bread so I came by the mill to get my grinding done before I came here and it made me late." I thanked him and he started home.[2]

Even as the Saints were struggling to survive at Quincy, Joseph Smith and a few others, including his brother Hyrum, were still imprisoned at Liberty. While there, the Prophet wrote a letter to the Saints instructing them to document the losses that they sustained in Missouri:

---

[1]Letter from Elizabeth Haven to Elizabeth Howe Bullard, 24 February, 1839, in Ora H. Barlow, *The Israel Barlow Story and Mormon Mores*, 143.

[2]*Our Pioneer Heritage*, 20:260. Reuben Allred was a son of Isaac Allred's brother James.

And again, we would suggest for your consideration the propriety of all the saints gathering up a knowledge of all the facts, and sufferings and abuses put upon them by the people of this State; and also of all the property and amount of damages that they have sustained, both of character and personal injuries, as well as real property.[3]

Spirits were raised considerably when Smith and his compatriots were allowed to escape and arrived at Quincy on 22 April 1839. Many of the Saints already had followed the counsel of the Prophet to record their Missouri experiences and grievances and in May began the process of filing official statements with local civil authorities. On 8 May, Allen Taylor appeared before Carlo M. Woods, clerk of the circuit court for Adams County, and filed the following claim:

State of Mo Dr [debtor?] To Allen Taylor May 8th 1839

Loss Sustaned in Caldwell Co
Expence of moveing to the State,	$50.00
Loss on land by Sale & improvements,	800.00
Loss on Crops & time,	100.00
Expence of moveing out of the State,	500.00
	$1,450.00

I hereby Certify the above account to be just and true according to the best of my Knowledge

Allen Taylor[4]

Many of the affidavits were similar in form and content to Taylor's. It is obvious that he, like other Mormons who were expelled from Missouri by proclamation of the governor, felt justified in asking that he be compensated for having moved to the state in the first place. Though Isaac Allred did not make that particular claim, the overall form and substance of his affidavit, which was filed on 18 May, resembled that of his son-in-law, Taylor:

---

[3]*D&C* 123:1–2.
[4]Clark V. Johnson, ed., *Mormon Redress Petitions; Documents of the 1833–1838 Missouri Conflict*, 361–362.

Quincy Ill May 1839
State of Missouri to Isaac Allred Sen Dr.

to the nesesity of removing from Clay to Caldwell Co in consequence of the non protection of Law in said state During 1836
$600.00
to being deprived of my citisonship in said state by the non protection of Law and the Govners Exterminating order of 1838
1,000.00
to Loss on land   1,000.00
to Loss on Grain and Cost of removing from said State   200.00
to Exsposur of myself & family's heath   500.00
$3,800.00 $3,300.00

I certify the above acount to Be Just Petitions, p. and true a cord-
ing to the Best of my Knowledg

Isac Alred[5]

William Taylor's widow, Elizabeth, also eventually filed a
claim which indicated that while they sold their land in Clay
County, though at a loss, they received essentially nothing for
their land in Caldwell County:

Hancock County Illenois January 6th 1840

A Bill of Damages a gainst the State of Missouri by Elizabeth
Taylor in Consequence of the Order of the Govenor to Expell from
the State forthwith from the State all people Comonley Called
Mormons
for the Loss of property in Clay County on the Sale of Land
$100[0] One thousand Dollars
for the Loss of Land in Caldwell County and Other Property
One thousand Dollars
for Mooveing from the State of Missouri and Sufferages Five
hundred Dollars

Elizabeth Taylor[6]

These petitions were among the 491 that Joseph Smith later
took to Washington, D.C., to present before Congress in an effort
to gain redress for their losses in Missouri. Smith eventually
gained an audience with President Martin Van Buren, who

[5]Ibid., 126.   [6]Ibid., 362.

ELIZABETH PATRICK TAYLOR
Courtesy of Shari Franke

seemed sympathetic but declined to help, saying, "Gentlemen, your cause is just, but I can do nothing for you."[7] Efforts to persuade Congress to grant redress also were rebuffed. At the same time the embarrassed Missouri congressional delegation began building its own defense, based on transcripts of a hearing held in Richmond, Missouri, where numerous anti-Mormons and ex-Mormons testified. Under the circumstances, it was clearly time to try to put Missouri in the past and to move on.

As a matter of fact, Joseph Smith had been preparing to move on even while he was imprisoned at Liberty. Whereas some church leaders questioned the wisdom of gathering en masse, Smith was adamant that the Saints must remain together as a group. While at Liberty, he received several letters from Isaac Galland, a land speculator who offered to sell twenty thousand acres at two dollars an acre. In March 1839, the Prophet wrote from jail to Bishop Edward Partridge in Quincy:

---

[7]*History of the Church*, 4:80.

It still seems to bear heavily on our minds that the Church would do
well to secure to themselves the contract of the land which is proposed to them by Mr. Isaac Galland, and to cultivate the friendly
feelings of that gentlemen, inasmuch as he shall prove himself to be
a man of honor and a friend to humanity.[8]

Galland proposed to sell land on both sides of the Mississippi:
in Hancock County, Illinois, on the east, and in the Half-Breed
Tract directly across the river in Iowa. The latter was a tract originally set aside by Congress as a refuge for the offspring of frontiersmen and Indians, but the land had been sold and resold to
the point that true ownership of the land was difficult to ascertain. Nevertheless, the terms offered by Galland—nothing down
and twenty years to pay, with properties that the Saints abandoned in Missouri as partial payment—were too attractive not to
accept.

The first purchase of about 170 acres of land, in the neighborhood of Commerce, about fifty miles north of Quincy, took
place on 30 April 1839, and soon the Saints were flocking to their
new gathering place. Isaac Allred rented, subject to sale, two
parcels of land in Commerce in 1839. It is likely that Allen Taylor, as well as his mother Elizabeth and her family, also moved to
Commerce in 1839.[9] Eventually all who had lost their property at
Far West, which included the Allreds and the Taylors, were
given free lots in the city.

The site of Commerce (later renamed Nauvoo by the Saints),
on a large bend of the Mississippi River at the head of the Des
Moines rapids, was among the most beautiful in that region. The
beauty of the area, however, could not disguise the fact that it was
swampland, full of mosquitoes and with water unfit for human
consumption. An early settler, Jesse Crosby, referred to the area
as "sickly," and later recorded that "Our enemies had been known
to say that we would die all of us if we attempted to settle
there."[10] Joseph Smith was well aware of these problems:

---

[8]*History of the Church*, 3:298.

[9]Land records in the Library of the Historical Department of the Church, Salt Lake City.
Isaac Allred rented both Lot 2, Block 50 from Joseph Smith, and Lot 1, Block 60 in 1839.

[10]Jesse W. Crosby, "History and Biography of Jesse W. Crosby," 7.

. . . the place was literally a wilderness. The land was mostly covered with trees and bushes, and much of it so wet that it was with the utmost difficulty a footman could get through, and totally impossible for teams. Commerce was so unhealthful, very few could live there; but believing that it might become a healthful place by the blessing of heaven to the Saints, and no more eligible place presenting itself, I considered it wisdom to make an attempt to build up a city.[11]

The swamps were a breeding ground for the *Anopheles* mosquito, a carrier of malaria (known as ague to the early settlers), and scores of Saints became ill and many died from the disease. Other communicable diseases, notably dysentery, typhoid, meningitis, scarlet fever, and diphtheria, were rampant. When Benjamin Johnson arrived in Nauvoo in the summer of 1839, he reported:

Nearly every one was sick. . . . Nearly all were down with typhoid or malarial fever which it almost seemed would sweep the place with death, for among all the families of the saints it was rare to find one who was able to wait upon and care for another.[12]

The severity of disease in Nauvoo forced the Saints to call upon the healing power of the priesthood. Eventually Joseph Smith also became very ill, but after several days he was prompted to arise and extend help to others. The Prophet also sent members of the Council of the Twelve Apostles to outlying areas to heal the sick. Others also engaged in efforts to heal, frequently without success, prompting Smith to rebuke those who continued to lay hands on the sick without the power to heal them, saying: "It is time that such things ended. Let the Elders either obtain the power of God to heal the sick or let them cease to minister the forms without the power."[13]

The success of the Prophet in healing the sick did not go unnoticed by others, and a non-member who had heard of the miracles asked Smith to come and administer to his dying twin babies. Joseph said that he could not go, but he gave Wilford Woodruff a red silk handkerchief and told him to administer to them, promising that when he wiped their faces with it they

[11]*History of the Church*, 3:375.   [12]Benjamin Johnson, *My Life's Review*, 60.
[13]Pratt, *Autobiography*, 254.

would be healed.[14] It is not known why Smith specifically used a red silk handkerchief for vicarious healing, but Woodruff's experience was by no means unique. As Heber C. Kimball recalled, "I have known Joseph, hundreds of times, [to] send his handkerchief to the sick, and they have been healed."[15] Among other similar accounts was that of Pleasant Green Taylor:

> On one occasion my sister was very sick. My mother sent me to see if the Prophet would come home and administer to her, but not having the time, he sent a red silk handkerchief with his blessing and promised that she should get well. The promise was fulfilled, for she was healed immediately.[16]

Perhaps the greatest ally in fighting malaria that first year was the cold winter weather that sent the insects into dormancy, but the hot summer weather was accompanied by the return of disease-bearing mosquitoes. The accompanying widespread sickness in the city left little room for celebration, and so the Fourth of July in 1840 was observed quietly in Nauvoo. Also, the memory of the rejection of the redress petitions in Washington was still too fresh to allow for much patriotism among the Saints. Three days after the quiet Fourth, an event occurred which was a portent of yet more trouble for the beleaguered Saints.

For several months crime had been rampant along the banks of the Mississippi, with some of the theft on the Missouri side by Mormon refugees who justified their actions by considering it to be the only method available to recoup some of their losses in that state. A rumor circulated that the leaders of the church did not consider robbing the Gentiles of Missouri to be a sin as long as it did not exceed the losses of the Saints in that state, and the Missourians began to blame every occurrence of theft on the Mormons.[17]

On 7 July, as James Allred and Noah Rogers drove a wagon to the riverbank near Nauvoo in search of firewood, they were

---

[14]Wilford Woodruff, *Leaves from My Journal*, 65.
[15]*Journal of Discourses*, 4:294.   [16]Taylor, "Record."
[17]The rumor persisted until Hyrum Smith, on 26 November 1841, felt compelled to issue an official denial; see *History of the Church*, 4:461-61.

accosted by an armed party of Missourians who took them to a thicket near the river where there was a cache of stolen goods. Two other Mormons, Benjamin Boyce and Alanson Brown, were already in custody, and the four captives were taken across the river to Tully where they were charged with theft. Allred was stripped of his clothing and tied to a tree where he was threatened repeatedly for most of the night.

Despite the threats, Allred refused to confess and was released. Rogers and Boyce did confess, but only after being beaten. Brown confessed in order to avoid a beating and escaped.[18] Though there was no evidence to convict any of the four kidnapped Mormons, suspicion lingered that Alanson Brown may have been involved in the thefts, and Governor Carlin of Illinois, who had previously supported the Saints and who had made a strong protest to Governor Boggs of Missouri over the kidnapping, was left sorely disappointed.

However, this did not prevent Governor Carlin, or any Illinois politician, from seeking the support of the Saints. At the time, Illinois was about equally divided between the two major political parties, the Whigs and the Democrats. Though Nauvoo was not yet an incorporated city, it was growing rapidly, and the power of the Mormon vote became increasingly evident to political leaders. Because of this, the Mormon leaders were able to obtain support of both parties in passage of a very liberal charter by the Illinois State Legislature, which made Nauvoo the sixth city in the state with an official charter.[19]

The Nauvoo Charter had an unusual feature empowering the municipal court to grant writs of habeas corpus, which were used later to free arrested persons, in particular Joseph Smith, regardless of the jurisdiction under which they were arrested. It also provided that the boundaries of Nauvoo, generous to begin with, could be easily enlarged. But the crowning provision of the charter gave the city its own militia, the Nauvoo Legion.

---

[18] *Times and Seasons*, 1:141–42.
[19] The others were: Chicago, Alton, Galena, Springfield, and Quincy.

The Legion was created by the city council on 3 February 1841. Though most local militias in the state were organized at the county level, the Nauvoo Legion was a city militia controlled directly by the mayor. Joseph Smith was the Legion's top officer, holding the rank of lieutenant general, the highest rank held by a military officer in the United States since George Washington. After Illinois officials approved his election, others discovered what Smith might already have known—namely that only a court-martial of his equals could remove him, and he had no equals in military rank in the entire country.

The Legion was divided into two cohorts, or brigades, on 1 May. Selected as second lieutenant to serve under Colonel Charles C. Rich in the First Regiment of the Second Cohort was Allen Taylor, with his brother-in-law William M. Allred as first lieutenant. Though another brother-in-law, Isaac Allred Jr., became an officer two years later, easily the most prominent member of Allen Taylor's extended family in the Nauvoo Legion was Hosea Stout.

In 1833, Stout was working in the lumber business in Putnam County, Illinois, when he encountered Charles Rich, who had come to proselytize in the area. Following several more encounters with prominent Mormons in the next few years, he was baptized in 1838 and moved to Far West. Stout became a member of the Danite Band and fought under Rich, along with William M. Allred, at the Battle of Crooked River.

After the Mormons at Far West surrendered, twenty-eight of their Danite warriors who had fought at Crooked River, including Stout and Rich, fled north into Iowa. Samantha Stout, Hosea's wife, was so weakened by malnutrition and exposure in her wanderings that she died in November 1839 and was buried in Lee County, Iowa. Stout moved onward to Nauvoo, where on 8 March 1840, he was appointed clerk of the High Council, the policy-making body of the church.[20] On 29 November 1840, exactly one year after the death of his wife, he married Allen Taylor's sister Louisa. Like his brother-in-law Taylor, Stout was

---

[20]James Allred was also a member of the High Council.

made a second lieutenant in the Second Cohort of the Nauvoo Legion and later was promoted to the rank of colonel.

In addition to creating the Nauvoo Legion, the city council responded to problems faced by all towns by appointing special officers and enacting laws. Two of the first laws passed guaranteed the rights of peaceful assembly and freedom of conscience to all religions. A forty-member police force under Captain Hosea Stout enforced the laws and labored the best they could to prevent crime. To help unemployed immigrants, the city also sponsored a public works program to build stores, hotels, homes, and eventually a temple.

There was no more important project in Nauvoo than building the Temple, the "House of the Lord." After all, the construction of a temple was one of the primary reasons for gathering. A revelation in 1833 stated: "I gave unto you a commandment, that you should build an [*sic*] house, in the which house I design to endow whom I have chosen with power from on high."[21] Oliver Cowdery stated the same sentiment more forcefully a year later:

> We want you to understand that the Lord has not promised to endow his servants from on high[,] only on the condition that they build him a house; and if the house is not built the Elders will not be endowed with power, and if they are not they can never go to the nations with the everlasting gospel.[22]

A temple was constructed in Kirtland and dedicated on 27 March 1836, but it was abandoned when the Saints left the city to go to Far West in 1838. Three more temples were planned in Missouri—at Independence, Far West, and Adam-ondi-Ahman—but persecution and violence had prevented their construction. A temple in Nauvoo was a necessity, and Joseph Smith stated publicly in July 1840: "Now brethren I obligate myself to build as great a temple as ever Solomon did, if the church will back me up."[23]

There was, of course, no doubt that the church would back

---

[21]*D&C* 95:8.

[22]Oliver Cowdery, Kirtland, Ohio to John F. Boynton, 6 May 1834, in Oliver Cowdery Letterbook.

[23]Joseph Smith sermon, 19 July 1840, recorded by Martha Jane Knowlton, as recorded in *Brigham Young University Studies* 19:394.

him in this important project. To provide funds to build a temple, a revelation was given at Far West in July 1838 that instructed members to tithe themselves, contributing their "surplus property" to the church at first, and afterwards one-tenth of their annual increase.[24] Construction on the Nauvoo Temple began in April 1841 and continued for the next five years. William M. Allred started his ox team with the first load of stone for the Temple, though Lorenzo Brown, with his swifter team of horses, delivered the first stones to the temple site.[25] Allred also stated that he "worked more or less on the Temple until it was finished," as did other members of the Allred and Taylor families, which was typical since they were expected to tithe their labor as well as their income, working one day in ten for the church, with much of this tithing labor directed towards the completion of the Temple.

As important to Joseph Smith as the construction of the Temple was the construction of the Nauvoo House, intended to be a permanent hotel wherein the Prophet and his family would have perpetual quarters and where "the weary traveler may find health and safety while he shall contemplate the word of the Lord."[26] In promoting and defending the project Smith stated: "The building of the Nauvoo House is just as sacred in my view as the Temple. I want the Nauvoo House built. It *must* be built. Our salvation depends upon it."[27]

Rather than using tithing proceeds to finance its construction, as was the case with the Temple, Joseph sold stock at fifty dollars a share to men in good church standing, making it a private profit-making venture, invested with the public interest but backed also by the church and the power of revelation. Not only was constant encouragement given from the pulpit for members to work on the hotel, but some, such as William Allred (the brother of Isaac Sr.), were actually directed by revelation to assist the project. Allred, who was bishop of the stake at Pleasant Vale, and Henry Miller asked Joseph Smith in March 1841 "to inquire

[24]*D&C* 119:1–4.
[26]*D&C* 124:23.
[25]William Allred, op. cit.
[27]*History of the Church*, 5:287

of the Lord His will concerning them." Smith recorded the following:

> I inquired of the Lord concerning the foregoing question, and received the following answer—Let my servants, William Allred and Henry W. Miller, have an agency for the selling of the stock for the Nauvoo House, and assist my servants Lyman Wight, Peter Haws, George Miller, and John Snider, in building said house; and let my servants William Allred and Henry W. Miller take stock in the house, that the poor of my people may have employment, and that accommodations may be made for the strangers who shall come to visit this place, and for this purpose let them devote all their properties, saith the Lord.[28]

Unfortunately, William Allred died in July, just four months after the revelation was given, and played little role in the construction of the Nauvoo House. Even with the firm and assertive support of Joseph Smith, the project progressed slowly due to competition for capital, labor, and materials not only from its great sister project, the Temple, but also with other private ventures, particularly house-building, in the rapidly expanding city.

And the growth of Nauvoo was truly astounding. Missionary success, particularly in the British Isles, along with constant encouragement for the new converts to emigrate, brought a steady stream of new residents to the city. The area encompassed by the original city plat was filled within a few months and various large landholders subdivided their property and induced the Nauvoo City Council to incorporate numerous additions into the city. The first and largest such addition was that of Ethan Kimball, in October 1839, and it was to the Kimball Addition that Isaac Allred moved in 1840, where he eventually owned and lived on part of lot 50, along the Carthage Road, as did his son-in-law, Allen Taylor.[29]

By late 1842, Mormons were living in about a dozen settlements on both sides of the Mississippi River near the Des Moines Rapids. A visitor to Nauvoo at this time wrote:

> The incorporated limits of Nauvoo contains, it is said, about seven

---

[28]*History of the Church,* 4:311. [29]Nauvoo Land Records, HDC.

thousand persons; the buildings are generally small and much scattered. The Temple and Nauvoo House, now building, will probably,
in beauty of design, extent and durability, excel any public building
in the state, and will both be enclosed before winter.

From all I saw and heard, I am led to believe that, before many
years, the city of Nauvoo will be the largest and most beautiful city
of the west, provided the Mormons are unmolested in the peaceable
enjoyment of their rights and privileges, and why they should be
troubled while acting as good citizens, I cannot imagine; and I hope
and trust that the people of Illinois have no disposition to disturb
unoffending people who have no disposition but to live peaceably
under the laws of the country, and to worship God under their own
vine and fig tree.[30]

Nauvoo did continue its phenomenal growth, and before long
it was, along with Chicago, one of the two largest cities in Illinois. By many accounts, though not all, it was becoming a beautiful city, particularly as wood-frame and brick houses replaced
frontier log cabins, and the Saints planted fruit and shade trees,
vines and bushes on their large lots. Life was exhilarating as converts continued to arrive in companies and the economy continued to grow. Though there were subtle signs of a gathering storm
in Nauvoo, the Saints had reason to believe that they had finally
found their Zion.

---

[30]*History of the Church*, 4:566.

Chapter VI

ASSASSINATION AT CARTHAGE

KASKASKIA, ILLINOIS, was a city located about two hundred miles downstream from Nauvoo, at the confluence of the Mississippi and Kaskaskia rivers. Originally settled by French traders in 1703 and named after the Indian tribe of the same name, Kaskaskia was first ceded to the British by the Treaty of Paris in 1763 and then was captured by U.S. troops during the American Revolution in 1778. At the time that John D. Lee was born in Kaskaskia in 1812, the city was the capital of the Illinois Territory; in 1818 it became the first capital of the newly-created state of Illinois. It remained a busy, important city for a number of years, retaining much of its French character, built around the church and the central square, but gradually declined in importance and was eventually inundated and totally destroyed by the shifting waters of the Mississippi.

Ralph Lee, John D. Lee's father, was a member of the Lee family of Virginia and a second cousin of General Robert E. Lee. He was a master workman who contracted and put up buildings and erected a fine home for himself. However, when the health of his wife Elizabeth failed, Ralph Lee began to drink to excess; when Elizabeth died in 1815 and Ralph was unable to care for his children, three-year-old John D. Lee, evidently supported by the money from his mother's estate, was put into the hands of a Negro nurse who spoke only French. After four years, John

JOHN D. LEE
Photograph taken December 26, 1857, three months after the massacre at Mountain Meadows. *Courtesy of Utah State Historical Society.*

Doyle, Lee's maternal grandfather died, and his uncle, John Conner, was put in charge of the estate. Lee then became a member of this household, a French-speaking child in an English-speaking home, where he remained, though by his account unhappy most of the time, until he reached the age of sixteen and set out on his own.

Though christened a Catholic, John D. Lee was fascinated with other religions and invited people of several faiths to preach in his home. In 1837 a young man named King passed through the area on his way to join the Mormons in Missouri when he met Lee, who invited him to stay at his home until spring arrived. Lee was attracted to the message offered by King and began to study the doctrines with "a prayerful heart."

In the meantime, a neighbor and friend, Levi Stewart, who had gone to Far West to investigate Mormonism at its gathering place, had been converted and returned with a copy of the *Book of Mormon*. John D. Lee had many conversations in the next few

months regarding the new religion but was not converted immediately. Later that year his second child, Elizabeth Adaline, died
of scarlet fever and Lee began to consider Mormonism more
intently:

> The night she lay a corpse I finished reading the *Book of Mormon*. I
> never closed my eyes in sleep from the time I commenced until I fin-
> ished the book. I read it after asking God to give me knowledge to
> know if it was genuine and of Divine authority. By careful examina-
> tion I found that it was in strict accord with the Bible and the gospel
> therein contained.[1]

His conversion thus assured, Lee determined to leave Illinois
and go to join the Saints at Far West where he and his wife were
baptized in June 1838, just a short time before hostilities broke
out that led to the Saints' expulsion from Missouri. After returning to their former home in Vandalia, Illinois, Lee left his wife
and family and, with Levi Stewart, departed on a short mission
to preach the gospel in Tennessee, where he baptized twenty-
seven persons.

During the next four years, Lee served three short missions,
including one to Kaskaskia, the place of his birth. Returning
home in October 1842, he spent November and December with
his family, but by mid-January 1843 he departed on yet another
mission, this time back to the branch of the church he had
helped establish in the vicinity of Murfreesboro, Tennessee.

Shortly after his arrival, Lee held a meeting that was attended
by few due to inclement weather. Among those who did attend
were John H. Redd and his brother-in-law John Holt, who had
traveled by horseback seventeen miles in the heavy rain. Holt's
son William had joined the Mormon Church the previous year,
which might explain the willingness of Redd and Holt to travel
so far in foul weather, though both men undoubtedly had
endured many harsh conditions in their careers.

John Holt was a seaman from North Carolina who had fought
in defense of Wilmington and Beaufort in the War of 1812. John

---

[1]John D. Lee, *Mormonism Unveiled, or The Life and Confessions of the Late Mormon Bishop,
John D. Lee*, 52.

H. Redd became acquainted with Holt around that time and introduced him to his sister Mary; shortly after the couple was married in 1814, Holt received a discharge from the navy, but Redd was just beginning his career, in which he became a sea captain. The title Captain stayed with him even after he gave up his career and moved inland to Tennessee with his wife Elizabeth to join John and Mary Holt at Murfreesboro.

Redd and Holt cautioned Lee not to preach in public, but he ignored the advice. Fearing for Lee's safety, Redd formed a party of ten men to escort and protect him. Lee preached publicly and soon met with success:

> After the fourth sermon I commenced to baptize members. The first one that I baptized at that place was parson John Holt, of the Christian faith. Then I baptized seven of the members of his church; then Captain Redd and his family. The unexpected success created great excitement in that section of country.[2]

The excitement described by Lee was manifested in antagonism and intimidation. A mob gathered and threatened to tar and feather him if he continued preaching. To circumvent the threat, John H. Redd invited Lee to preach at his home and let it be known that he would not tolerate any misbehavior:

> Captain J. H. Redd ... told the people that he did not want any person to come into his yard unless they came intending to behave; that if there was any violence used there some one would get hurt. I preached at his house that afternoon. A fearful storm raged during most of the time, but this was fortunate, for it kept the mob away. While I was preaching a drunken wag interrupted me and called me a d—d liar. Captain Redd was sitting near me with two large pistols, which he called his peace-makers. This insult was not more than out of the fellow's mouth when Captain Redd caught him by the neck and rushed him out of the house into the rain. The coward begged hard for himself, but he was forced to go out and sit under a porch during the rest of the sermon. Captain Redd was a kind-hearted, generous man, but would not stand abuse.[3]

Within the next two weeks, Lee also baptized Wilson D. and Harvey A. Pace, whose future paths would cross repeatedly with

---

[2]Ibid., 136.   [3]Ibid., 137.

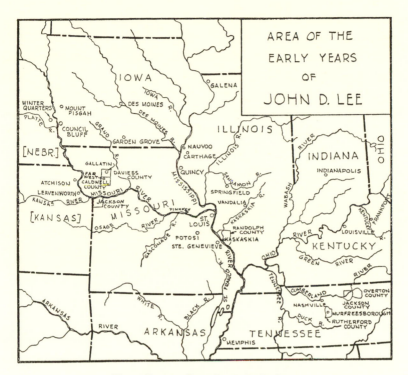

From Juanita Brooks, *John D. Lee*,
The Arthur H. Clark Company, 1962.

those of the Redd family (another family member, James Pace, evidently was baptized prior to this time). Also baptized were Venus and Chaney, two of Captain Redd's slaves.

While in Rutherford County John D. Lee generally stayed at the house of Captain Redd, sharing meals, assisting in harvesting wheat, and "reading and writing also instructing such as came with inquiring minds."[4] Before leaving the area, Lee called the members together and organized them into a branch of the church, calling it the "Friendship Branch of Rutherford," at which time John Holt was ordained an Elder and John H. Redd "Teacher and Clerk."[5]

---

[4]John D. Lee, "Missionary Journal of John D. Lee," entry of 17 July 1843. See also *Mormonism Unveiled*, 143.　　　　　[5]Lee, "Missionary Journal," entry of 6 August 1843.

The Nauvoo to which Lee returned in late summer had the appearance of a successful, rapidly growing city. Many log cabins were replaced with brick or wood-frame houses and business was expanding with shops and commercial buildings on all sides. But this was the City of Joseph, and without a doubt the major attraction was Joseph Smith himself.

The vast majority of the citizens of Nauvoo were Mormons, and to them Joseph was a prophet of God. But he was much more than that, as witnessed even by those who did not believe in him as a prophet, such as Josiah Quincy, who became the mayor of Boston the year following his visit to Nauvoo and who wrote the following:

> It is by no means improbable that some future text-book, for the use of generations yet unborn, will contain a question something like this: What historical American of the nineteenth century has exerted the most powerful influence upon the destinies of his countrymen: And it is by no means impossible that the answer to that interrogatory may be thus written: *Joseph Smith, the Mormon Prophet.*[6]

Joseph Smith was widely revered by the citizens of Nauvoo. He was their spiritual and temporal leader, but he also had a very human side. William M. Allred recollected how the Prophet sometimes needed to put aside his religious and civic duties:

> I have played ball with him many times in Nauvoo. He was preaching once, and he said it tried some of the pious folks to see him play ball with the boys. He then related a story of a certain prophet who was sitting under the shade of a tree amusing himself in some way, when a hunter came along with his bow and arrow, and reproved him. The prophet asked him if he kept his bow strung up all the time. The hunter answered that he did not. The prophet asked why, and he said it would lose its elasticity if he did. The prophet said it was just so with his mind, he did not want it strung up all the time.[7]

Besides playing ball, the Prophet had a well-known fondness for wrestling, which was a popular sport in his time. This is somewhat interesting in light of a resolution drawn up by lead-

---

[6]Josiah Quincy, *Figures of the Past.*
[7]William Allred, in the *Juvenile Instructor*, 27:471.

ers of the Quorum of Seventies at Far West in 1837 that stated: "We discard the practice of ball-playing, wrestling, jumping and all such low and degrading amusements. . . ."[8] Nevertheless, Smith often engaged in wrestling, taking on most challenges and delegating a few others. Once, for example, a large, drunken man stumbled into a meeting where the Prophet was speaking:

> The man interrupted by using foul language which became louder and louder with insults. He shouted that he was a better man than the prophet and would show everyone. He loudly challenged the Prophet to a wrestling match. At first the Prophet tried to ignore the man, but as the insults became louder and more abusive, President Smith turned to one of his companions, Allen Taylor, and said, "Allen, come up and throw this man." Allen did not hesitate, he felt sure he could do what the Prophet had asked of him. He immediately tackled his opponent, threw him, and pinned him to the floor. Defeated, the bully got to his feet and made a fast exit.[9]

Joseph Smith also took part in other recreational activities such as duck hunting, but it is clear that even while relaxing in such activities he was often called upon to act as a prophet. Joseph Taylor, Allen Taylor's older brother, wrote of a time when he went to inquire of the Prophet if his brother John, who had been imprisoned in Missouri for about six months, would ever come home:

> As the Prophet Joseph only lived about three miles from our house I got on a horse and rode to his home. When I reached there, Sister Emma Smith said that he and his son Joseph had just gone up the river near Nauvoo to shoot ducks. I rode up to them, when the Prophet inquired about my mother's welfare.
>
> I told him that Mother was very sad and downhearted about the safety of her son John; and she had requested me to come and ask him as a man of God whether my brother would ever return home. He rested on his gun, and bent his head for a moment as if in prayer or deep reflection. Then, with a beautiful beaming countenance, full of smiles, he looked up and told me to go and tell Mother that her son would return in safety inside of a week. True to the word of the Prophet, he got home in six days after this occurrence.[10]

---

[8]*Messenger and Advocate*, May 1837.
[9]Juanita Kossen, "Sketch of the Life of Captain Allen Taylor."
[10]Joseph Taylor, in the *Juvenile Instructor*, 27:202.

With Joseph Smith as the prophet and leader of the city, out-
wardly everything seemed to be going well in Nauvoo, but the
bustling air of prosperity could not hide signs of developing
trouble. William M. Allred, in writing his memoirs, summed up
the year 1843 in one sentence: "It seems that we had nothing but
hard work, hard living and constant persecution."[11] While an
oversimplification, there was indeed much hard work, often
combined with low wages and rather poor living conditions, but
most important to the Saints that year was the return of persecution, particularly as manifested in the kidnapping of Joseph
Smith.

It all started the previous year with an assassination attempt
on former governor Lilburn Boggs, the archenemy of the Saints,
in May 1842. Missouri authorities accused Joseph Smith of the
attempted murder and twice tried to extradite him back to Missouri, though Smith was able to establish his whereabouts in Illinois on the day of the shooting.

Even before the extradition attempts, bodyguards were
selected to protect the Prophet. While in Nauvoo, only fourteen
men were listed as officially ordained bodyguards, though many,
including Allen Taylor, evidently served to some extent in that
capacity.[12] None of the bodyguards, however, were with Joseph
Smith in June 1843, as he traveled with his wife Emma to vacation
at the home of her sister, Elizabeth Wasson, about two hundred
miles north of Nauvoo near Dixon, Illinois. What happened next
was widely misunderstood by the Saints at the time, including
Reddick Allred, who wrote in his diary:

> When the enemy began to see the greatness of his achievements and
> the rapid gathering of our people under the leadership of the Prophet,
> mobs began to rate and Gov. Boggs sent a demand for him and they

---

[11]William Allred, op. cit.

[12]*History of the Church*, 7:135. James Allred, an uncle of Allen Taylor's wife, was one of the
ordained bodyguards. There is, however, no date given for this listing (it was included in
the *History of the Church* in an entry from late 1844). Many others, including Allen Taylor, claimed to have served to some extent as a bodyguard of the Prophet, which in Taylor's case is quite conceivable given his relation to Allred as well as to his brother-in-law
Hosea Stout, who was chief of police and, by many accounts, one of Joseph Smith's
bodyguards.

sent a posse to kidnap him while he was on a visit to Dickson [Dixon] but in this they failed as our people were on the lookout.[13]

In fact, the event to which Allred referred was a third attempt by Missouri officials to return Joseph Smith for trial, but in this instance the action was instigated not by former Governor Boggs but by John C. Bennett, once the mayor of Nauvoo and former friend of Smith, who had been cut off from the church and was seeking revenge. This time the charge was treason, not attempted murder as previously, and Governor Thomas Ford of Illinois agreed to a writ of extradition, which was carried to Dixon by Sheriff Joseph Reynolds of Jackson County, Missouri, and Constable Harmon Wilson of Hancock County, Illinois. In the absence of bodyguards and caught off guard by Reynolds and Wilson, who represented themselves as Mormon elders who wanted to see the Prophet, Smith was arrested. Though the arrest appears to have been legal, it was perceived by many Mormons to be a kidnapping and a posse set out from Nauvoo in great haste towards Dixon to rescue Smith.

Even before the posse arrived, two Mormons filed charges against the arresting officers for false imprisonment and threatening the Prophet's life, and the three indicted men—Smith and the two officers—headed towards Judge Stephen A. Douglas' court in Quincy to seek resolution of the case. However, Smith was able to convince his friends that the Nauvoo court had the power to try his case, and after being ushered back into town by the posse that had been sent to rescue him, the Prophet promptly was released by the court on a writ of habeas corpus.

Nauvoo was alive with jubilation, but the celebration could not completely overshadow the undercurrent of rising dissension among some of the faithful. The doctrine that was responsible for this was that of celestial marriage, or plurality of wives. Rumors about the existence of polygamy in Nauvoo had been spreading for months, but it was not until the revelation regarding the doctrine was read to the High Council on 12 August 1843,

---

[13]Reddick Allred, op. cit., 5:301.

that the public in general became aware of the practice. William Law, second counselor in the First Presidency, and two members of the High Council in particular looked upon Joseph Smith as a fallen prophet as a result of the revelation.

Accompanying the rumblings of discontent within the church were threats from non-Mormon neighbors. Perhaps the major cause was the fear of the Mormon's potential political power, since they tended to vote as a group and thus could determine the outcome of any election. In addition, the growing size of the Nauvoo Legion, at the time about four thousand strong, gave cause for others to fear that the Mormons might challenge the authority of the state.

In an effort to quiet accusations against himself on the political front and to distract attention from the matter of plurality of wives, Joseph Smith, on 29 January 1844, declared himself to be a candidate for the presidency of the United States. Joseph realized that he had no real chance of winning the election, but he felt that entering the race would help gain publicity and respect for the church. Speaking to the Twelve Apostles and his brother Hyrum, the Prophet declared that they "must send every man in the city who is able to speak in public throughout the land to electioneer and make stump speeches. . . ."[14] The campaign was to begin in earnest after the April conference of the church, at which time General Conferences would be scheduled "all over the nation" with Joseph himself attending as many as possible.

Immediately before the April conference, John H. Redd, his wife Elizabeth, and his sister and brother-in-law, Mary and John Holt, arrived in Nauvoo. Their first order of business was to obtain a patriarchal blessing—a lifetime blessing of guidance, warning, encouragement and reassurance—from the Patriarch of the church, Hyrum Smith, which they did on 3 April 1844. More than simply obtaining a patriarchal blessing, it is possible if not likely that the primary motive for their journey to Nauvoo was to attend the April conference.

It was well known throughout the church in February and

---

[14]*History of the Church*, vol. 6, p. 188

March that Joseph Smith was a candidate for president. The April conference was attended by as many as twenty thousand people, far exceeding the population of Nauvoo, which at the time was approaching twelve thousand. Speakers at the conference endorsed and the congregation unanimously affirmed Joseph's candidacy. More than three hundred elders volunteered to preach the gospel and campaign for the Prophet and were appointed by the Council of the Twelve to serve in different states. Among those appointed to serve in this mission were John H. Redd and his friend John D. Lee, who were sent to Kentucky, and John Holt, who was assigned to North Carolina, the state of his birth.[15]

In spite of the public relations efforts of the church that centered on Joseph Smith's presidential candidacy, opposition to the Saints intensified in the early months of 1844. Political fears and economic jealousies from the outside were troublesome enough, but the greatest problem was the apostasy developing within the church. William Law, second counselor to Joseph Smith, and his brother Wilson led a conspiracy to expose Joseph as a fallen prophet. Other leaders joined in and their followers grew to number approximately two hundred.

At the April conference, the conspirators sought the downfall of the Prophet but were unsuccessful. The leaders of the conspiracy were exposed in the *Times and Seasons* and were excommunicated from the church. They next took the course of publishing an opposition newspaper called the *Nauvoo Expositor*, which was published on 7 June. William Law considered Joseph Smith a fallen prophet, not a false one, and the newspaper was filled with accusations supporting Law's viewpoint.

---

[15] *Times and Seasons*, vol. 5, p. 505. John H. Redd is mistakenly listed as John H. Reid. The Church Historian's Office has determined this to be the case as is listed in the index of the *Journal History of the Church*, listing for 15 April, 1844. A further insight into the editorial misspelling is found in a letter of John D. Lee to the editor of the *Times and Seasons*, dated 28 February 1844 and printed in vol. 5, p. 461, which reads: "DEAR SIR: Information came to me recently, through a letter written by brother Reid and Holt, Rutherford county, Tenn. . . ." This is clearly a reference to John H. Redd, with whom Lee had lived in Rutherford County, and his brother-in-law, John Holt, both of whom were baptized by Lee.

The city council convened immediately and decided that the newspaper was a public nuisance that, if not stopped, would incite mob action. Joseph Smith, who was the mayor of Nauvoo, ordered the city marshal, John Greene, to destroy the press and burn any remaining newspapers. According to William M. Allred, this was not the first time such an action was taken by the Nauvoo city government:

> There was a saloon put up right by the Temple. The city council declared it a nuisance. I was ordered out with my company (with others) as a guard while the order was executed. They took a team and drawed it away to a steep gulley and tipped it over down the hill, bottles and all. I was also present when the *Nauvoo Expositor* was destroyed.[16]

The order to destroy the newspaper was carried out within hours, even though the demolition of the press was a clear violation of property rights, as was, of course, the prior destruction of the saloon by the Temple. This time, however, the non-Mormon public became very aroused and enemies of the church proclaimed the destruction of the *Expositor* a violation of freedom of the press. Citizens' groups in Hancock County called for the removal of the Saints from Illinois. Nowhere was the attack more vehement than in the *Warsaw Signal*, where Thomas Sharp, an incessant critic and foe of the Mormons, called for citizens to arise, stating that "war and extermination" were inevitable.[17]

The extreme danger of the situation was apparent to Joseph and Hyrum Smith. Joseph immediately wrote to Governor Thomas Ford to apprise him of the situation and Hyrum wrote to Brigham Young to have him summon home the apostles and the elders on political missions. Then, on 18 June, Joseph stood in full uniform on the framework of an unfinished building opposite the Mansion House and made his last speech to the Nauvoo Legion. Drawing his sword and presenting it to heaven he said prophetically, "I call on God and angels to witness that I have unsheathed my sword. This people shall be free or my blood shall be spilt on the ground."[18]

---

[16]William Allred, op. cit.   [17]*Warsaw Signal*, 12 June 1844, p.2.
[18]William Allred, op. cit.

Joseph's guards and the Nauvoo Legion were mobilized and the city was placed under martial law. Non-Mormons in surrounding communities were concerned about the actions in Nauvoo. As a result of the turmoil, Governor Ford went to Carthage on 20 June in an attempt to neutralize the situation. The Governor wrote a letter to the Prophet in which he insisted that only a trial of the city council members before a non-Mormon jury in Carthage would satisfy the people, promising complete protection for the defendants if they would surrender.

In counsel with his closest friends, Joseph decided that the best course of action was to leave Nauvoo: "The way is open. It is clear to my mind what to do. All they want is Hyrum and myself; then tell everybody to go about their business. . . . We will cross the river tonight, and go away to the West."[19]

Reddick Allred was more specific, writing that Joseph "crossed the river having in view the intention to go to the Rocky Mountains to find a location for the Saints where they could dwell in safety. . . ."[20] Joseph's first priority may have been to save himself, a natural reaction in light of the situation. Governor Ford, who later admitted that he had received frequent appeals "to make a clean and thorough work of the matter, by exterminating the Mormons, or expelling them from the State," emphasized the threat to Joseph.[21]

Late at night on 22 June, Joseph and Hyrum, accompanied by Willard Richards and Orrin Porter Rockwell, crossed the Mississippi River in a skiff. Unusually heavy rains had caused flooding up and down the river, destroying most of John D. Lee's hometown, Kaskaskia. The boat was so leaky and the river so high that it took nearly the entire night to get to the other side. However, several of the Prophet's friends in Nauvoo, including his wife Emma, sent word across the river begging the men to return, assuming that the Smith brothers were guilty of nothing and thus surely would be acquitted. Joseph might also have been fighting his conscience, considering, according to Reddick Allred, that "some half-hearted saints followed him [across the

---

[19]*History of the Church*, vol. 5, p. 545–46.   [20]Reddick Allred, op. cit., 5:302.
[21]Thomas Ford, *A History of Illinois, from Its Commencement as a State in 1818 to 1847*, 345.

river] and accused him of cowardice for leaving the Saints at the mercy of the mob."[22]

Joseph realized what others apparently did not, namely that a return to Nauvoo would be in essence a death sentence. To those who beckoned him to return he replied, "If my life is of no value to my friends it is of none to myself."[23] The next day Joseph and Hyrum returned to Nauvoo.

On 24 June, Joseph was charged with treason for having declared martial law in Nauvoo. That evening, Joseph and Hyrum Smith rode from Nauvoo to surrender at Carthage. By the Mansion House, Joseph turned to a group of men, among whom was William M. Allred, and said, "Boys, if I do not come back, take care of yourselves, for I go as a lamb to the slaughter."[24] As he passed his farm on the eastern outskirts of the city, he declared, "If some of you had got such a farm and knew you would not see it any more you would want to take a good look at it for the last time."[25]

There was great commotion in Carthage as Joseph and Hyrum surrendered and were ushered to the Carthage Jail, accompanied by eight of their friends. At the jail Joseph gave to James Allred the sword he had unsheathed during his final speech to the Nauvoo Legion, saying, "Take this—you may need it to defend yourself."[26] Soon afterward, Joseph's friends, with the exception of John Taylor and Willard Richards, were forced to leave the jail.

Governor Ford had offered protection for the prisoners and knew of the potential for conflict in Carthage but was unaware of a plot to kill the Prophet and foresaw no possibility that any harm would come to him. But as the governor was in Nauvoo on 27 June addressing the Saints, a large group of men, with blackened faces to hide their identity, rushed the jail. Joseph and the others fought off the attackers with a cane and fired shots from a pistol that had been smuggled to them but they were no match for the mob. One shot fired through the door struck Hyrum Smith in the face, mor-

[22]Reddick Allred, op. cit., 5:302.   [23]History of the Church, vol. 6, p. 549.
[24]William Allred, op. cit. Also, History of the Church, vol. 6, p.558.
[25]History of the Church, vol. 6, p. 558.   [26]Eliza Munson, "Early Pioneer History," 2.

tally wounding him. John Taylor was wounded five times, but the bullet that might have killed him hit his watch in his vest pocket. Joseph, seeing that there was no safety in the room, tried to jump from the open window but was shot. Exclaiming, "Oh Lord, my God!" Joseph fell to the ground outside where he was dragged up against a wall and shot several more times, killing him. Miraculously, Willard Richards remained unscathed.

The day after the news of the tragedy reached Nauvoo, Allen Taylor's mother and his sister Sarah were among those who went to the jail and saw the blood which had been spilt on the floor. The bodies of Joseph and Hyrum Smith were brought back to Nauvoo where, on 29 June, about ten thousand people viewed them. Governor Ford feared a Mormon uprising, and indeed many were "so enraged at the mob that they wanted to go out and slay them." But Willard Richards, who had pledged his life and honor that there would be no uprising, calmed the crowd, saying, "Brethren, think! Think! Think! Think before you act."[27]

John Taylor was at Carthage for a few days recovering from his wounds when James Allred arrived with a wagon to carry him back to Nauvoo, but the ride in the wagon was too bumpy and painful for the wounded Taylor. A sleigh on which a bed rested was rigged up and tied to the back of Allred's wagon, and Taylor rested on the bed while the sleigh was dragged through the tall grass of the prairie back to Nauvoo.[28]

John Taylor made a steady recovery and, though bedfast, helped Willard Richards run the church, but the greatest concern for the Saints was the loss of their prophet, Joseph Smith. Without him there was a major leadership void which could not be filled immediately: Sidney Rigdon, the first counselor in the First Presidency, had moved to Pittsburgh due to a conflict with the Prophet; William Law, the second counselor, had been excommunicated in the aftermath of the *Expositor* affair; and all of the apostles with the exception of John Taylor and Willard Richards were on missions in the East.

The apostles and other missionaries, including John H. Redd,

[27]William Allred, op. cit.   [28]*History of the Church*, vol. 7, p. 117–18.

who had been sent on missions after the April Conference, were recalled to Nauvoo, but it was not until August that most of them received word of the Prophet's death and were able to return. Brigham Young arrived from New England on 6 August and found that Sidney Rigdon had preceded him. In a speech to a large assembly on 8 August, Rigdon asserted that he, as the only remaining counselor in the First Presidency, should assume the leadership of the church.

After Rigdon finished, Brigham Young arose to address the crowd; many of those present, including Pleasant Green Taylor, thought they saw Joseph Smith standing in front of them, as Taylor's son later recorded:

> He, as well as hundreds of others, arose to his feet and felt sure that Joseph had been resurrected; and even after Brigham began to speak, he still thought it was the Prophet Joseph who was speaking to them.[29]

William M. Allred, who also was present, recorded the event with a slightly different slant:

> After Rigdon got through Brigham got up and spoke with such power that it convinced nearly all that were present that the mantle of Joseph had fallen on him. I was perfectly satisfied.[30]

Most of the Saints, like Allred, were "perfectly satisfied" that the leadership of the church should be given to the Quorum of the Twelve Apostles, with Brigham Young at its head. The Twelve met in council the day after they were sustained and began to set in order the organization and affairs of the church.

One of the most immediate changes, beginning on 18 August, involved the expansion of the seventies quorums, in part because of a decision that all elders under the age of thirty-five become seventies. In addition, Brigham Young announced at the October conference that if a person desired to preach the gospel he would be ordained to the office of seventy.[31] Among those ordained to

---

[29]Taylor, op. cit.   [30]William Allred, op. cit.

[31]The Seventies in the LDS Church are an ordained office in the Melchizedek Priesthood; they are elders with a special call and ordination "to preach the gospel, and to be especial witnesses unto the Gentiles and in all the world." See *D&C* 107:25. As the name might suggest, up to 70 seventies formed a quorum.

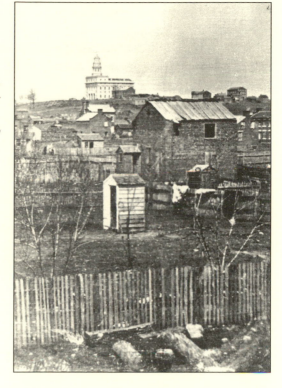

Nauvoo, 1846
Photograph by Charles William Carter
of 1846 daguerrotype.
ourtesy of the Church Archives, The Church
of Jesus Christ of Latter-day Saints.

the office were John H. Redd, Allen Taylor and his brothers
Pleasant Green and Joseph, and several sons of Isaac Allred.[32]

One of the most important buildings in Nauvoo, the Seventies Hall, was completed in December 1844, under the direction
of John D. Lee, primarily as a meeting place for various quorums
of the seventy. But without a doubt the most important building
was the Temple. Other projects were discontinued in an attempt
to rush the Temple to completion. Brigham Young made it clear
that time was of the essence, saying at the October conference,
"The first thing we have got to do is to build the Temple where

---

[32]"Index, General Record of the Seventies, Book B: 1844–1847," HDC. The sons of Isaac
Allred who were ordained seventies were: James Riley, Paulinus Harvey, Reddick Newton, Reddin Alexander, and William Moore. John H. Redd and Allen Taylor were both
in the Seventh Quorum. Isaac Allred was a High Priest.

we can receive those blessings which we so much desire. Never mind mobocrats, but let us do what God has commanded us."[33]

Time indeed was of the essence, for the leaders of the church already knew that the Saints would have to abandon Nauvoo. Throughout the remainder of the year and into 1845 the city continued to grow. New homes, gardens, and farms were established. But the spectacular growth only increased the antagonism of the church's enemies. Intensified hostilities led the Quorum of the Twelve Apostles to announce on 24 September that the exodus of the Saints from Nauvoo would take place the following spring as soon as the grass on the prairies was tall enough to sustain their livestock.

All that remained was the completion of the Temple, which was vital to the Saints in order to provide the opportunity for as many as possible to receive their endowments, a course of instruction, ordinances, and covenants given only in dedicated temples. Rooms in the Temple were dedicated as they were completed and by early December they were prepared for ordinances. In the first group of six couples to receive their endowments were James and Elizabeth Allred.[34] Work in the Temple continued at a feverish pace, on many occasions both day and night. Isaac and Mary Allred received their endowments on 17 January; three days later Allen and Sarah Lovisa Taylor did likewise.[35]

After the murder of the Prophet the primary mission of the Saints had been to complete the Nauvoo Temple in order to do their sacred ordinance work. This mission soon would be completed and now it was time to move on—once again—in search of the elusive Zion.

---

[33]*History of the Church*, vol. 7, p. 292.   [34]Norton Jacob, "Autobiography."
[35]Nauvoo Temple Endowment Register.

Chapter VII

Exodus

NAUVOO WAS A BEEHIVE of activity during the final months of 1845, as the Saints built wagons and gathered provisions necessary for the journey to the west. Ironically, in many ways the city had never seemed so prosperous. The citizens of Nauvoo made a determined effort to complete the Temple, their homes, and their shops, and to cultivate their farms, even though they knew they would have to abandon everything in a few months.

Anticipating a spring exodus, church leaders organized the Saints in twenty-five companies of one hundred families each, led by captains of hundreds, fifties, and tens. Though the evacuation was planned in considerable detail, nobody anticipated that it would begin in the middle of winter. But when reports, unfounded in fact but encouraged by Governor Ford, reached Nauvoo that federal troops planned to arrest the Mormon leaders, the decision was made for them to leave the city long before the grass was green.

The weather in early February 1846 was exceptionally mild as the evacuation began under the direction of chief of police Hosea Stout. The first wagons rolled out of Nauvoo on 4 February; two days later Bishop George Miller crossed the river with his family, aided by Reddick Allred and a team outfitted by his father and his brother-in-law Allen Taylor.[1] In the next days Stout then arranged for his wife and other members of her fam-

---

[1]Reddick Allred, op. cit., 5:303.

Hosea Stout
Exactly one year after the death of his first wife,
Stout married Allen Taylor's sister Louisa.
Courtesy of Utah State Historical Society.

ily, including her mother and brother, Elizabeth and Pleasant
Green Taylor, to be among the first to leave.[2]

The exiles were ferried across the river on a makeshift fleet of
vessels—virtually anything that would float—and set up camp at
Sugar Creek. Once in Iowa the Saints were greeted by increasingly cold and bitter weather. Many had no tents or adequate
shelter from the elements. By the time Brigham Young arrived
on the Iowa side on 15 February, the mud had become so deep
that his teams had to be yoked double to pull the wagons up the
hill to the Sugar Creek camp.

As the temperature continued to plummet, on about February
25, the Mississippi River froze over. Many wagons that had lined
up at the river front waiting to be ferried to Iowa seized the
opportunity and crossed the frozen river. What seemed to some

[2]Taylor, op. cit; Juanita Brooks, ed., *On the Mormon Frontier: The Diary of Hosea Stout,*
1:113–114. Pleasant Green Taylor crossed the Mississippi on 8 February and Hosea and
Julia Ann Taylor Stout, along with Elizabeth Taylor, went on 9 February.

to be a blessing from heaven only added to confusion at Sugar Creek, for the early departure from Nauvoo already had upset a carefully-planned order of travel. As it warmed, rain began and continued for about eight weeks, soaking everything and saturating the prairies, turning them into shallow lakes and quagmires. And so, after traveling for just one week, the companies made an extended stop at Richardson's Point, only about fifty-three miles from Nauvoo.

The independent and competitive spirit of ambitious men such as Bishop George Miller exacerbated the general disorder. Reddick Allred, who remained with Miller's company for several weeks before returning to the main camp to help his own family, remembered:

> I was gone about two months, enduring much hardships in the heavy storms of rain falling like a flood. President Young traveled with the main camp, but Bishop Miller kept ahead showing his bull-headedness. I went back to visit President Young's camp and he said to me, "Tell Bishop Miller the nearer the root, the sweeter the grass."[3]

On 24 March, Hosea Stout reported that more than half of his men were out of provisions and there was no feed for the animals. Two days later Brigham Young found it necessary to regroup the camp into three companies of one hundred families, with captains of hundreds and fifties for general command. In addition, one commissary was created for contracting work to help buy provisions and a second, in which James and Isaac Allred were in charge of the fifth and sixth fifties, to distribute food in camp.[4]

Travel was more orderly following the reorganization, but nothing could overcome the wet spring weather. Almost constant rain created interminable mud, leading Brigham Young to comment in late March that they had passed through only one mud hole that day "which was about six miles in length." On 6 April, Hosea Stout wrote:

---

[3]Reddick Allred, op. cit., 5:303.
[4]William Clayton, *An Intimate Chronicle, The Journals of William Clayton*, 266.

This was of all mornings the most dismal dark and rainy. . . . This day capped the climax of all days for travelling. The road was the worst that I had yet witnessed up hill & down through sloughs on spouty oak ridges and deep marshes raining hard the creek rising. The horses would sometimes sink to their bellies on the ridges, teams stall going down hill. We worked and toiled more than half the day and had at last to leave some of our wagons and double teams before we could get through.[5]

Traveling across Iowa with Hosea Stout was his brother-in-law, Pleasant Green Taylor. Food was scarce and Taylor was sent out by Stout to hunt for game and also to take some books to sell in order to buy food. Stout rejoiced when Taylor and Jesse D. Hunter came home one night without killing any game but selling three books, the proceeds of which were used to buy bacon, "which was a great relief to us for we were suffering for want of something to eat."[6]

Even before the Nauvoo exodus began the Rocky Mountains had been chosen as the destination for the Saints, though the general membership had not been told of the decision. Leaders were called to a conference on 17 April to determine who could make the trip to the mountains that year. Hosea Stout was among those who were chosen to go, but in his destitute state Stout declined.

On the morning of 22 April Stout's pregnant wife, Louisa, gave birth to a daughter, also named Louisa. "This was my first born in the wilderness as some of the old prophets once said," Stout wrote, "and from the situation of our dwelling might be called a 'Prairie chicken.'"[7] In deference to his wife's condition, sick and with a newborn child, Stout waited until the next day to travel onwards. Three days later his older children, Hosea and Hyrum, came down with whooping cough.

Stout and others soon were out of provisions and were frustrated that "the people would not sell flour when they knew we were starving and some sick."[8] When Benjamin Jones, who had gone to local settlements to peddle belongings in order to buy

[5]Hosea Stout, op. cit., 149.   [6]Ibid., 153–54.
[7]Ibid., 155.   [8]Ibid., 158.

food, didn't return, James Allred and Green Taylor, as he was called, were sent after Jones, leaving Stout destitute for help in herding cattle as he was scarcely able to walk.[9] More than a week later Stout, still without food, went with Jones into the woods to talk over their feelings when word was sent that his son Hyrum was dying. Little Hyrum died that afternoon in his father's arms, the second child of his to be lost in such a manner. The dejected Stout wrote:

> I shall not attempt to say anything about my feelings at this time because my family is still afflicted. My wife is yet unable to go about and little Hosea my only son now is wearing down with the same complaint and what will be the end thereof. I have fearful foreboding of coming evil on my family yet. We are truly desolate and afflicted and entirely destitute of any thing even to eat much less to nourish the sick, & just able to go about myself. Arrangements being made to bury him this evening.[10]

With so much suffering, hunger, and sickness, with wagons and equipment in disrepair, and with no prospects for better weather, the dream of reaching the Rocky Mountains later that season was fading. A plan was forged to establish farms or way stations along the road. Hundreds of acres were planted at a place named Garden Grove because of a grove of timber in the middle of the prairie, but the conditions made life difficult for even the hardiest of souls. Hosea Stout's brother Allen recorded:

> About these times the rattle snakes bit a good many of our animals and there was a great deel of sickness in camp on account of the great exposure the saints were forced to undergo.... There was great want of bread in camp, so that we were oppressed on every hand but we cried to the Lord who herd our Prares and we wer fed by his all bountiful hand but some showed out theire evil harts by there meen intreegs and shelfishness.[11]

By the time the Saints established Garden Grove, they were in uncharted prairie wilderness. A second, larger settlement called Mount Pisgah was made about forty miles west of Garden

---

[9]Ibid., 158.   [10]Ibid., 160.
[11]Allen Joseph Stout, "Reminiscences and Journal."

Grove and served as temporary church headquarters. In June the Saints continued on to western Iowa, experiencing much easier travel as the roads dried out and feed for the animals was readily available.

After four months of travel following the exodus from Nauvoo, they entered Indian land, but staying there would require permission from the government. The leaders hoped that there was still time for some of the Apostles and others to press on to the West before the onset of winter storms, but the more immediate concern was where the main body of refugees would spend the winter. Answers to both concerns began to come into focus with the arrival in camp of Captain James Allen of the United States Army.

It all started with the annexation of Texas by the United States in 1845. Then, in 1846, President James K. Polk set his expansionist eyes on the acquisition of New Mexico and California. Mexican and American troops had a skirmish on 24 April 1846, and three weeks later Congress declared war. Though many Americans were excited about the possibilities brought about by the war, the Mormons, who were not supported by the government in their struggles in Missouri and Illinois, at first were not very sympathetic. Hosea Stout recorded a typical reaction to the news of the war on 27 May 1846:

> In the midst of the rain & gross darkness Pleasant Green Taylor, my wife's brother came to the tent wet thoroughly.... He said that his mother and all his folks were eight miles from here.... He said also that there was a war between the United States and Mexico and a great excitement in the state about raising troops to March to the relief of General Taylor in Texas.... I confess that I was glad to learn of war against the United States and was in hopes that it might never end untill they were entirely destroyed for they had driven us into the wilderness & was now laughing at our calamities.[12]

Unbeknownst to most of the Mormon exiles, Brigham Young had authorized Jesse C. Little in January 1846 to meet with national leaders for the purpose of seeking government aid for

---

[12]Hosea Stout, op. cit., 163–64.

the migrating Saints. Little arrived in Washington, D.C., just eight days after war had been declared and on 3 June met with President Polk. The day before this meeting the President met with his Cabinet and discussed his concerns regarding the Mormons, as he recorded in his diary:

> Col. [Stephen W.] Kearny was also authorized to receive into service as volunteers a few hundred of the Mormons who are now on their way to California, with a view to conciliate them, attach them to our country, and prevent them from taking part against us.[13]

President Polk, afraid that the Mormons might shift their allegiance to British interests in the Oregon territory, authorized the raising of a battalion of five hundred men who were to serve under Col. Kearny, commander of the Army of the West. Kearny then appointed Captain James Allen to enlist soldiers from the encamped Saints in southern Iowa, but Allen was greeted with suspicion and disbelief by the destitute Saints who worried more about their own survival on the plains than the war with Mexico.

What the Mormons did not know was that Captain Allen's presence was undoubtedly a result of the solicitation of help from the federal government made by Jesse Little on behalf of Brigham Young. Meeting with other leaders, Young recognized several advantages of government service: Desperately needed capital for the exodus could be procured as recruits were paid in advance for their term of enlistment; members of the battalion could keep their arms at the end of their enlistment; and, significantly, the Mormons would be permitted to make temporary settlements on Indian lands.

It was with a touch of irony that Brigham Young in early July tried to clear the air of the prejudice against the federal government, which had been promoted by him a few months earlier in order to keep the Saints unified during their exodus from Nauvoo. The Mormons were, naturally, suspicious of the government that had ignored their repeated calls for help or intervention in both Missouri and Illinois. Young was persuasive, but equally

---

[13]James K. Polk, *Polk: The Diary of a President, 1845–1849,* 108–9.

important was the affable nature of Captain Allen, who was recruiting men at Council Bluffs. As Hosea Stout recorded on 5 July 1846:

> From Mother [Elizabeth] Taylor's I went, leaving my wife there to see Captain James Allen. . . . He was a plain non assuming man without that proud over bearing strut and self concieted dignaty which some call an officer-like appearance. I came up and commenced a conversation with him. . . . I was much pleased with his manner as a gentleman notwithstanding my prejudice against, not only him but also the government which he was sent here to represent.[14]

Recruiting continued for nearly three weeks, and in the end an estimated 543 men were mustered into the Mormon Battalion at Council Bluffs, Iowa Territory. Brigham Young then selected Mormon officers for each of the five companies. Particularly well-represented in the Battalion was the family of Isaac Allred, whose sons, Reddick and James Riley Allred, were joined in Company A by his nephews, James T. S. Allred and Reuben W. Allred; another nephew, Thomas C. Ivie, enlisted in Company C.[15] Isaac Allred's son-in-law Allen Taylor also volunteered, despite having five young children to care for, including a month-old girl, but it was "deemed advisable for him to remain and help the Saints," so his brother Joseph went in his stead (also in Company A).[16] Before leaving Iowa the men were promised by Brigham Young, "Go and you shall have no fighting to do— you shall go before and behind the Battles."[17]

On 21 July 1846, the Mormon Battalion began their historic march. With so many able-bodied men gone it was no longer possible for a group to reach the Rocky Mountains that year, and energies were directed toward finding a suitable winter way station. A site was chosen on the west bank of the Missouri River for their "Winter Quarters," a place not only to spend the winter

---

[14]Hosea Stout, op. cit., 175.
[15]Norma Baldwin Ricketts, *The Mormon Battalion, U.S. Army of the West 1846–1848*, 16; 21–25.
[16]Obituary of Allen Taylor, *Journal History of the Church*, 29 December 1891.
[17]Reddick Allred, op. cit., 5:304.

but a center for planning, regrouping, and preparing for the following year. Reuben Allred, before he joined the march of the
Mormon Battalion, set up a ropewalk by the river to make two
huge ropes from local hemp that then were stretched across the
Missouri to provide a ferry for transportation of materials and
equipment to build the new city, the first in Nebraska.[18] The
ferry opened for public use on 1 July, carrying wagons, families,
and supplies across the river day and night.

Winter Quarters was organized in what had become a familiar pattern, dividing families into groups of tens, fifties, and hundreds. Twenty-four police and fireguards were hired to work in
shifts around the clock, with Hosea Stout chosen as captain of
the guard. After a few weeks the leaders decided that the Nauvoo Legion should be reorganized in order to help the police
prevent spies from entering and leaving camp. The men voted
unanimously to reinstate all former captains of the Legion
before electing new ones, including Isaac Allred's sons Redden
and William M. Allred. In addition, Stephen Markham and
Hosea Stout were elected colonel and lieutenant colonel of the
first battalion of infantry.[19]

Thomas L. Kane, a non-Mormon visitor who had been
directly involved in the negotiations in Washington, D.C., which
led to the call of the Mormon Battalion, was impressed with the
activity on the Iowa side of the river opposite Winter Quarters:

> [The bottomlands] were crowded with covered carts and wagons;
> and each one of the Council Bluff hills opposite was crowned with its
> own great camp, gay with bright white canvas, and alive with the
> busy stir of swarming occupants. In the clear blue morning air, the
> smoke streamed up from more than a thousand cooking fires.
> Countless roads and bypaths checkered all manner of geometric fig-
> ures on the hillsides. . . . From a single point I counted four thousand
> head of cattle in view at one time. As I approached the camps, it
> seemed to me the children there were to prove still more numerous.[20]

---

[18]Gail Geo. Holmes, "A Prophet Who Followed, Fulfilled, and Magnified," in Susan Easton Black and Larry C. Porter, ed., *Lion of the Lord*, 133.

[19]Ibid., 136, 139. See also Stout, op. cit., 204, entry of 10 October 1846.

[20]Thomas L. Kane, *The Mormons: A Discourse delivered before the Historical Society of Pennsylvania, March 26, 1850*, 25–26.

While most of the Saints were self-sufficient, many were unable to provide for themselves. Brigham Young was very concerned about these people, both in Iowa as well as in Nauvoo. Four days before the departure of the Mormon Battalion, ninety men at Council Bluffs, including Allen Taylor and James Allred, were appointed as bishops to take charge of the families left behind by the soldiers.[21] Young asked volunteers in the Battalion to leave their pay for the benefit of their families and directed the bishops to keep an account of all monies and properties received by them.

Two weeks later, on 8 August, the Pottawattamie High Council met to discuss the duties of bishops regarding the welfare of the poor. A committee of seven, including Allen Taylor, was appointed to check on the condition of the poor in the different camps.[22] This was just shortly after plans had been made across the river in Winter Quarters to send companies back to Nauvoo to "bring on the poor, to fulfill the covenant . . . that we never would cease our exertions till all were gathered."[23]

About three thousand had left Nauvoo in the winter and another ten thousand in the spring, but nearly a thousand Saints remained there, too poor or sick to leave. In early September Orville Allen departed Winter Quarters with a relief company of about a dozen men to rescue the Saints in Nauvoo. Allen's company was in transit when word arrived in camp that Nauvoo was in a state of siege and surrender, endangering the lives of those still in the city. Non-Mormons, becoming ever more restless while awaiting the complete evacuation of Nauvoo by the Saints, first carried out a series of lynchings on farms near Nauvoo and then attacked the city itself. Only about 150 able-bodied men were left to defend the city, and after five days of fighting the Mormons were forced to surrender unconditionally, ending the "Battle of Nauvoo."[24]

[21]Pottawattamie High Council Minutes, 24 July 1846.

[22]Ibid., 8 August 1848.

[23]*Journal History of the Church*, 17 July 1846.

[24]William G. Hartley, "The Pioneer Trek: Nauvoo to Winter Quarters," *Ensign*, June 1997, 31–42.

Refugee camps were scattered along the Mississippi riverbank in eastern Iowa near Montrose. Most of the exiles had little food and only blankets for shelter. In response to the grave situation, on 2 October 1846, the Pottawatamie High Council, under the leadership of its president, James Allred, met and decided to send more men and teams back to help gather the poor:

> Voted that all men who go 1st this fall with teams to assist the poor, be instructed to meet at Keg Creek Bridge on Wednesday evening next in reddiness [sic] to proceed on their journey. Voted that Jno. [John] Murdock take the oversight of all teams and men who go from the East side of the Mo. River and appoint others as he shall deem best.[25]

In contrast to Allen's rescue mission, this time the men were mainly farmers and hay cutters from the Iowa side of the river rather than from Winter Quarters. Allen Taylor was appointed by Murdock to assist in rescuing the Saints at Nauvoo and they, with their companies, were on their way just before Captain Allen arrived at Montrose.

The impoverished, hungry Saints that Captain Allen found were not in good shape to travel, but on 9 October flocks of exhausted quail flopped into the camp in such large numbers that "every man, woman and child had quails to eat for their dinner."[26] That same day Joseph Heywood, John Fullmer, and Almon Babbitt—the three trustees appointed by Brigham Young to sell off Nauvoo properties and pay remaining obligations after the exodus from the city—brought shoes, clothing, molasses, pork, and salt to the camp. The first of the "poor" Saints finally were ready to begin their journey.

Allen Taylor and James Murdock arrived at Montrose by the end of October to round up the rest of the refugees. With each day it became more evident why it had been "deemed advisable" that Taylor "remain to help the Saints" rather than go with the Mormon Battalion. In a remarkably short period of time his company overtook the Orville Allen Company:

---

[25]Pottawattamie High Council Minutes, 2 October 1846. The notes mistakenly identified James Murdock as John Murdock.
[26]Thomas Bullock, Will Bagley ed., *The Pioneer Camp of the Saints*, 76.

Sunday 15 November 1846—Father Fisher called us up before dawn of day, and we heard Allen Taylor's Camp, who was near us. We have been 37 days [on the road] and they 17, in coming to this place from the Mississippi, being more than half as quick again.[27]

Allen Taylor's company undoubtedly was smaller than Orville Allen's, which would have been a factor in facilitating travel, but the short amount of time necessary to move his company was noteworthy nevertheless. Taylor and his company evidently were taking steps to seal off the rear lest they be followed by their enemies, creating a problem for Orville Allen's trailing company:

Tuesday 17 November 1846—A muddy morning . . . Brother Harmon's cattle had been driven up for a start, but thro' the negligence of the driver were allowed to stray away again which delayed us till 12 o'clock, when we had to go 3 miles round the ridge road (on account of the bridge on the shorter road being burnt up, supposed by Allen Taylor's Company, who said they should encamp there and burn it).[28]

As the rescue teams returned to western Iowa, their leaders were surprised to see a new city with several hundred houses. John D. Lee, who just a few days previous had returned from a mission to Santa Fe, New Mexico, to bring back Mormon Battalion pay, was equally amazed:

I was astonished when I looked around and saw what serious enterprise and industry had brought to pass within 6 weeks past. A city of at least 400 houses had been erected in that short space of time, through the ingenuity and industry of the Saints. No other people but the Saints of God has ever been known to accomplish as much in so short a time.[29]

This main settlement, Winter Quarters, was built on Indian lands on the west bank of Missouri River, now Florence, a suburb of Omaha, Nebraska. With houses ranging from two-story brick homes to sod huts, Winter Quarters housed almost four thousand Saints by the end of November 1846. Hosea Stout moved into his new house on 24 November, though it wasn't much of a

---

[27]Ibid., 94.   [28]Ibid.
[29]John D. Lee, *Journals of John D. Lee, 1846–1847 and 1859*, 17.

house, with "Neither door nor windows not even but a few of the craks [*sic*] was yet stoped up and a hard North wind blowing."[30] It was the first day that his "only living child [daughter of Louisa Taylor] now 7 months & 2 days old ever was in a house."[31]

Though many dwellings were primitive, it was far better than the conditions endured by those who left Nauvoo in the winter and struggled for nearly five months to cross Iowa. In addition to those who settled at Winter Quarters, approximately twenty-five hundred Saints established dwellings on Pottawattamie Indian lands on the east side of the Missouri River during the winter of 1846–47. Never in their short history had the Saints been so widely scattered or so poorly housed. This was the sixth home for many of the Taylors and the Allreds since joining the church—Salt River, Clay County, Far West, Quincy, Nauvoo, and now southwestern Iowa—and hardly the most comfortable. Most of the settlements were in an area known as the Missouri Bottoms but were widely called the "misery bottoms" by the Saints, due to sickness and poor living conditions. Wilford Woodruff wrote, "I have never seen the Latter Day Saints in any situation where they seemed to be passing through greater tribulations or wearing out faster than at the present time."[32]

The hardships were compounded by the absence of so many men: Reddick, James Riley, James T. S. and Reuben Allred were among the five hundred still marching with the Mormon Battalion; Pleasant Green Taylor and his brother William, after working with their brothers to build a home for their mother, were but two of the many who went to Missouri to seek employment in order to buy provisions; and, even at this difficult time, men still were being sent on missions for the church.

But not all was sorrow and misery. There were many social diversions, such as singing, dancing, concerts, games, hunting,

---

[30]Hosea Stout, op. cit., 213.
[31]Ibid., his other three children as well as one wife died on the way to Winter Quarters. By the time winter was over little Louisa died, as did one of Stout's two remaining wives; only his wife Louisa, sister of Allen Taylor, remained of the family which seven months prior consisted of three wives and four children.
[32]Woodruff, "Journal," 17–21 November 1846.

fishing, and riding horseback. Women often came together in neighborhood groups to gather food, quilt, braid straw, comb each other's hair, wash clothes, and knit. Above all, the hope and vision of their new Zion remained vital as they recited the words of a popular hymn, written three months earlier by William Clayton to celebrate the birth of a daughter:

> We'll find the place which God for us prepared,
> Far away in the West;
> Where none shall come to hurt or make afraid;
> There the Saints will be blessed.
> We'll make the air with music ring
> Shout praises to our God and King;
> Above the rest these words we'll tell
> All is well! All is well![33]

[33]William Clayton *Come, Come Ye Saints*, 15 April 1846.

Chapter VIII

POTTAWATTAMIE

SOUTHWESTERN IOWA had few white settlers prior to the arrival of the Mormons in the spring of 1846. A sizeable area on both sides of the river was known as "Council Bluffs," a name given in reference to a council held in 1804 on a bluff by Lewis and Clark with Oto/Missouri Indians. In 1846 the land was occupied mostly by the Pottawattamie-Ottawa-Chippewa Federated Tribe of Indians, who previously had surrendered their lands in Illinois and elsewhere to the government and were removed to Iowa.

The Pottawattamies had the rights to the land along the Missouri in Iowa and were pleased with the Mormon refugees, though, as Thomas Kane noted, "They would have been pleased with any whites who would not cheat them, nor sell them whisky, nor whip them for their poor gipsy habits, nor bear themselves indecently toward their women." In addition, Kane remarked, the Indians admired "those who sacrifice, without apparent motive, their worldly welfare to the triumph of an idea."[1]

In response to the Mormon appeal to settle temporarily on Pottawattamie lands, the Indians held a solemn council under the auspices of an officer of the United States. After the smoking of peace pipes and the exercising of metaphoric expression was completed, the renowned and scholarly Pottawattamie chief Pied Riche arose and said:

---

[1]Kane, *The Mormons*, 56.

My Mormon Brethren,

The Pottawattamie came sad and tired into this unhealthy Missouri Bottom, not many years back, when he was taken from his beautiful country beyond the Mississippi, which had abundant game and timber, and clear water everywhere. Now you are driven away, the same, from your lodges and lands there, and the graves of your people. So we have both suffered. We must help one another, and the Great Spirit will help us both. You are now free to cut and use all the wood you may wish. You can make all your improvements, and live on any part of our land not actually occupied by us. Because one suffers and does not deserve it, is no reason he shall suffer always, I say. We may live to see all right yet. However, if we do not, our children will.[2]

The main staging area for settlement at the Missouri River was a camp near Council Bluffs called the Grand Encampment which, as Hosea Stout observed, stretched east about nine miles.[3] Though Reuben Allred's ferry was in operation both day and night, only a limited number of the thousands of emigrants who were waiting could cross the Missouri each day. Soon there was insufficient wood, grass, and water to support the remaining settlers as well as their livestock, and thus many of them had to seek new campsites that had access to those necessities.

Much of the surrounding area is undulating with hills and dales of rich grassland broken by picturesque valleys. Numerous streams flow through these beautiful prairies, generally in a southwesterly direction, emptying into the Missouri River. Though the soil was excellent, the supply of timber was limited, and many settlements were hastily constructed along creeks such as the Pigeon, Honey, and Mosquito, and in other scattered areas where substantial groves of trees were found.

Nearly as many emigrants remained in Iowa among the Pottawatamies during the winter of 1846–47 as were in Winter Quarters. In sharp contrast to Winter Quarters, which grew quickly into a city of nearly five thousand people, the settlements

[2]Ibid., 59.
[3]Hosea Stout, op. cit., 174, entry of 5 July 1846. Stout wrote that the outer camps were about twelve miles from the ferry across the Missouri, which was, in turn, about three miles from the main camp.

in Iowa were much smaller and widely scattered. The largest of the communities in Iowa was Miller's Hollow, which was established by Bishop George Miller about six miles northeast of Grand Encampment near Mosquito and Indian creeks. The other, much smaller Iowa settlements were not villages or even hamlets but merely a collection of farmhouses, often in a grove or on a creek, with a church and school and perhaps a mill.

About eighty branches of the church were established in these small settlements between 1846 and 1852, many with colorful names such as Plum Hollow Branch, Indian Mill Branch, and Prairie Chicken Point. The earliest of the settlements were on Mosquito Creek, an appropriately named stream according to Mary Richards: "Thursday [August] 6th [1846] . . . came home & went to bed. But the misskateos [mosquitoes] haveing taken possesion of our tent we was not permited to sleep all night."[4]

A few miles north of Mosquito Creek was Pigeon Creek, described by Wilford Woodruff as a stream about fifteen feet wide and one to ten feet deep, "with a hard blue clay bottom well supplied with good fish."[5] Along this stream was found some of the finest farming land in Iowa. Isaac and James Allred and a number of their children settled there, as did Allen Taylor, his mother Elizabeth, and other members of the Taylor family, while preparing for the trek to the valley of the Great Salt Lake.[6] The branch, presided over by Isaac Allred and known as Allred's Branch or Allred's Camp, was located about eight miles east of Winter Quarters and eight miles north of Miller's Hollow.

Throughout the summer, refugees continued to arrive at the Missouri. In the late summer and autumn of 1846 a strange disease that the Saints called "black canker" broke out in some of the camps along the lowlands of the Missouri River. It swept the "misery bottoms" like the black plague that devastated Europe in the Dark Ages. At one time more than a third of the camp occupants lay stricken. Many others were still weak from the ordeal of

---

[4]Mary Haskin Parker Richards, *Winter Quarters, The 1846–1848 Life Writings of Mary Haskin Parker Richards*, 87.
[5]Woodruff, "Journal," entry of 18 July 1846, HDC.
[6]Reddick Allred, op.cit.; Taylor, op. cit.

crossing Iowa after their flight from Nauvoo. John Loveless, who arrived at Council Bluffs in early June and located himself on the Little Pigeon at Allred's Branch, wrote:

> I witnessed scenes of suffering, destitution and heartrending distress that would have melted the heart of [the] adamant, and caused a man, yew, even the Saints of God to curse and swear eternal vengeance against the perpetrators of all this horrid misery.[7]

But there was neither energy nor time that could be wasted in contemplating revenge against those who had caused the Saints to flee Nauvoo. The first order of business was to build lodging and prepare for the coming winter and the upcoming trek across the plains. Typical was William Lampard Watkins, who wrote:

> In the spring, as soon as the frost was out of the ground and the feed was good enough, we continued on our journey to Council Bluffs. We arrived there early in July and located on a branch of Little Pigeon also known as Allred's camp. Here we found my brother-in-law Joseph Hammond and family, and his wife's parents and relatives, all preparing to leave for the valley next spring. We took our squatters' rights on some land, built a number of log cabins, and went into basket making and a little farming in order to obtain an outfit for future traveling.[8]

In the late summer and fall the refugees cut and stacked thousands of tons of prairie hay, gathered and preserved hundreds of barrels of wild berries, and salted or dried the meat of wild game. Scattered upon Pottawattamie lands, the Mormons sustained themselves through the harsh winter of 1846–47, called by Thomas Kane "the severest of their trials."[9] It didn't help that many men were away in service with the Mormon Battalion, though, ironically, their absence probably helped many Saints survive the winter as battalion pay was used at home to purchase food and other necessary provisions.

Above all and in spite of hardships, sickness, and death, the first thought for most was of the final exodus to the mountains.

---

[7]Autobiography of John Loveless, *Our Pioneer Heritage*, 2:224.
[8]Diary of William Lampard Watkins, *Our Pioneer Heritage*, 19:392.
[9]Kane, *The Mormons*, 63.

Not all were united, however, in their choice of who should lead the migration. As the head of the Quorum of the Twelve, Brigham Young was the de facto leader, but neither he nor anyone else had replaced Joseph Smith as president of the church. Several, such as Sidney Rigdon, James J. Strang, and William Smith, the Prophet's only surviving brother, had made prior claims to church leadership and had been excommunicated. Others, such as William Marks, former president of the Nauvoo Stake, refused to follow Young's leadership and also were excommunicated.

Brigham Young realized the danger inherent in this dissension and sought the will of the Lord on how to deal with the problem. On 11 January 1847 he told of a dream he had the previous night in which he discussed with Joseph Smith "the best means of organizing companies for emigration."[10] Hosea Stout recorded that day in his journal, "President Young spoke of the order which he contemplated going into for our journey in the spring but nothing I think is yet definite on the subject."[11] Three days later, after much thought, Young presented to the church something very definite, "the Word and Will of the Lord concerning the Camp of Israel in their journeyings to the West."[12]

The document was accepted by assembled priesthood quorums as revelation. While it did not specifically address the problem of dissension, it said that the trek was "under the direction of the Twelve Apostles," thus firmly establishing Young, the president of the quorum, as the leader of the exodus. Hosea Stout wrote of emotions that must have been shared by many:

> Such was the "Word & Will" of the Lord at this time . . . and my feeling can be better felt than described for this will put to silence the wild bickering and suggestions of those who are ever in the way & opposing the proper council. They will now have to come to this standard or come out in open rebellion to the Will of the Lord. . . .[13]

Most were very anxious to begin the journey, though it was not practical for thousands to travel at once to an unknown area where, as the famed Jim Bridger would offer to wager Young, it

---

[10]*Manuscript History of Brigham Young*, comp. Elden J. Watson, 11 January 1847.
[11]Hosea Stout, op. cit., 226.   [12]*D&C* 136.

was not entirely certain that even corn would grow. The original idea was to handpick a company of 144 men that would establish a base in the mountains for further migration.[14]

Brigham Young clearly was in charge, but there was still an undercurrent of dissent. Exactly two weeks after Young and his pioneer camp began the long journey across the plains, Hosea Stout visited Allen and Pleasant Green Taylor at Pigeon Creek "to engage them to take care of some cattle and horses which may be detained, belonging to the dissenters who are going away."[15] Regarding the number of dissenters who left the church at this time, John D. Lee wrote:

> . . . the ferry is thronged continually with waggons to cross, that the scattering has become so general that bro J Taylor and P P Pratt put a vetoe on any teams crossing without a certificate from Pres. I. Morley to show his approval.[16]

The decision to cross the plains was difficult even for some who had remained faithful. On July 1 Lee was visited at Winter Quarters by his friend John H. Redd, who had returned from Nauvoo to his plantation in Rutherford County, Tennessee, rather than join the trek across Iowa. On 4 July Lee recorded: "Left Bro. John H. Redd considerably difficulted in his mind with reference to removing W[est]."[17] The next day Redd began the return trip to Tennessee, still not having reached a decision.

In the meantime the long march of the Mormon Battalion was reaching a conclusion. The battalion celebrated the Fourth of July at Fort Moore in Los Angeles and was discharged officially on 16 July.[18] True to Brigham Young's promise they had

[13]Hosea Stout, op. cit., 229.

[14]One man dropped out and three women—wives of Brigham Young—his brother Lorenzo Young, and Heber C. Kimball, as well as two children were added to the company for a total of 148.   [15]Ibid., 253.

[16]Lee, *Journals of John D. Lee, 1846–47 and 1859*, 162.   [17]Ibid., 185.

[18]Isaac Allred's sons Reddick and James R. were among those who were in Los Angeles for July Fourth, as was his nephew Richard Ivie; James Allred's sons James T. S. and Reuben W. Allred became ill along the way and spent the winter in Pueblo, Colorado, along with other battalion members of the "sick detachment." Joseph Taylor and Thomas Ivie were among fifteen men chosen to escort Brigadier General Stephen W. Kearney from San Pedro to Monterey to confront John Fremont, the temporary governor of California who refused to recognize General Kearney as the new governor. See Ricketts, *The Mormon Battalion*, 61–162.

REDDIN AND REDDICK ALLRED
Courtesy the International Society, Daughters of Utah Pioneers

seen no fighting. Seventy-nine of the 317 men who completed the march re-enlisted for another six months; a few others either decided to stay in California or to rejoin their families by retracing their route. The remaining 223 men prepared to leave Los Angeles under the direction of Levi Hancock, who, as was the pattern, divided the group into hundreds, fifties and tens. James Pace, John H. Redd's old friend from Rutherford County, Tennessee, and Andrew Lytle were appointed captains of the two hundreds; Reddick Allred, William Hyde, Daniel Tyler, and Jefferson Hunt were chosen to lead the four fifties.

Reddick Allred's fifty left Los Angeles on 23 July, traveling steadily northward through the San Joaquin Valley until they reached Sutter's Fort on the Sacramento River. While still camped there in late August they received news that the pioneers were settling in the Salt Lake Valley.[19]

[19]Ricketts, *The Mormon Battalion*, 172. The news came from C. C. Smith, who had traveled with Samuel Brannan, to Green River, Wyoming, where they met the pioneer company.

As a matter of fact, an advance company of pioneers scouted the Salt Lake Valley on 22 July and camped in the valley that night. The next day a work party of 42 men and 23 wagons under the direction of Apostle Orson Pratt entered the valley, and on 24 July the main body of the pioneers arrived, including Brigham Young, who was suffering from mountain fever. "President Young," Wilford Woodruff recorded in his journal, "expressed his full satisfaction in the appearance of the valley as a resting place for the Saints, and was amply repaid for his journey."[20] Thirty-three years later Woodruff remembered the moment in a more dramatic fashion from which legend was born:

> [Brigham Young] was enwrapped in vision for several minutes. He had seen the valley before in vision, and upon this occasion he saw the future glory of Zion and of Israel, as they would be, planted in the valleys of these mountains. When the vision had passed, he said: *It is enough. This is the right place, drive on.*[21]

The intention of the pioneers was to survey the valley and to lay the foundation for the arrival of families at Salt Lake later that summer. On 29 July they were joined by a group of Saints from Mississippi and members of the Mormon Battalion, who for health reasons spent the winter in Pueblo, Colorado, rather than traveling with the battalion to California.[22] With this addition there were more than four hundred persons in the valley, but for many, the stay in the valley was not long. The first group of pioneers left for Winter Quarters on 17 August, while Brigham Young and the second company departed on 29 August. Most of the pioneers, along with a number of Battalion members, returned to Winter Quarters, but preparations already had been made for the arrival of large company of families, including 566 wagons and 1,553 persons.

Before leaving the valley Brigham Young wrote a letter addressed to "Capt. Jefferson Hunt and the officers and soldiers of the Mormon Battalion." After only two weeks the pioneers in the Salt Lake Valley were destitute and Young worried that an

[20]Woodruff, "Journal," entry of 24 July 1847.   [21]Woodruff, Wilford, *Utah Pioneers*, p. 23
[22]Reuben Allred and his wife Ezadie Ford, and James T. S. Allred and his wife Elizabeth Manwaring were among the Battalion members to enter the valley at this time.

influx of people would strain the meager resources of those who had just settled there. The letter recommended that those men with adequate means proceed to Salt Lake while others were asked to remain in California and labor until spring. In response to the letter, about half of the men returned to Sutter's Fort to find employment, while the other half, including the principal leaders (Hancock, Lytle, Allred, Pace, Hyde, Hunt, and Tyler), commenced their journey to the East, arriving in the Salt Lake Valley in mid-October.

Those whose families were not in the valley stayed just two days before leaving on 18 October for Winter Quarters, traveling separately in companies led by James Pace and Andrew Lytle. Inherent in commencing the journey at such a late date was the risk of bad weather, and the group reached Fort Bridger in a severe snowstorm. One hundred and fifty miles below Fort Laramie after another storm, the men had to break trail through deep snow. As they reached the Loup River, conditions worsened dramatically:

> At daylight one morning we found ourselves under a foot of snow and a hundred miles from timber, nothing to burn but wet buffalo chips and without tents. The day before we got to the Loup Fork. I found the head of Brother Rainey's mule; a company a week ahead of us had eaten the animal but left the head. I cut out the brains and I got help to eat the meat. We got to the Loup fork too late to cross, so we camped, but when we got up in the morning it was snowing hard and the river was full of floating ice and we could not cross. It snowed all day so we lay in camp, divided all the flour and meat we had and ate it up. It was 5 days before the ice block dissolved enough for us to cross, during which time we lived on rawhide.
>
> On the 5th day of our slow journey down the river, one of Captain Lytle's mules got down and I told the boys to lift it up and I would cut its throat and we would eat it, which was done and all partook.[23]

During the last ten days before they reached Winter Quarters, the only food they had to eat was Captain Lytle's mule. Weather conditions continued to be nearly intolerable:

The snow was from one to two feet deep and when night came we

---

[23]Reddick Allred, op. cit., 5:307.

thought of the saying, "Would to God it was morning," (having to sleep on the snow until our bones ached) and in the morning say, "I would to God it was night," anticipating a hard day's tramp through the snow.[24]

Captain Lytle's group arrived at Winter Quarters on 18 December 1847, two months to the day after they left the Salt Lake Valley. Brigham Young greeted and invited Reddick Allred to stay the night with him, but he ended up staying with Sister Henry, a "good old friend." Though provided a good bath, clean underclothes, and a good feather bed, Allred awakened his hostess in the night with heavy groans. Asked if his supper had given him stomach pains, Allred replied, "I have had none, but it is this bed that hurts me."[25]

The journey of four thousand miles was over, and finally it was time for Reddick Allred to rejoin his family:

> December 19, 1847. I crossed the Missouri River and went eight miles to Little Pigeon, Allred's settlement, where I found my wife and daughter living with father, all well and overjoyed at the safe return of their soldier boy and husband. It was several days before they would allow me to eat what I wanted, and even then I was much distressed with my victuals. Father had kept my wife and child as one of his family and we remained with him all winter. Father was presiding over this Branch of the Church.[26]

Many others were crossing the Missouri to Iowa at the time Allred returned to his family. A decision had been made to vacate Winter Quarters, primarily in response to pressure from the Bureau of Indian Affairs, which initially had given permission to reside only temporarily on Omaha lands, but also with the expectation that it would "accelerate the departure of the saints generally."[27] By this time many of the residents of Winter Quarters had already moved or were moving to Miller's Hollow, whose name soon would be changed to Kanesville in honor of Thomas Kane, or to other Iowa settlements.

Another very important decision had been reached in early December. For more than three years the church had been without

---

[24]Ibid.   [25]Ibid.   [26]Ibid.
[27]*Journal History of the Church*, 25 November 1847.

a president; in early December the Twelve unanimously decided to organize a First Presidency with Brigham Young as the president of the church. A log tabernacle, sixty feet long and forty feet wide, was built in haste at Miller's Hollow to accommodate a "Jubilee" conference, which was convened on Christmas Eve day. After several days of dancing and numerous addresses and messages from church leader, the new First Presidency was sustained.[28]

This action gave the members a new sense of security. Apostle George A. Smith led the congregation in the shout of praise: "Hosanna, Hosanna, Hosanna to God and the Lamb. Amen! Amen! and Amen!"[29] The rejoicing continued into mid-January, at which time a "Jubilee" of five days' duration was celebrated through dance and feasting. Reddick Allred recalled:

> After we rested a while, President Young proclaimed a jubilee in the Log Tabernacle at Kanesville and invited the returned soldiers. As Brother William Hyde and I were approaching, President Young said to President [Heber C.] Kimball and others (pointing to us), "These men were the salvation of this Church." We all had a free dance and enjoyed it very much.[30]

Once the celebration ended, all thought was turned to the upcoming season. For those in Pottawattamie this meant preparation for spring planting. For many in Winter Quarters it was a season of emigration, which had as its major purpose the evacuation of Winter Quarters. Understandably this was the principal topic of discussion on April 6, the first day of General Conference.

It has been stated that those residents of Winter Quarters who had the means emigrated in 1848, while those who didn't joined their fellow Saints at Pottawattamie. In reality it was not quite so simple, for few families by themselves had the necessary means to cross the plains. At the General Conference, Joseph Young, Brigham's older brother, arose and said:

> I feel that I want to make a few remarks on our emigration. I have had opportunity to know about the circumstances of the brethren in

---

[28]Hosea Stout, op. cit., 291–292.   [29]Nels Anderson, *Desert Saints*, 73–74.
[30]Reddick Allred, op. cit., 5:310. Heber C. Kimball was the First Counselor to Brigham Young in the First Presidency. According to President Young, the Jubliee was convened by the Seventies, not by himself (see *Journal History of the Church*, 20 January 1848).

Winter Quarters; there is not one man out of ten there who have got
provisions or teams enough for their journey. . . . I have said that if a
good many would draw lots and put their teams, wagons, etc.
together they could get off. Put your and mine together and one of
us can go. Otherwise there is nobody in camp who can go.[31]

Brigham Young took to heart the suggestion of his brother
and arranged the loan of sixty teams from the Pottawattamie
Saints. He found it best, however, to give to another the responsibility for the teams:

No man need give a team to any other man and think I will be responsible for it. . . . Brethren, don't put teams out at random. When you
send a team, send a good confidential driver who will take care of it
and return it safe so that you shall not be deceived. . . . It is moved and
seconded that Allen Taylor take charge of the teams coming back.[32]

The goal that summer was to gather the Saints to the Great
Basin in ever-increasing numbers. Though Brigham Young issued
a "General Epistle" to the membership of the church calling upon
Latter-day Saints throughout the world to gather to Winter
Quarters to get ready for the journey to Salt Lake City, the vast
majority of the two thousand who were ready to make the journey
in May 1848 were already living along the Missouri. "Both sides of
the river thronged with Emigrating waggons & roling out contin-
ually," wrote John D. Lee. "Every exertion is making to go West."[33]

By mid-May great numbers of Saints were encamped on the
Elkhorn river southwest of Winter Quarters. Brigham Young
and his family departed May 26:

On the 26th I started on my journey to the mountains, leaving my
houses, mills and the temporary furniture I had acquired during our
sojourn there [Winter Quarters]. This was the fifth time I had left
my home and property since I embraced the gospel of Jesus Christ.[34]

The plan for the overland expedition called for the formation
of three companies, each to be led by a member of the new First
Presidency—Brigham Young, Heber C. Kimball and Willard
Richards. On the last day of May, Young and Kimball com-

[31]Ibid., 6 April 1848.   [32]Ibid.
[33]Robert Glass Cleland and Juanita Brooks, *A Mormon Chronicle: The Diaries of John D. Lee,
1846–1876*, 1:28 (entry for 16 May 1848).

menced organizing the people in their companies into hundreds, fifties, and tens and appointing the officers necessary to manage to journey (Richards' company was formed a month later on June 30). It was a stirring sight to behold the nearly two thousand people who were camping on the Elkhorn, as Thomas Bullock wrote:

> If any person enquire, "Is Mormonism down?" he ought to have been in the neighbourhood of the Elk Horn this day, and he would have seen such a host of waggons that would have satisfied him in an instant, that it lives and flourishes like a tree by a fountain of waters; he would have seen merry faces, and heard the song of rejoicing, that the day of deliverance had surely come.[35]

With a total of 397 wagons and 1,229 people, Young's was by far the largest of the companies and had to be divided into several groups in order to avoid overcrowding at campsites and water holes. On May 31 Lorenzo Snow, William Perkins, Zera Pulsipher, and Allen Taylor were chosen to be captains of hundreds. "Hundred" was a misnomer in this case, since Allen Taylor's company actually numbered 190 wagons and 597 souls, comprising nearly half of Brigham Young's entire company, and twice as large as any other "hundred" of the 1848 emigration season. Perkin's company, on the other hand, was comprised of only fifty-seven wagons, primarily because John D. Lee, who had been chosen by Brigham Young to be captain of the second fifty of the Perkins unit, was generally disliked at the time and nobody wanted to go with him.[36]

The companies started out in order, at one-day intervals, with Lorenzo Snow in the lead and Allen Taylor in the rear. Cattle were able to swim across the river, but wagons had to be ferried, which was a slow, painstaking process, even though the Elkhorn ferry was a substantial improvement over the conditions endured by the 1847 pioneers. A wagon could cross the river every five minutes, and thus it took several days for all of the wagons of the Kimball and Young companies to be ferried across.

---

[34]*Manuscript History of Brigham Young*, entry of 26 May 1848.

[35]Letter of Thomas Bullock, 10 July 1848, printed in *The Latter-Day Saints' Millennial Star*, Vol. X, No. 20, 15 October 1848.

[36]Juanita Brooks, *John Doyle Lee, Zealot—Pioneer Builder—Scapegoat*, 130. Snow had ninety-nine wagons in his "hundred," while Pulsipher had only fifty-one.

A wide variety of animals accompanied each of the groups. Taylor's company, for example, had 30 horses, 16 mules, 615 oxen, 316 cows, 63 loose cattle, 134 sheep, 66 pigs, 282 chickens, 19 cats, 31 dogs, 3 goats, 8 geese, 6 doves, and 1 crow.[37] Snow's company also included two beehives. It is easy to imagine how difficult it would be to control such a menagerie, particularly at nighttime when the wolves started to howl: "The wolves kicked up a regular rumpus during the night; as quick as they commenced howling the dogs barked, the cattle lowed, and men shouted to call their loose cattle together."[38]

The 1848 emigration differed little in its route or its encounters on the trail from the 1847 companies. The make-up of the group was very dissimilar, however, consisting of regular families rather than a small, handpicked party of able-bodied men. Fortunately the three main leaders, Brigham Young, Heber C. Kimball, and Willard Richards, had traveled to the Salt Lake Valley and back to Winter Quarters in 1847 and had experience in crossing the plains. This was especially important since, for a variety of reasons, the Mormons never used professional guides; they preferred to "trust in the Lord," but this time experience bred more self-reliance.

The 1848 company, much larger than the 1847 pioneer company, was unwieldy and at first very slow moving. Brigham summoned his captains on the evening of June 6 and suggested that they "perfect their organizing," forming smaller companies that would travel double-file. It was decided that the wagons would be numbered and would move in order, though slower teams would start an hour earlier than the others.[39] To help maintain order, Hosea Stout, who was traveling in Allen Taylor's company, was appointed captain of the guard.[40]

The organizational summit must be considered a success, for the very large company ultimately moved at almost the same speed as the much smaller pioneer company the year before. Brigham Young realized how important it was to train leaders

[37]*Journal History of the Church*, 16 June 1848, entry of camp clerk Thomas Bullock.
[38]Ibid., 4 June 1848.
[39]Ibid., 6 June 1848.
[40]Brooks, *On the Mormon Frontier*, vol. 1., p.314, entry of 6 June 1848.

for future seasons of emigration, and he proved to be the consummate leader and teacher. Brigham was never above helping to repair a broken wagon wheel, helping to set a broken leg, or traveling at the rear of the train, the most unpopular of all positions due to the dust created by the hundreds of wagon teams in front. After reaching the Loup Fork, he braved the river's quick current and shifting quicksand and "crossed & recrossed back & fourth, untill he Saw all over safe."[41]

After the crossing, the camp moved down the river near a stand of trees and formed an oblong ellipse, which Brigham Young had learned in 1847 was practical both to corral the livestock and to guard against attack from the Indians. Allen Taylor's hundred failed to make the proper formation and he quickly was taught a lesson: "Pres. Young ordered Allen Taylor and [captain of fifty] Daniel Garn not to rest until every wagon was put into a correct line or corral with ours, showing it for a pattern."[42]

The crossing of the Loup Fork was close to the ninety-eighth meridian, almost immediately at the beginning of the Great Plains, a vast high plateau of semiarid grassland over which cold winters and warm summers prevail, with low precipitation and humidity, much wind, and sudden changes of temperature. This was a different world than most of the Saints had experienced. As Taylor's company moved on from the river, Hosea Stout recorded: "The ground soft & unpleasant travelling. The day was very hot. One ox of John Alger melted and died."[43]

The unfavorable conditions slowed the progress of the company to about ten miles a day. Grass was scarce for the animals and wood and drinking water were also limited. Hosea Stout recorded, in his typically colorful manner: "Had to use the Bois de vache or Buffalo chips for fuel which were damp which made rather an unfavorable impression on our women relative to being entirely confined to them before we get to our journey's end."[44] Stout also wrote of another event that left an unfavorable impression:

---

[41]Cleland and Brooks, *Mormon Chronicle*, 39 (entry of 15 July 1848).

[42]*Journal History of the Church*, 15 July 1848, entry of Thomas Bullock.

[43]Brooks, *On the Mormon Frontier*, vol. 1, p. 316 (entry of 19 June 1848).

[44]Ibid., 316 (entry of 22 June 1848).

Tonight about dark a skunk made us a visit Locating himself under my waggons. We endeavored to drive it away without exciting it but knowing the Power it held over us seemed perfectly tame while we had only to deal mildly with it. At length it went under Judge Phelps waggon & laid down in his harness where we were obliged to let it be in peace.[45]

Skunks were an occasional encounter, but the buffalo were everywhere. Stout wrote, "Saw 1000's [*sic*] of Buffalo today which moved as black clouds in the prairie. It is a sight not to be described & only to be realized by sight."[46] Unfortunately, despite Brigham's instructions to the contrary, there was wanton killing of the buffalo by company members:

> The hunting fever seized on the brethren and they, regardless of the previous arraingements [*sic*], to let hunters kill our meet often ran and left their teams pursuing & shooting at the buffalo all day. Many were killed & left out, & but few brought into camp.[47]

As Captain Taylor's company came within view of Chimney Rock, the most famous and recognizable landmark of the entire trail, they encountered a large company of Sioux, which Stout described as "very friendly and altogether the best looking and neatest Indians I ever saw."[48] As they reached Chimney Rock four days later a meeting was held, at which time Young's and Kimball's companies each were divided into four smaller companies to facilitate travel, which was becoming ever more difficult in such large groups.

Travel may have been easier in smaller groups, but hardships still abounded as the Saints encountered sandy roads and choking dust, as well as frequent drenching rains and hail storms. They had been traveling upstream and therefore uphill the entire route, causing fatigue and also bringing on colder weather at the higher altitudes. In early August, beaten down and worn out, they finally made it to the Sweetwater River, 764 miles from Winter Quarters.

The grass at the Sweetwater was greener and more plentiful

---

[45]Ibid., 317 (entry of 30 June 1848).
[46]Ibid., 317 (entry of 1 July 1848).
[47]Ibid., 317 (entry of 30 June 1848).
[48]Ibid., 318 (entry of 12 July 1848).

than had been encountered since the beginning of the journey, but several animals still died each day of starvation or water poisoning. In the midst of all the hardships spirits were buoyed greatly when, on August 17, an advance team from Salt Lake met the companies with "the joyful information that a large number of teams and waggons were on the way."[49] With this welcome news the sixty teams borrowed from the Pottawattamie Saints were unyoked in preparation for their return to Iowa, as Brigham Young reported:

> I arrived at the last crossing of the Sweetwater on the 20th and tarried to return the borrowed teams and wagons. . . . Elder Kimball and I returned from this point, 48 men and boys, 59 wagons, 121 yokes of cattle, 44 mules and horses in charge of Allen Taylor to Winter Quarters.[50]

An epistle from Presidents Young and Kimball to the Pottawattamie Saints, along with sixty-one letters and a list of returned wagons, cattle, and other animals were given to Allen Taylor, whose return company was organized on August 29 and departed the next day. On September 6, one mile below the upper ford of the Platte River, Taylor wrote to Young:

> I am sorry that my report is rather unpleasant on account of losing cattle. . . . As we were encamping on Sweetwater under the gravelly bluffs it happened that some of our cattle strayed off. . . . I have had men out hunting for the lost cattle all the time till now, but all in vain; there is 9 head gone as yet. . . . Three oxen have died. . . .[51]

The news didn't get any better for some who were awaiting their borrowed teams, for several men had died and ten of the wagons did not return. In a letter dated October 20, 1848, Orson Pratt wrote:

> Conference voted to send an express to the mountains. . . . At the Horn, they met Captain Allen Taylor with fifty waggons and the return teams which went on in the spring company; they left President Young on the Sweetwater at the Upper Crossing. Four deaths had occurred on the road. About twenty cases of mountain fever had

---

[49]Ibid., 323 (entry of 17 August 1848). [50]*Journal History of the Church*, 20 August 1848.
[51]Ibid., 6 September 1848.

occurred, but all recovered, or were recovering. A number of oxen had died of poison.[52]

Fortunately, the conditions that greeted Taylor and his company were better than expected, as Pratt continued in his letter:

> It has been very healthy throughout Pottawattamie County; no deaths within our knowledge; few have had the ague or fever. Our late crops have come in well and we abound in such things as the land produces. Wheat, corn and potatoes are raised in sufficient quantities to last the people two years, if preserved for the food of men; but no doubt the worn-out cattle, which have returned from the mountains, and many others, will feast largely on the two latter articles.[53]

As was the case throughout Pottawattamie County, Allred's Branch was thriving. Two hundred ninety-four acres were planted there in 1848, including 47 acres with wheat, 191 acres with corn, 37 acres with buckwheat, and 19 acres with turnips and other vegetables.[54] No fruits or berries were under cultivation, but there were plenty of wild strawberries, red and black raspberries, and, a few miles away, Pottawattamie plums.[55] Of the forty church branches in the county that were asked to give an account of their farming operations in 1848, only seven reported more extensive plantings than Allred's Branch.[56]

After the autumn harvest it was time for the Pottawattamie Saints to prepare for the upcoming winter. For Allen Taylor, Isaac Allred, and many members of their families, it would be the final winter in Iowa. Taylor already had been successful in helping rescue the "Poor Saints" from Nauvoo, in captaining the largest single company of Saints yet to cross the plains, and in returning borrowed wagons and teams from the Sweetwater back to Iowa. Finally it would be his turn to go to Zion, and nobody could have been better prepared.

---

[52]Ibid., 20 October 1848. According to an entry of 14 October 1848, nine or ten cattle died and five were lost along the way in addition to the ten wagons that were not returned.
[53]Ibid.   [54]Ibid., 10 October 1848.
[55]Clarance Merrill, "Autobiography," reprinted in *Our Pioneer Heritage*, 9:321.
[56]*Journal History of the Church*, 10 October 1848. The largest planting was at the Blockhouse Branch near Kanesville with 775 acres, followed by the Big Pigeon Branch with 480 acres.

Chapter IX

THE ALLEN TAYLOR COMPANY

IN THE FALL OF 1847, about three weeks before Reddick Allred and other ex-soldiers from the Mormon Battalion left Sutter's Fort in Sacramento to rejoin their families in Iowa, John Sutter sent James Marshall to the Coloma Valley on the American River, about forty miles east of the fort, to build a sawmill. After a site was located, Peter Wimmer with his family and a number of laborers from the disbanded Battalion were summoned to construct the mill.[1]

On 24 January 1848, while checking to see that the tailrace of the mill had been flushed clean of silt and debris, Marshall looked down through the clear water and saw what appeared to be gold. One of the Mormons, Azariah Smith, recorded in his journal: "This week Mon. the 24th, Mr. Marshall found some pieces of (as we suppose) Gold, and he has gone to the Fort, for the purpose of finding out."[2] Marshall and Sutter tested the nuggets with nitric acid and determined them to be gold.

Sam Brannan, who presided over a group of Mormon settlers that went by ship to San Francisco in 1846, got wind of the strike

---

[1] James Wilson Marshall, "Account of the First Discovery of Gold." The former battalion members were: James Barger, Ira Willes, Sidney Willes, Alexander Stephens, William Coons, James Brown, Henry Bigler, Azariah Smith, William Johnston, and Israel Evans. Bigler, Smith, Stephens, Brown, Barger, Johnston, and Peter Wimmer were present when Marshall discovered gold. Several of Wimmer's family members and possibly Peter himself were Mormons.

[2] Azariah Smith, David Bigler, ed., *The Gold Discovery Journal of Azariah Smith*, entry of 30 January 1848.

and went first to Sutter's Fort and subsequently to Mormon Island in the American River, where the Mormon miners showed him their gold and gave him the church's tithe.[3] Brannan, an entrepreneur who founded California's second newspaper, the *California Star*, immediately recognized that by publicizing the gold strike, he could make a greater profit by selling his goods to the flood of men who came in search of gold than by joining them in the fields. When published reports in the *California Star* and the *Californian* failed to stir excitement in San Francisco, Brannan, a great believer in the power of publicity, ran down the streets of San Francisco holding a bottle of gold dust in one hand and waving his hat with the other while shouting, "Gold! Gold! Gold, from the American River!"[4]

Soon afterwards San Francisco was nearly deserted for the gold fields, and the Gold Rush was on, though the news didn't reach the East Coast and Europe in time for the 1848 emigration season. But 1849 was a different story, as great masses—more than thirty thousand across the plains and many by sea to San Francisco—made their way to California to seek riches in gold country. At least five thousand of these Forty-niners, as the gold seekers were called, made Kanesville, Iowa, the staging area for their journey west.

The Pottawattamie Saints were not untouched by the news of gold. The *Frontier Guardian*, a Kanesville newspaper established by Orson Hyde to serve the Mormons who remained in Iowa, reported in its second edition, "Considerable excitement has prevailed here since last Fall, concerning an extensive Gold Mine, as thought by some to have been discovered in the Bluffs. . . ."[5] Despite the gold fever in Iowa, few Mormons joined in the rush to California—not surprising, considering that they were emigrating for religious reasons rather than for economic gain. But it was surprising that far fewer Saints made the trek to Utah in

---

[3]Brannan noted that the miners paid a 10 percent assessment, not as tithing but based on the "right to the discovery." See Will Bagley, *Scoundrel's Tale*, 256.
[4]Hubert Howe Bancroft, *History of California*, 6:56.
[5]*Frontier Guardian*, 21 February 1849.

1849 than in most other years, despite the encouragement they were given:

> To the oft repeated question, "shall I go to the [Salt Lake] Valley?" We answer, we advise every person to go, who is able to take with him the amount of provisions requisite, and means to purchase a supply for the remaining part of the year.... We believe that the blessing of Heaven will attend every man in leaving this place as soon as he is able; and that whoever delays after that time will be the loser by it....[6]

Many did delay, but not for lack of desire—Forty-niner Riley Senter, passing through Kanesville on his way to California, noted that the Mormons were "all anxious to get off to the mountains."[7] But, after a particularly severe winter, supplies were running low and surplus grain had been consumed by the livestock, causing many to wonder if enough food remained to last until the fall harvest.[8] Moreover, most of the Saints were in destitute circumstances, lacking the necessary means to undertake the long journey west.

Economic conditions changed rapidly in 1849 as a result of the Gold Rush. The Saints prospered greatly from selling farm products and livestock and providing skilled labor to the flock of Forty-niners. William Lampard Watkins, a resident of Allred's Branch about eight miles north of Kanesville, recorded:

> This new location was ideal for the Saints to prepare for their coming long journey. Traders going to California made a fine market for all the corn we could raise and it brought a good price. A great many began to make improvements and much business was done in Kainsville [Kanesville]. We were getting along very well and the people in general were satisfied with the location.[9]

There was ample reason to be satisfied, for the Mormons began enjoying prosperity previously not experienced in Iowa. Many farmers and merchants reaped great rewards as food and

---

[6]Ibid., 21 March 1849, quote of George A. Smith and Ezra T. Benson.
[7]Riley Senter, *Crossing the Continent to the California Gold Fields*, reprint from the Exeter, California, *Sun*, 1938.   [8]Ibid., 7 March 1849.
[9]Diary of William Lampard Watkins, *Our Pioneer Heritage*, 19:393.

supplies were sold to the California emigrants at a premium and replenished with goods from Missouri purchased at a lesser price.[10] For some the new prosperity may have come too late to be able to make the trip to Salt Lake City that year; others may have decided to postpone the journey in order to share in the newfound economic gain. Regardless, in 1849 about one thousand fewer Saints crossed the plains than in the previous year.

Those who did choose to make the journey knew exactly what preparations were necessary, for the *Frontier Guardian*, in its second edition, issued instructions to the Saints planning to emigrate during the 1849 season.[11] Companies would go, the newspaper instructed, whenever fifty wagons were assembled, provided they were properly equipped and supplied. Since the winter on the Missouri had been so severe, it was assumed that the winter in the Salt Lake Valley also had been harsh (a correct assumption), and a greater amount of provisions, particularly flour, was advised. And a cricket infestation in Salt Lake in 1848 brought an unusual request:

> Take turkeys, geese and ducks to the Valley instead of chickens. They have a plenty of chickens there already. But turkeys! turkeys! are the birds to eat up and destroy the crickets. Pigs will eat them also. Take the latter by all means.[12]

Though at least one independent Mormon company had crossed the plains in the spring, the first organized company was formed in late May under the leadership of Orson Spencer, who had been in charge of the British mission and had just recently arrived in Kanesville.[13] Nearly three weeks passed following the departure of Spencer's company on 6 June before another company was formed, the delay due in great part due to poor weather. Daniel Stillwell Thomas left his log cabin on the fifteenth of June to join the trek and found that due to heavy rains "the water

---

[10]*Frontier Guardian*, 16 May 1849.   [11]Ibid., 21 February 1849.
[12]Ibid.

[13]The independent company of fifty-seven Saints departed Kanesville on 19 April, captained by Howard Egan, who had gone to the Rocky Mountains and back both in 1847 and 1848; the primary mission of the company was to take a printing press to the Salt Lake Valley.

was so high it was almost impossible to get to the ferry."[14] Travel to the ferry seemed even more difficult for William Blood:

> In June 1849, soon after Brother Lambert's family came to our house, we left our home and started for Winter Quarters, nine miles from where we lived. The river and the sloughs were very high. In crossing the sloughs we had to cut two logs and fasten them together, just the distance apart of the width of a wagon, then cut two grooves in each log for the wagon wheels to fit into, then hitch one team to each log. In this way the wagon was prevented from sinking too deep into the mud, and the water was kept out of the wagon boxes. Thus we were nearly three weeks making the journey to Winter Quarters with our two wagons.[15]

In a meeting on 24 June near little Pigeon Creek, George A. Smith declared it best to organize on the Iowa side of the river primarily "on account of trouble with indians," though there was little trouble of the sort at the time on the opposite side of the river.[16] At the meeting, by Smith's motion, Allen Taylor was appointed Captain of Hundred.[17] The company quickly was organized and crossed the Missouri using the original ferry built by Reuben Allred, who was, coincidentally, a member of Taylor's company.

Once across the river, company members confirmed the appointment of Allen Taylor as Captain of Hundred and elected Reddick Allred and Enoch Reese Captains of Fifty. In addition, Andrew Perkins was elected President of the camp, with Isaac Allred and Absalom Perkins as his counselors and David Moore as clerk.[18] With the completion of the organization, according to William Blood, "All things were prepared for the journey, but we remained in camp on July 4 and respected the day of the independence of our nation."[19]

That they would respect the Fourth of July at all was a drastic change of heart compared to the previous year, when Hosea Stout, expressing feelings shared by many, wrote: "Today is our

---

[14]E. Kay Kirkham comp., *Daniel Stillwell Thomas, Utah Pioneer of 1849*, 21.
[15]Ivy Hooper Blood Hill, *William Blood, His Posterity and Biographies of their Progenitors*, 14.
[16]George A. Smith, "Minutes of a meeting of The Company of Saints, 24 June 1849."
[17]Ibid.   [18]Ibid., 47–8.   [19]Hill, op. cit., 14.

Allen Taylor
Courtesy of Michael Macfarlane

Nation's annaversary [*sic*] or birth day of her liberty while we are fleeing exiles from her tyranny & oppression."[20] Margaret Judd, who with her family stayed with Allen Taylor after the expulsion from Far West in the winter of 1838, recalled that, for those in camp, it was a day "not entirely to celebrate, but to wash and do mending and various other things that were necessary."[21] It was a different story, however, for those who remained in Allred's Branch, as reported in the *Frontier Guardian*:

> Fourth of July—Dinner at Allreds' Branch.
> Mr. Editor—Sir: The citizens began to assemble about 10 o'clock, A.M. Several salutes were fired in honor of the day, by direction of Capt. Joseph Taylor. The committee which had been previously chosen, had found a shade, under which a long table was soon constructed, and our ladies (God Bless them,) soon had it covered with white linen, and then the way the cakes, pies and chicken fixens was displayed along the table was enough to make a man's mouth water—

[20]Brooks, *On the Mormon Frontier*, 1:317 (entry of July 4, 1848).
[21]Margaret Judd Clawson, "Rambling Reminiscences of Margaret Gay Judd Clawson," *New Era*, May 1974, 46.

in fact there was a splendid feast. . . . Col. Jesse Haven was called on for a speech . . . at the close of which the Washington Song was sung by Capt. Wm. M. Allred and lady. . . . No spirituous liquors were on the ground, but a barrel of good beer, manufactured by our friend, John Walker, Esq., was tapped to good advantage.[22]

As the sun rose the following morning, Reddick Allred's fifty began the journey towards the Salt Lake Valley. As was often the case, "fifty" was just an approximation of the number of wagons in the group rather than an actual sum; Allred's company actually consisted of seventy-two wagons and 246 persons, along with the typical assortment of animals, including turkeys, ducks, geese, and pigs, as had been advised by the *Frontier Guardian*. Enoch Reese's fifty, comprised of sixty-five wagons and 199 persons, was still organizing and did not depart until the next day.[23]

The first challenge came almost immediately, where the rain-swollen Elkhorn River was one hundred feet wide and swift enough to tear the ferrying raft from its guiding rope. Fortunately, Christopher Merkley, a member of Enoch Reese's fifty, was experienced in such matters and was chosen by Captain Taylor to take charge of the ferry.[24] A site was chosen upstream, a new ferry was constructed and, after a delay of three days, the first fifty crossed the river and was joined the next day by the sixty-five wagons of the second fifty.[25]

While the Taylor Company was crossing the Elkhorn, the final three Mormon companies of the season, under Silas Richards, Ezra T. Benson, and George A. Smith, were preparing to depart from Winter Quarters. Together the four companies totaled more than one thousand, but in stark contrast to 1848, they were hardly alone on the north side of the Platte. "The amount of emigration is immense, beyond all estimate," reported the *Millennial*

---

[22]*Frontier Guardian*, 11 July 1849. In addition to William M. Allred and Joseph Taylor, Pleasant Green Taylor also remained at Allred's Branch for another year. It is readily evident from this and many other sources that the "Word of Wisdom," an 1833 revelation to Joseph Smith which among other things advised against the use of tobacco and alcohol, was not strictly followed for many years.

[23]Moore, op. cit., entries of 4, 5, and 6 July 1849, 48–49.

[24]Christopher Merkley, *Biography of Christopher Merkley*, 29.

[25]Moore, op. cit., 50.

Star. "It is predicted there will be extreme distress and privation among the emigrating caravans."[26] With this in mind it was deemed important by Allen Taylor to communicate with the trailing Mormon companies. To accomplish this a hole was bored in a good-sized pole into which letters were inserted. The pole then was set into the ground creating a "post" office, as it was good-naturedly called.[27]

The post office proved to be an effective front-to-back line of communication for the Mormon companies, though in the first days after crossing the Elkhorn there was little news worthy of communicating. June rains had given way to July heat, bringing with it a plentitude of mosquitoes but also great beauty to the prairie. "The plains here . . . are covered with rich, luxuriant pastures and beautiful flowers of different odors, colors and variegated hues," wrote William Appleby, clerk of the G. A. Smith Company that was traveling several days behind Taylor.[28]

The beauty of the plains and the excitement of the trip, however, could barely mask the monotony encountered by the pioneers. "In traveling as we did, one day was very like another," wrote Margaret Judd.[29] Each day was spent on the trail, going as far as was reasonable; at night the men took care of the cattle while the women prepared the food. To break the tedium, at the end of the day a bonfire was made while the young folks sang, told stories, played, danced, and made their "own amusements," as Mary Jane Lyttle recalled: "Lovers strayed in the moonlight not too far from camp and I suppose repeated the old old but ever new story."[30]

Through the first ten days of the journey the closest thing to a noteworthy event for the entire company was when Allen Taylor was called upon to settle a complaint of the tens who were tired

---

[26]*Millennial Star*, 1 September 1849, reprinted from the *Cleveland Herald*, 15 May 1849.

[27]Moore, op. cit. 11 July 1849, 50.

[28]William Appleby, "Church Emigration of 1849, Fourth Company," in *Church Emigration Book*, 23 July 1849.

[29]Clawson, op. cit., 46.

[30]Mary Jane Lyttle Little, "Memories of Mary Jane Lyttle Little," copied into the Alfred Douglas Young journal, 38.

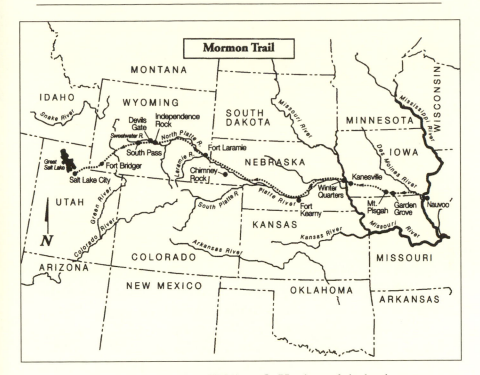

Used by permission of William G. Hartley and the book
*My Best for the Kingdom: History and Autobiography of
John Lowe Butler, a Mormon Frontiersman.*

of traveling each day in the rear. There was no mention, perhaps
not even a thought, of the "elephant," a very popular expression
among the overlanders alluding to the perils and hardships they
had to survive in order to reach their destination. But then, during the night of 16 July, there was a stampede in Enoch Reese's
fifty. The following night there was another stampede, worse
than the first but merely a prelude to what was to come:

> July 18th—In the morning, after the cattle were all yoked, and most
> of them chained together, we had another stampede, which was
> truly awful to behold; cattle rushed from the coral [*sic*], chained
> together, from 2 to 3, 4 and 5 yoke, and were literally piled up in

heaps . . . two men badly and two slightly hurt. Through the course of the day, we had some six or eight stampedes, and it was with extreme difficulty that we got them quieted . . . during this operation I think I saw some of the tracks of the "big elephant."[31]

Three men were injured in the stampedes, one of whom nearly broke his back.[32] "He was a gold digger going to California who had overtaken us and was traveling with our company for a while," Margaret Judd later reminisced.[33] From that time forth there was no doubt that stampedes were the "elephant" of the Allen Taylor Company. To prevent further mayhem, the company began traveling in separate tens, even in Indian country, reasoning "that it was more dangerous traveling among stampedes than among Indians."[34]

The company reunited to cross the Loup Fork which, with its soft banks, quicksand, and shifting sandy bottom, always presented a problem, especially in the driving rain encountered on 21 July. A frustrated Allen Taylor again appointed Christopher Merkely to find a ford in the river.[35] Merkely, though sick from exposure to the raw conditions, succeeded and the difficult crossing was made, but already it was evident that the most dreaded and memorable events of the journey would be those that led James Parshall Terry to exclaim, "This was a summer of stampedes."[36]

Terry, who had gone to the Salt Lake Valley and back to Iowa in 1848, was writing with the authority of experience. In that year, he wrote, at night the wagons circled and each head of cattle was tied outside, while in 1849, in the Enoch Reese fifty, at dark all horses and cattle were placed inside the enclosed wagons.[37] And

---

[31]Martha M. Morgan, *A Trip Across the Plains in the Year 1849*, 8. Martha Morgan and her husband Jesse were non-Mormons who were traveling with the Allen Taylor Company to "California via Salt Lake." Though the diary was published by and under the name of Martha Morgan, it was in fact written by her husband Jesse, who died in California in 1850.

[32]Moore, op. cit., 52.   [33]Clawson, op. cit., 49.

[34]Ibid., 53.

[35]Merkley, op. cit., 29.

[36]James Parshall Terry, "Biographical Sketch of James Parshall Terry,"11.

[37]Ibid.

that, according to Reddick Allred, was the source of the early nighttime stampedes:

> Captain Taylor, having crossed the plains the year before as captain of Prest. Young's company, was of great service. He advised us to tie our stock by the head outside of the wagons as they were corralled at night, which I strictly observed, but Capt. Reese did not, with the result that he had not been out a week until his cattle stampeded in the night smashing down wagons to get out.[38]

Cattle also stampeded in the daytime, and not only in Allen Taylor's Company. Early in the morning of 26 July cattle belonging to a group called the California Enterprise Company stampeded in a severe hailstorm, stranding the company. Unbeknownst to them, on 27 July near the Wood River the Taylor Company found fifty-one head of oxen and steers, and two days later, near Fort Kearny, retrieved another fifty.[39] The California company searched in vain for more than a week, but on the fourteenth day after the stampede, the Taylor Company reached the stranded travelers and returned all of the lost livestock.[40]

It was difficult to comprehend just how far and how fast the stampeding cattle had traveled. "They went about 130 miles in 48 hours, which appeared to me almost incredible," wrote Riley Senter, a member of the California company.[41] Others estimated, probably correctly, that they actually had gone the distance in just thirty-six hours.[42] Regardless, the members of the California company were grateful for the return of the cattle and sent to the Mormons a copy of resolutions they had made:

> *Resolved*, That we return our united thanks to Capt. Allen Taylor, the other officers and members of the train of Latter-day Saints for their kindness and gentlemanly conduct in stopping and procuring for us our teams which broke from our carrel [*sic*] on the morning of the 25th of July, a part of which were discovered on Wood river, some 130 miles from where they left our camp. Also, their vigilant exer-

---

[38]Reddick Allred, op. cit., 5:310–11.
[39]Appleby, op. cit., 2 and 4 August 1849. Riley Senter, op. cit., wrote that ninety-seven head of cattle stampeded.
[40]Senter, op, cit.   [41]Ibid.
[42]*Journal History of the Church*, 12 August 1849.

tions in rescuing a number from the hands of some individuals near Fort Childs, who were determined to detain them, in which, had they succeeded, we would have suffered great inconvenience, since our teams are our main dependence here.[43]

By the time the stray cattle were returned to their owners, the Taylor company had entered buffalo country. "All along up the Platte River for two or three hundred miles we saw thousands of buffalo every day," wrote William Blood. "They were so numerous they could not be counted. Large herds were scattered all over the prairie as far as the eye could see.... I saw more buffalo that summer than I have ever seen of tame cattle in my life."[44]

The pioneers did more than just look at the buffalo. Each family or individual had brought with them the prescribed provisions, but as food supplies began to run out hunters were appointed to kill buffalo. "All thought buffalo meat better than any other kind they had ever eaten," noted Riley Senter,[45] though enthusiasm waned with a steady diet of the meat:

> After swallowing buffalo beef for a few days it affected us all very badly; a big dose of salts was not in with it. I don't wish any one particular harm, but when I see some of our swell dandies now a days, I often wish they could have a few good meals of the old boiled buffalo. I tell you it would take the stiffening out of them.[46]

On occasion the buffalo would stampede, a fearsome event—especially at night—creating "an awful sound of tramping and bellowing," causing the ground to shake and the wagons to tremble but, for the most part, inflicting no real damage.[47] When the buffalo got too close the cattle became agitated; as William Blood wrote, "They seemed to give our oxen a wild spirit."[48] But the worst stampede of the journey started not with thousands of buffalo but rather with a small number of cattle, in broad day-

---

[43]Copy of resolutions made by the California Enterprise Company, Thos H. Owen, Captain, 7 August 1849, printed in the *Frontier Guardian*, 26 December 1849. The newspaper said of Captain Owen, "Judge Owen is well known in Illinois and other states. He is an honorable and high-minded man, if he is a Democrat."

[44]Hill, op. cit., 15.   [45]Senter, op. cit.

[46]Richard Warburton, "A Journal of Events Encountered by Richard Warburton While Crossing the Plains in '49," in *Heart Throbs of the West*, 10:437.

[47]Clawson, op. cit., 49.

light, and ended with the realization of the Saints' worst fear—the loss of human life.

There is no way of knowing what would have happened had Absalom Perkins remained a member of Enoch Reese's Fifty, in which he was a captain of ten. After a series of stampedes, Reese's company divided and traveled in two separate divisions.[49] Perkins, whose teams were especially wild spirited, asked to join Reddick Allred's company, perhaps thinking that only a change of company would help calm his animals. Allred consented and only after the fact realized that he had made a tragic oversight in assigning the order of travel.

It happened on the afternoon of 15 August when the company in which James Parshall Terry was traveling took its turn in the lead.[50] Allred told Perkins to fall in the rear, which he soon learned "was bad policy for their stock remembering their fright started to run while moving."[51] Terry, driving some distance ahead, "heard a great noise" and looked back to find the whole wagon train in bedlam.[52] Perkins' cattle had been frightened by a horse and bolted, running toward the front of the train and drawing other teams into the stampede. Thomas Judd, caught amid the chaos, whipped his staid old oxen to keep them going along, fearing that they might turn suddenly and cause the wagon in which his family was riding to capsize.[53] "In a short time," Allred wrote, "teams were running in every direction, excepting a few at the head."[54]

Parshall Terry, one of those at the head of the train, jumped out of his wagon and took the lead ox by the horn to keep the team quiet.[55] Reddick Allred stood by his team, "talking kindly and they did not move."[56] The stampeding cattle ran until they were exhausted, causing extensive damage. "It was frightful to behold," wrote Reddick Allred, "especially when we gathered up the wounded."[57] In the stampede several were injured and three

[48]Hill, op. cit., 15.

[50]Terry, op. cit.

[52]Terry, op. cit.

[54]Allred, op. cit., 311.

[56]Allred, op. cit., 311

[49]Merkley, op. cit., 30.

[51]Allred, op. cit., 311.

[53]Clawson, op. cit., 50.

[55]Terry, op. cit.

[57]Ibid.

were badly wounded, including Margaret Hawk, who died that night.[58]

In the aftermath of the chaos, on the morning of August 18, Captain Taylor called a meeting of the company. The cause of the stampede was obvious to all and Taylor, wanting to prevent further trouble, told Perkins "to take the lead for a few days until his spirited animals got cooled down."[59] The solution was simple and just, though there was without doubt more contention in the company at that meeting than at any other time during their journey west. "The Mormons quarreled like fiends, and I think besmeared about three-fourths of an acre of ground," observed non-member Jesse Morgan from his Gentile vantage point, "but Perkins' Ten went ahead."[60] Having Perkins in the lead achieved its desired effect. "They had several stampedes after but they had the road before them and no one was hurt that I know of," wrote Daniel Stillwell Thomas.[61]

Already they were within sight of Chimney Rock, a slender column rising nearly five hundred feet above the Platte River that, together with the bluffs leading to Scott's Bluff, appeared to Morgan "more like the work of art than of nature."[62] The landscape was unlike anything that most had ever experienced. It was a definite and welcome change from the monotonous and flat Platte valley, but it also marked the beginning of a higher, drier country that would put increasing strain on the livestock.

About thirty miles past Scott's Bluff and almost exactly halfway between Kanesville and the Salt Lake Valley, the Taylor company encountered the first Indians they had seen since beginning their journey. "They were Sioux and ostensibly very friendly," wrote Jesse Morgan.[63] "They were all dressed alike in new buckskins, leggings and coats, feathers in their hair, and they carried bows and arrows," William Blood described a large company of Sioux. "They seemed to be about six feet in height. They looked grand and noble as they marched past in single file."[64] William Appleby

[58]Ibid., 25 August 1849.   [59]Kirkham, op. cit., 21.
[60]Morgan, op. cit., 18 August 1849, 12.   [61]Kirkham, op. cit., 22.
[62]Morgan, op. cit., 20 August 1849, 13.   [63]Ibid., 24 August 1849, 13.
[64]Hill, op. cit., 14.

concurred, writing, "They were the finest, noblest, best looking and neatly dressed Indians I ever saw."[65]

The Mormon company stopped for four hours to trade with the Sioux, "giving flour, meal, powder, lead and cloths, for buffalo robes and moccasins."[66] The Indians traded commonly with overland emigrants and, to the surprise of many, were very shrewd. "The Indian is a financier of no mean ability and invariably comes out A1 in a bargain," wrote Forty-niner Catherine Haun of her company's experience in dealing with the Indians earlier that summer. "Though you may, for the time, congratulate yourself upon your own sagacity, you'll be apt to realize a little later on that you were not quite equal to the shrewd redman—had got the 'short end of the deal.'"[67]

Following the brief encounter with the Sioux, the Saints were less than a day's travel from Fort Laramie, a point at which trail conditions suddenly changed. From the Missouri River the Oregon Trail followed the south bank of the Platte River while the Mormon Trail remained on the north side, but at Fort Laramie the trails merged, bringing much greater competition for camping spots that had adequate feed for the livestock.

The climb along the Platte was steadily uphill along a relatively gentle grade, but Fort Laramie marked the end of the high plains and the beginning of a much more arduous upgrade haul to the Rocky Mountains. "From this place we began to see the destruction of both life and property," noted Jesse Morgan.[68] Many pioneers overestimated the amount of cargo they could haul and were forced to jettison the excess as their oxen began to fatigue, creating a giant junkyard:

> We here find great quantities of stuff thrown out by those going in the fore part of the season—old boxes, casks, trunks, beans, and clothing and various things. The thing in the greatest plenty is old iron in various shapes.
>
> Everything that it was thought could be spared was left, caused generally by the strife to get thru as early as possible. We find a great

---

[65]Appleby, op. cit., 26 August 1849.   [66]Morgan, op. cit., 24 August 1849, 13
[67]Catherine Haun, "A Woman's Trip Across the Plains in 1849," 23.
[68]Morgan, op. cit., 27 August 1849, 14.

many wagons that were left. Some sold for $10 and even as low as $2.50, while others who could get nothing offered burned them with the stuff on board.[69]

As the month of August reached a climax the Allen Taylor Company came within view of the Rocky Mountains. The pioneers were astonished to see a mountain white with snow at that time of year. Though they were becoming exhausted from the rigors of the long journey, they were still more than a month away from reaching Zion and it was no time to take it easy, particularly as they prepared to cross the mountains. "Here Captain Taylor pushed us hard," recorded Jesse Morgan.[70]

Allen Taylor was fully aware of the fine line he was walking in pushing the company and the livestock at this time. Even before reaching Fort Laramie, as Margaret Judd recalled, "The cattle were tired and footsore and the traveling was very hard so Father told us that morning we must all walk."[71] Catherine Haun, crossing the region earlier in the summer, wrote:

> The poor animals were never well fed and the road now was over rough, steep mountainous grades . . . the wretched creatures sweltered under the hot rays of the midday sun as they trudged over miles of bleak plains with never a tree to shelter them. . . . [72]

On 3 September Taylor wrote in a letter to Brigham Young of the poor pastures and the weakened condition of the cattle and meekly called for help:

> . . . many in our companies feel sanguine that they can go to the Valley without help, should they be so providential as to keep their cattle alive through the alkali regions. Many of us, however, would be glad of a little help and indeed will undoubtedly require it before we can climb the mountain heights. We expect, however, that Geo. A. [Smith] is heavy laden, having much Church property, etc., and will need the most help. . . . We do not expect to dictate to you what shall be for us, or what shall be for Geo. A. but we look to you for dictation, for counsel and for help.[73]

In the two preceding emigration seasons enough Saints had

---

[69]Senter, op. cit.   [70]Morgan, op. cit., 29 August 1849, 14.
[71]Judd, op. cit., 50.   [72]Haun, op. cit.
[73]*Journal History of the Church*, 3 September 1849, letter of Allen Taylor to Brigham Young.

traveled from Kanesville to the Salt Lake Valley and back that all were fully aware of the dreaded alkali region mentioned by Taylor. "One of the greatest curiosities are the alkali lakes," wrote Riley Senter. "They are of quite frequent occurrence and are dangerous to cattle, as many die on the way from drinking the water."[74] James Parshall Terry concurred, writing, "Between North Platte and Sweet Water I have seen cattle drop down in the yoke and be dead in a few minutes from drinking alkali water. I have seen the road strewn so thick with dead animals that in places a person could step from one to another."[75]

Each passing day brought with it the death of more cattle. Wolves, always plentiful and brazen, became increasingly troublesome as they preyed on the weakened livestock. To Jesse Morgan, travel in this area was "nothing but a continual scene of rocky mountains, sandy barren plains, destruction of cattle, wagons, and other property." As a sort of exclamation point Morgan added, "Here the Rattlesnake has taken up his abode."[76]

Taylor's company clearly could have used relief, but the arrival of a group of twenty-one wagons and a large number of oxen from the Salt Lake Valley on 16 September was merely a teaser, as they were bound for George A. Smith's company, that company being more in need of assistance. Fortunately, travel became much easier as the company crossed the Continental Divide at South Pass. For eight hundred miles the journey had been mostly uphill; now, at last, it was downhill. Furthermore, the weather was splendid for travel: Though they were in the midst of the mountains on the first day of autumn, Jesse Morgan recorded, it was "so warm that we experienced no inconvenience in traveling in our shirt sleeves."[77]

The weather held until the first of October when the company reached Fort Bridger, but conditions deteriorated the next day and by daybreak on 3 October there was snow already shoe deep and steadily falling.[78] At South Pass, where the Richards, Ben-

---

[74]Senter, op. cit.   [75]Terry, op. cit., 114–15.

[76]Morgan, op. cit., 13–14 September 1849, 15.

[77]Ibid., 22 September 1849, 17.

[78]Ibid., 3 October 1849, 19. Morgan's ten was camped about fifteen miles west of Fort Bridger.

son, and Smith companies were camped, blizzard conditions lasted for about thirty hours and resulted in the deaths of sixty-two cattle.[79] But in the relative comfort of Fort Bridger, protected from the harsh elements, Allen Taylor's wife Sarah Lovisa gave birth to a baby girl, Clarissa Elvira Taylor.

In such a large company—446 persons, according to David Moore's count—it is unlikely that Clarissa Taylor was the only baby born during the journey, but to Allen Taylor she was the most important, and a day or two of rest was justified before continuing onwards.[80] Taylor had pushed his company hard and they had made good time for a large company—Silas Richards' company, in comparison, departed Winter Quarters just four days after the Taylor company but was still two weeks away from Fort Bridger. But as they entered the mountains they "split up into smaller companies for convenience for food and camping."[81] The fragmented groups were no longer under the constant direction of Captain Taylor.

It was just over a hundred miles from Fort Bridger to the Salt Lake Valley, but this portion of the journey was anything but easy. By 1849 the trail was well established, yet the rugged terrain and the creeks, filled with boulders and willows, complicated travel over the last thirty-six miles in the narrow canyons leading to the Salt Lake Valley. Sixteen-year-old William Riley Judd, son of Thomas Judd, was driving a team for a widow and her little girl, who "nearly drove [him] crazy with questions," as they neared the valley. "I told them that when we got to Emigration Canyon the wagon would tip over," Judd recounted. "She told me if it did, she would tell Brigham Young. This was intended for a joke, but lo and behold, when we got to the canyon the wagon actually tipped over and broke the bows. . . . [I] failed to find out if she told Brigham Young."[82]

Every day for nearly a week beginning on 12 October, portions

[79]Appleby, op. cit., 4 October 1849.

[80]When Taylor was at Fort Bridger, Jesse Morgan was about a day's travel ahead and yet reached the Salt Lake Valley four days before Reddick Allred's company, in which Taylor was traveling. See Morgan, op. cit., 19–20.

[81]Allred, op. cit., 311.

of the widely scattered company reached Salt Lake; Allen Taylor, Reddick Allred, and members of their families arrived on October 16. The journey was long and arduous, though the vast majority arrived safely: Whereas nearly two thousand people died while crossing the plains in 1849, that number included only two members of the Allen Taylor Company—Margaret Hawk and a young son of Joseph Egbert.[83] But the minimal loss of life in no way lessened the hardships suffered by the pioneers, as James A. Little summarized: "The difficulties that ordinary emigrants passed through in crossing this thousand miles of desert can never be understood except by those who pass through them."[84]

Salt Lake City in 1849, when the new emigrants arrived, was not especially prosperous, despite a good harvest. James Little found "a destitute but cheerful people, struggling with the sterile elements for existence."[85] But the timing of the Gold Rush couldn't have been better, as thousands of Forty-niners detoured through Salt Lake to replenish supplies and provisions.

The Mormons bargained shrewdly, knowing well that this was the last stop for the California bound emigrants. "They were, at the time of which we speak, masters of the situation into which their enemies had forced them," wrote James Little of the Saints in Salt Lake.[86] "What!" said Brigham Young, "sell bread to the man who is going to earn his one hundred and fifty dollars a day, at the same price as you do the poor laborer, who works hard here for one dollar a day? I say, you men who are going to get gold to make golden images . . . pay for your flour!"[87] John Hawkins Clark, whose company rested in the Salt Lake vicinity for nine days on its way to California, observed from the other side, "Visiting Salt Lake valley and city was something like taking in the Irishman's show; it cost nothing to get in, but a great deal to get out."[88]

---

[82]William Riley Judd, *Treasures of Pioneer History*, 3:174.
[83]John D. Unruh, *The Plains Across*, 516 n. 75. Egbert's son died on July 27.
[84]Little, op. cit., 15:97.
[85]James A. Little, *From Kirtland to Salt Lake City*, 206.
[86]Ibid., 207.   [87]Sermon published in the *Deseret News*, 20 July 1850.
[88]John Hawkins Clark, as quoted in Unruh, op. cit., 312.

Clark was at least half-correct. In 1850, John H. Redd finally decided to go west and joined the company led by James Pace, his old friend from Tennessee. Traveling in another company were Joseph and Pleasant Green Taylor, who had accumulated the necessary means to enable them to join the members of their family who had crossed the plains the previous year. Approaching the Salt Lake Valley, Pleasant Green was taken by an unexpected sight: "We came in by way of Parley's Canyon, found my brother Allen collecting toll, this being a toll road, and he had been placed there for that purpose."[89]

The route was new, surveyed and cleared by Parley P. Pratt and called the Golden Pass Road. Though longer than the old road by nine miles, it afforded easier travel than the established trail. The toll was nominal—an average of about one dollar per wagon—but was resented by the non-Mormons, as now it cost them to get in as well as to get out of Salt Lake City.[90] A portion of the proceeds was used for road maintenance, but the traffic was sufficient—nearly six thousand wagons in 1850—to net Pratt a profit of about fifteen hundred dollars.[91] It was a small, rather insignificant slice of the total economy, but it was an unmistakable indication of a message that would continue to echo throughout the Salt Lake Valley: After failures in Jackson County, Far West and Nauvoo, *this* Zion would be a success, even if the Gentiles had to pay for it!

[89]Pleasant Green Taylor, "Record."
[90]J. Roderic Korns and Dale L. Morgan, *West from Fort Bridger: The Pioneering of the Immigrant Trails across Utah, 1846–1850*, 260.
[91]Unruh, op. cit., 318.

Chapter X

GATHERING TO ZION

WITHIN DAYS OF THE SAINTS' ARRIVAL in the Salt Lake Valley, Brigham Young vowed "to have every hole and corner from the Bay of San Francisco to the Hudson Bay known to us."[1] Party after party of explorers was sent out in every direction to explore other areas for possible colonization. Young soon realized that the location they had chosen for Zion had more potential than was apparent upon the arrival of the first pioneers in the Salt Lake Valley. But even with the rich harvest of 1849, were it not for the economic riches generated by the Gold Rush, Brigham would not have been able to formulate and realize his master plan of expansion and colonization in the Great Basin and beyond.

Young's dream of a place of peace and isolation had expanded to one of an extensive ecclesiastical empire, including the development of a "Mormon Corridor," a series of Mormon colonies stretching from Salt Lake to southern California that would guarantee free access to the sea. But colonizing the vast area would require far greater numbers than had arrived in the first three seasons of emigrations, so church leaders formulated a simple, three-pronged plan to bring more people to the Rocky Mountains: first, convince more church members to emigrate; second, expand the missionary program throughout the world; and, finally, create a system to help pay the cost of the journey for those who otherwise couldn't afford it.

---

[1]S. Kent Brown, Donald Q. Cannon, and Richard H. Jackson, op. cit., 96.

At the end of 1849 there were still about ten thousand Saints in the Missouri Valley near the old site of Winter Quarters, hundreds more in the eastern states and Canada, and about thirty thousand in England. A number of epistles from the church leaders, increasingly strong in their tone, were sent to these members to encourage them to emigrate as soon as possible. But the dream of colonies throughout the West would require still more emigrants than the number of existing members could provide, and so an active and extensive proselytizing campaign was inaugurated by increasing both the numbers of missionaries and the countries to which they were sent.

It was recognized that many, particularly in the Missouri Valley, would need financial assistance to emigrate, and so on 9 September 1849, a committee of five, including John D. Lee, was appointed to gather contributions to "bring the poor" from Kanesville and Winter Quarters.[2] Subsequently the Perpetual Emigrating Fund was launched. In theory as well as practice, voluntary donations were secured, loaned to those in need, and then replenished by the émigrés after their arrival in the Valley:

> When the Saints thus helped arrive here, they will give their obligations to the Church to refund to the amount of what they have received, as soon as circumstances will permit; and labor will be furnished, to such as wish, on the public works, and good pay, and as fast as they can procure the necessaries of life, and a surplus, that surplus will be applied to liquidating their debt, and thereby increasing the Perpetual Fund.[3]

The vast majority of the Saints who arrived during the first two years of settlement in the Rocky Mountains remained in the Salt Lake Valley, though a few small towns such as Bountiful, Farmington, and Kaysville were established a few miles to the north. But with the anticipated influx in increasing numbers of emigrants, many of whom would be aided by the Perpetual Emigrating Fund, Brigham Young's vision of colonization became more focused, with his eyes directed southward:

[2]Ibid., 9 September 1849.
[3]The First Presidency to Orson Hyde, October 16, 1849, *Millenial Star*, XII (1850), 124.

We are about to establish a colony of about thirty families in the Utah Valley, about fifty miles south. We hope soon to explore the valleys three hundred miles south and also the country as far as the Gulf of California with a view to settlement and to acquiring a seaport.[4]

The Utah Valley was a logical place to commence the colonization, since it was fertile, attractive, and not too distant. The initial thirty-three families arrived on the Provo River in October 1849, forming the nucleus of what would become the city of Provo. Initial Indian resistance was overcome in a two-day skirmish called the Battle of Fort Utah, and within a year the population had grown to 2,026 and the foundation had been laid for settlements on each of the eight streams in the valley.[5] A short time later, fifty families were called to settle Sanpete Valley, south of Utah Valley.

The colonizers included new émigrés as well as previously-arrived families. In the winter of 1850–51, John H. Redd, his brother-in-law John Holt, and William Pace, each of whom had arrived that summer in the James Pace Company, provided the nucleus for a settlement in the Utah Valley along the Spanish Fork River known as the Lower Settlement or Palmyra.[6] In December 1850 Allen Taylor and other members of his family, including his mother, Elizabeth, moved to Kaysville.[7] In the spring of 1852 Brigham Young advised James Allred to select a place for a settlement where he could locate with his numerous posterity and kindred and preside over them. Allred complied and, along with his brother Isaac and many members of their families, chose a site in the Sanpete Valley that was called the Allred Settlement—as was their settlement twenty years earlier in the Salt River Valley in Missouri.[8]

At the time these new colonies were being formed, there were still eight thousand Saints remaining at the camps in Iowa and Missouri. Apostles Ezra T. Benson and Jedediah M. Grant, who

---

[4]*Journal History of the Church*, 9 March 1849.
[5]Leonard J. Arrington, *Great Basin Kingdom*, 86.
[6]William G. Hartley, *My Best for the Kingdom*, 257.
[7]Hosea Stout, *On the Mormon Frontier*, 384.
[8]Andrew Jenson, *Encyclopedic History of The Church of Jesus Christ of Latter-day Saints*, 852.

were appointed to clear out these camps as soon as possible, explicitly told the members, "We wish you to evacuate Pottawattamie and the states and next fall be with us."[9] The First Presidency also issued a call to the many thousands of church members scattered throughout the world to "come home to Zion":

> When a people, or individuals, hear the Gospel, obey its first principles, are baptized for the remission of their sins, and receive the Holy Ghost by the laying on of hands, it is time for them to gather, without delay, to Zion; unless their Presidency shall call on them to tarry and preach the Gospel to those who have not heard it; and generally, the longer they wait the more difficult it will be for them to come home; for he who has an opportunity to gather, and does not improve it, will be afflicted by the devil.[10]

Many chose not to "be afflicted by the devil," and as a result about ten thousand Mormons migrated to the Great Basin in 1852, the vast majority of whom were among the remaining Saints at the camps in the Missouri Valley. With those camps mostly empty, beginning in 1853 attention was focused on gathering the many thousands of church members in Europe, but there were still many Saints in Canada and the eastern states who were primed and ready to go to the Rocky Mountains. Among those who decided to go in 1853 was the Imlay family of Chesterfield Township, Burlington County, New Jersey.[11]

James Havens Imlay was born in Imlaystown, New Jersey, on 6 April 1815—fifteen years to the day before Joseph Smith met with five others in Fayette, New York, to organize the Mormon Church. His father, John, disappeared when James was a young boy—perhaps, it has been speculated, a soldier who was killed in the final days of the War of 1812—and when his mother, Rebecca, died on 4 September 1819, James became an orphan and went to live with an uncle, Thomas Imlay.

The first Mormon missionaries began preaching in New Jersey when James Imlay was still a teenage boy living in his uncle's

---

[9]*Frontier Guardian*, 14 November 1851.

[10]"Seventh General Epistle of the Presidency . . . ," *Millenial Star*, XIV (1852), 325.

[11]Chesterfield was the residence at the time of the 1850 United States Census. There is no record of any subsequent residence before the Imlays left New Jersey in 1853.

JAMES HAVENS IMLAY AND
WIFE ANN ELIZA
Courtesy of Dellas Imlay

house. By the late 1830s some of the church's ablest missionaries, including Erastus Snow, Wilford Woodruff, Jedediah Grant, and Orson and Parley Pratt had established about a half-dozen Mormon congregations in central New Jersey.[12] One of their most important converts was William Appleby, a schoolteacher in Recklesstown and Clerk of Chesterfield Township, who was baptized in 1840 and almost immediately became a tireless and enthusiastic missionary.[13]

In the winter of 1840–41 Erastus Snow traveled through central New Jersey, visiting several branches of the church and preaching the gospel to "crowded and attentive audiences" at Toms River, New Egypt, and Recklesstown.[14] Snow at one of those meetings apparently introduced James H. Imlay and his wife, Anna Eliza

[12]William Sharp, "The Latter-day Saints or 'Mormons' in New Jersey," 3.
[13]In 1853 Recklesstown had a population of about eighty. See Thomas Baldwin and J. Thomas, *A New and Complete Gazetteer of the United States.*
[14]Snow, Erastus, Autobiography, typescript, 64.

Coward, to the Mormon faith. The Imlays probably also attended
meetings held by William Appleby on Sunday evenings in his
schoolroom.[15] Appleby met with considerable success in his missionary endeavors, baptizing twenty-six in a matter of a few
months, including the Imlays (who were baptized in early 1841 by
Appleby and confirmed by Apostle Orson Hyde), and establishing a branch of the church in Recklesstown.[16]

Within a few years, attrition due to emigration as well as
excommunication left the church in New Jersey in a depleted
and somewhat disorganized state. When William Appleby
returned to New Jersey in October 1848 after preaching in
Delaware and Pennsylvania, he found that seven of the twenty-
six he had baptized in Recklesstown had been "expelled from the
Church."[17] Shortly thereafter he visited Toms River, where he
found some members still in the faith but others "cold not having had any meetings in two or three years."[18] Appleby reorganized the branch and helped to revive the church throughout the
state before going west in 1849 as clerk of the George A. Smith
Company.

Thanks to Appleby's efforts, the church in New Jersey
remained vital through the next few years until the winter of
1852–53, when a group of Saints from throughout the state made
preparations to follow Brigham Young's admonition to gather at
the top of the mountains. The party, comprising "a large number
of persons from Toms River and other places in the state," left
Toms River on 5 April 1853—eight days before Brigham Young
issued his Ninth Epistle, urging members to "come home as fast

[15]William I. Appleby, *Autobiography and Journal, 1848–1856*, 53. The name Recklesstown,
named after Joseph Reckless, was changed to Chesterfield in 1897 after an influential resident, Anthony Bullock, became convinced by a friend that "the 'reckless' part of the
name sounds ridiculous." See Henry Charlton Beck, *More Forgotten Towns of Southern
New Jersey*, 204.

[16]James H. Imlay's obituary, *Deseret News*, 20 July 1890. See also Appleby, op. cit., 46, 53.
The baptism took place either in January or early February 1841, since Orson Hyde was
in the Pennsylvania, New Jersey, and New York area from October 1840 until 13 February 1841, when he sailed for Liverpool and didn't return to the United States until 1842.
See Howard H. Barron, *Orson Hyde, Missionary, Apostle, Colonizer*, 116–117.

[17]Appleby, op. cit., 53.

[18]Ibid., 51.

as possible."[19] James Havens Imlay decided to join the company despite the fact that his uncle Thomas Imlay offered him a considerable amount of money to give up the church and stay in New Jersey.[20]

Departing from Toms River, they made their way to Philadelphia, boarded a train to Pittsburgh, and took river steamers to Missouri. In Kansas City they purchased mules and wagons and began the trek west—about a month earlier than any of the organized Mormon companies of 1853.[21] Nearly halfway through their 130-day journey, on 5 June on the plains of Nebraska, Anna Eliza Imlay gave birth to a baby girl, who was given the unique name of Margaret Nebraska Imlay. The immense joy of this occasion was countered when, five days later, their twenty-two-month-old daughter Rachel Rebecca died. There was no choice but to bury little Rachel by the side of the road and move steadily onward.

The New Jersey Saints arrived in the Salt Lake Valley on August 11, about a month after colonial expansion to the south had been halted temporarily due to an altercation between an Indian and James Ivie, a nephew of Isaac Allred. Relations between the Ute Indians and the Mormons already were strained when, on 17 July, a Ute man and his wife were trading in Utah Valley near Springville at Ivie's home and began to quarrel. Ivie intervened in the dispute and in the ensuing skirmish whacked the warrior on the head with the barrel of a rifle, cracking his skull with a single blow. Though the Indian died a few days later, the incident may have escaped wide notice had not the man been a relative of Walkara (also known as Walker), chief of the Utes. Under the circumstances, however, the death was enough of a spark to detonate hostilities that became known as the Walker War.[22]

The Indians took immediate retribution by killing a settler,

---

[19]Theodore McKean, "Autobiography," 9; James R. Clark, ed., *Messages of the First Presidency*, 2:118. Nearly the entire Toms River branch emigrated, leaving no branch of the church in that area for nearly a hundred years. See Heber J. Grant, Conference Reports (*Deseret News*), October 1934, 3.

[20]Imlay, Hugh Anthony and Nella Covington Imlay, *The Imlay Family*, 36.

[21]Walker, op. cit., 111.   [22]Jenson, op. cit., 919–19.

Alexander Keel, a few miles south of Palmyra in Payson. The conflict quickly spread to the Sanpete Valley where, after a raid on 19 July, a dozen families moved from the Mt. Pleasant Settlement to the Allred Settlement. A fort was hastily constructed, but the day after the fort was completed, on 28 July, about four hundred Indians of the Walker band raided the Allred Settlement and drove off two hundred head of livestock and thirty horses, nearly all that the colony owned. Realizing the danger, the Allred Settlement was abandoned as all 118 settlers moved to Manti.[23]

The residents of Palmyra in the Utah Valley also suffered losses as the Indians drove off livestock and destroyed fences, buildings and crops. John H. Redd's sawmill on the Spanish Fork River was burned down, a loss of six thousand dollars. That was, unfortunately, but a prelude to a far greater tragedy, when his son John Holt Redd was thrown from a horse and died on 25 November 1853. Coming just two years after the loss of their youngest daughter, Redd's wife Elizabeth was bereft, went to bed, and died broken-hearted within three days.[24]

The Walker War lasted until the following year and posed enough danger that a "Spanish" wall, twelve feet high and six miles in length, was built around the city of Salt Lake. But despite the temporary lull in colonization in the south the expansion of the Kingdom proceeded unabated. Emigrants, many aided by the Perpetual Emigrating Fund, continued to arrive in unprecedented numbers and missionary efforts continued to increase throughout the world.

Hosea Stout celebrated the New Year of 1853 by preparing to travel to China to open missionary activities in the Orient. Unbeknownst to Stout, as he traveled by ship from San Pedro, California, to San Francisco, his wife Louisa was seriously ill in Utah; on 9 January, while Hosea was aboard a steamer anchored at San Luis Obispo, Louisa Stout died.[25] Stout and his companions, still unaware of Louisa's fate, continued their journey to

[23]Jenson, op. cit., 826.   [24]Ibid., 215.
[25]Hosea Stout, *On the Mormon Frontier*, 467, entry of 11 January 1853.

San Francisco and on to Hong Kong, where they arrived on 27 April. Their missionary efforts were completely rebuffed, however, and, frustrated by the difficult foreign language, the trio began the return trip home after only six weeks in China.

While en route home, on 23 August, Stout received news of his wife's death. Disconsolate, Hosea could not bring himself to describe the extent of his despair. "Why should we attempt to depict the feeling which such sad news brings to the heart as this morning beclouds my hopes when I learned that Louisa was no more," he wrote.[26] When Stout finally arrived in Salt Lake on 8 December he found that his children were being tended in Kaysville by his mother-in-law, Elizabeth Taylor, but after 210 days of babysitting her grandchildren, Mother Taylor declined to offer further help and charged Stout a dollar for each day she cared for his children. In order to pay his debt, it was necessary to sell his farm, and with that Hosea Stout hit rock bottom:

> It is impossible for me to describe my feelings when contemplating the sad dilema [*sic*] I am placed in at this time when dark clouds of more misfortune & sorrow hang heavily over my head yet. & I can not see one bright ray of future happiness. . . ."[27]

Stout did recover, but the mission had been a total failure and the idea of missionaries in China was put to rest. A second missionary endeavor, in India, suffered a similar fate, but the third new missionary effort of 1853, nearly half a world away on the African continent, met with success.

It actually started at a conference in Salt Lake City on 28 August 1852, at which 106 elders were called to serve missions throughout the world, including Hosea Stout to China and twin brothers Reddick and Reddin Allred to the Sandwich Islands (Hawaii). At the conference, Jesse Haven, William Walker, and Leonard Smith were called to open missionary activity in South Africa. The three elders responded without hesitation, despite the term of the mission call:

When we were appointed on our mission, [Apostle] George A.

---

[26]Ibid., 488, entry of 23 August 1853. [27]Ibid., 510–11, entry of 31 March 1854.

WILLIAM WALKER
With Jesse Haven and Leonard I. Smith, one of the first three Mormon missionaries sent to South Africa. *Courtesy of the Church Archives, The Church of Jesus Christ of Latter-day Saints.*

Smith said, "We are going to send you on a short mission not to exceed seven years;" so I expect if I live as long as that, I then shall be permitted to go home.[28]

Two weeks later, on 15 September, Haven, Walker, and Smith departed the Salt Lake Valley with about seventy elders bound for various fields of labor. The long, arduous journey began on horseback and proceeded on foot as the animals became weak and exhausted. The missionaries arrived at the Missouri River in about six weeks and, after a short pause, resumed their trip, first by steamer to St. Louis, Cincinnati, and Pittsburgh, and then by train to Philadelphia and New York. Sailing by way of Liverpool, the three missionaries arrived at Cape Town on 19 April, 1853, filled with faith but also with apprehension:

> . . . we left our homes without purse or scrip and have no other dependence, only in God. We are now landed in a strange land amongst strangers. Without home and without friends and without

---

[28]Jesse Haven, "Daily Journal of Jesse Haven," 1856.

money, which gives me feelings not easy to express when I reflect upon my feelings and qualifications.[29]

The Mormon elders arrived without fanfare, unannounced and unnoticed. Within a week, however, they had created a stir through their proselytizing and encountered a mob that shouted, made "hideous noises," and threw stones at the trio.[30] Newspapers quickly took notice and the *Cape Town Frontier Times*, on 26 April 1853, published a report of their arrival and activities.[31] News of the Mormon elders, often sensationalized or absurd, soon reached other areas, including the Eastern Cape, nearly four hundred miles from Cape Town:

> In the year 1853, all the newspapers of South Africa were filled with stories of a strange doctrine being preached in Cape-town by men from America. It was making a stir in that city, and a few had accepted and been baptized. One story was to the effect that a man had been baptized who was so wicked his sins made the water so heavy as it flowed past a waterwheel, it had broken several of the cogs.[32]

Residents of the Eastern Cape didn't have to wait long to see first hand what all the fuss was about, for in December 1853 William Walker and John Wesley, a former Methodist minister from Cape Town who had been baptized by Walker, arrived in Grahamstown. The elders met with "great opposition, birchbats and rotten eggs being hurled at them," and William Walker's carriage was thrown by a mob into the Kat River, never to be recovered.[33] But despite their notoriety, it is not likely that George Prince, who moved his family from Oliphant's Hoek to a remote location in the District of Bedford, knew of the missionaries.

The relocation of the Prince family to an area about fifty miles northwest of Oliphant's Hoek, at the base of the Kagaberg

---

[29]William Holmes Walker, *The Life Incidents and Travels of Elder William Holmes Walker*, 11.

[30]South African Mission Historical Report, 26 April 1853.

[31]*Cape Town Frontier Times*, 26 April 1853; Letter of Jesse Haven to the First Presidency, June 1854.

[32]Eli Wiggill, Diary, in *An Enduring Legacy*, 8:191.   [33]Ibid.

mountain and near—or perhaps in—the valley of the Mancazana River, occurred after and as a result of the Eighth Frontier War that ended in 1853. It all had to do with the Kat River Settlement and Sir Andries Stockenström, a South African leader who had been instrumental in the legislation of an 1828 ordinance that made "Hottentots and other free people of colour" equal before the law with Whites.[34] In 1829 Stockenström, who had been promoted to the rank of commissioner-general of the eastern part of the Cape Colony, set aside about four hundred square miles of fertile land that had formerly been occupied by Xhosa, on the upper reaches of the Kat River, as a settlement for the Khoikhoi.[35]

In the frontier wars that began in 1834 and in 1846, the men of the Kat River Settlement, both Dutch and Khoikhoi, fought alongside the British and colonial forces against the rebellious Xhosa.[36] But in 1850 the British Governor, Sir Harry Smith, decided that the Kat River land was too good for non-whites and sent troops to evict hundreds of people, accusing them of being squatters. When, as a result, the Eighth Frontier War erupted on Christmas Day 1850, Smith appealed in vain for the help of the Kat River men, but this time the Khoi, as well as some of the Dutch settlers, took the field with the Xhosa instead.[37]

After the rebellion was subdued and the war ended in 1853, the government yielded to the clamor among the British immigrants and began taking the fertile and rich grazing-lands of Kat River Settlement from the rebel Dutch and Khoi and giving them to white farmers.[38] Stockenström, greatly disheartened by the war and the failure of his policy concerning the Khoikhoi, returned home to his farm on the western edge of the Kat River Settlement in hope of reconstructing some sort of residence for his family. "I soon found that I had not the means to do so," he wrote, and resorted to selling off considerable portions of his vast farm.[39] On a portion of this land arose the town of Bedford, and

[34]Thompson, *A History of South Africa*, 60.   [35]Ibid., 62.
[36]*Illustrated History of South Africa*, 134.   [37]Ibid., 135.
[38]Ibid., 137.
[39]Sir Andries Stockenström, *The Autobiography of the Late Sir Andries Stockenström*, 2:312.

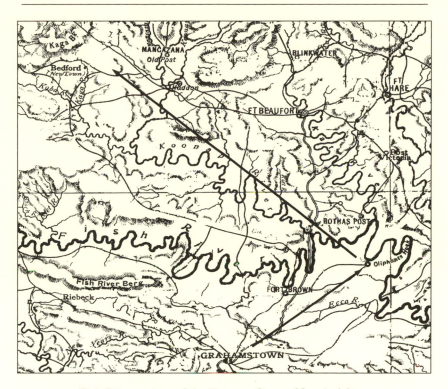

Fish River region of the Eastern Cape of South Africa,
showing the movement of George Prince's family.
Adapted from the 1856 Military Map of Henry Hall.

subsequently the western portion of the Kat River Settlement,
including former rebel land, was designated as the District of
Bedford.

Eli Wiggill, who lived in the District of Bedford less than a
day's travel from George Prince, recalled that, after the war ended,
"All the farmers were notified to make lists of their losses and, as
compensation, were given farms."[40] Henry Talbot, another close
neighbor, wrote, "the government gave father and myself a farm
for services done in the war of 1851."[41] George Prince was not a
man of means, and thus it was likely this type of land grant that

---

[40]Wiggill, Diary, 189.
[41]Henry James Talbot, "The Life of Henry James Talbot in South Africa."

enabled his move to Mancazana and the fertile grazing lands of the Bedford district, noted as one of the finest regions in the eastern frontier.[42]

Thomas Pringle, a Scottish poet who was among the area's earliest white settlers, wrote of an excursion into the valley of the Mancazana:

> The aspect of the country, though wild, was rich and beautiful. It was watered by numerous rivulets, and finely diversified with lofty mountains and winding vales, with picturesque rocks and shaggy jungles, open upland pastures, and fertile meadows along the river margins, sprinkled as usual with willows and acacias, and occasionally with groves of stately geelhout. Many of the mountain sides and kloofs were clothed with forests of large timber.[43]

Pringle further described the lower reaches of the valley, at the base of the Kagaberg, near the old, deserted Mancazana post:

> The scenery through which we passed was in many places of the most picturesque and singular description.... It appeared like a verdant basin, or *cul de sac*, surrounded on all sides by an amphitheatre of steep and sterile mountains, rising in the back-ground into sharp cuneiform ridges of very considerable elevation; their summits being at this [winter] season covered with snow, and estimated to be from 4,000 to 5,000 feet above the level of the sea. The lower declivities were sprinkled over, though somewhat scantily, with grass and bushes. But the bottom of the valley, through which the infant river meandered, presented a warm, pleasant and secluded setting, spreading itself into verdant meadows, sheltered and without being encumbered, with groves of mimosa which we observed in the distance herds of wild animals—antelopes and quaggas—pasturing in undisturbed quietude.[44]

The Mormon missionaries considered extending their efforts into the pristine interior but as late as Christmas 1854 still were concerned by rumors that another Frontier War was imminent.[45] The rumors proved to be unfounded and, after laboring in Fort

---

[42]Henry Hall, *Manual of South African Geography* (Cape Town: S. Solomon, 1866), 35.

[43]Thomas Pringle, *Thomas Pringle in South Africa, 1820–1826*, 62. Geelhout was a type of tree also known as Yellow-Wood; kloof is an Afrikaans word for ravine.

[44]Ibid., 17–18. The quagga was a mammal closely related to horses and zebras and is now extinct.

[45]Walker, op. cit., 44, entry of 25 December 1854.

Beaufort and Grahamstown for nearly thirteen months, William Walker and John Wesley ventured into the rugged area of the old Kat River, north beyond the valley of the Mancazana, that was dominated by the seventy-eight-hundred-foot-tall Winterberg.

On 30 January 1855, the two missionaries separated and Wesley "started for Mancazana."[46] A week later, on 4 February, Wesley and Walker rejoined at Winterberg to hold a Sunday meeting, after which Walker was going to return to Fort Beaufort but was forced to delay one day due to the death of his horse.[47] It was at this time that George Prince's dream of being visited by two men who were bearing an important message was fulfilled.

When she first learned of the dream, Sarah Prince reportedly responded, "You're as visionary as Abraham of Old, George."[48] It is impossible to gauge the sincerity of her statement, but as George and Sarah sat in the shade of their thatched house one afternoon, two men—most certainly Wesley and Walker— approached. "Sarah, these are the two men," George told his wife, in reference to the dream, and went to meet the Mormon elders.[49] Convinced that they bore the truth, he was converted immediately and within a few days was baptized, as were his wife Sarah and son Francis. William Walker recorded the events in his diary:

> Feb. 11th. Held meeting and had a good attendance and good attention, after which Mr. And Mrs. [George] Weigle [Wiggil] had offered themselves for baptism.... When Mr. James Wm. Tomson presented himself . . . we confirmed them as members of the Church. George Weigle and wife, James Wm. Tomson and Br. Prince, who had previously been baptised by Br. Wesley.
> Feb. 12th. Instead of returning to Fort Beaufort I went with Br. Wesley to Mancazana. We found Br. Prince's children sick with whooping cough, one very bad. By request we administered to him.
> Feb. 13th. After giving instructions we confirmed Sarah Prince, age 37 years. Also her son [Francis], age 14 years, as members of the Church. We also blessed 5 of Br. Prince's children.
> Feb. 14th. We administered to all Br. Prince's children. Were much better....[50]

---

[46]Ibid., 44, entry of 30 January 1855.   [47]Ibid., entry of 4 February 1855, 44.
[48]Juanita Kossen, "History of Francis Prince and Ann Elizabeth Imlay."
[49]*Treasures of Pioneer History*, 6:270.
[50]Walker, op. cit., 45, entries of 11–14 February 1855.

As was always the case in the early days of the church, new members were encouraged to emigrate to Zion immediately after their baptism. In November 1854 Jesse Haven organized a Perpetual Emigrating Fund at the Cape of Good Hope and admonished the Saints in South Africa to sell their possessions and proceed to Utah. The rare wealthy convert was especially valued for the help he or she could provide to the cause, as Leonard Smith wrote:

> There have been seventy (70) baptised here in this [Eastern Cape] Conference though some have fallen away. I have baptised one man worth $15000 or more. I counseled him to buy a ship to take the Saints from this land. He's quite willing to do it, and has tried to buy one but has not been successful as yet.[51]

Jesse Haven, William Walker, and Leonard Smith, expecting to serve as many as seven years in South Africa, could not have anticipated that a new member might purchase a ship that would enable the missionaries to leave for home as early as 1855. But the stage was set for an early departure when an epistle from the First Presidency was received, stating that elders who labored in countries where the climate did not agree with their health were at liberty to return home when they pleased without awaiting a replacement.[52] In March 1855, Haven, still in Cape Town, inquired into booking passage to England but decided that first he should visit his fellow missionaries in the Eastern Cape.[53]

Upon Haven's arrival at Port Elizabeth in June, the three elders met to discuss plans for their departure. Realizing that their missions soon would conclude, the missionaries redoubled their efforts to accomplish as much as possible in the time that remained, concentrating on the areas around Grahamstown, Fort Beaufort and Port Elizabeth. In late August Haven departed for Bedford in the company of John Wesley, who had been "appointed to preside over the Saints in and about Bedford, Winterberg, and Mancazana districts."[54] For Haven it was a memorable, if not entirely positive, experience:

[51]Leonard I. Smith, letter to George A. Smith, 26 October 1855, in Evan P. Wright, "A History of the South African Mission, Period I, 1852–1903."
[52]Wright, op. cit., 106.   [53]Haven, Journal, March 1855.
[54]Letter of Jesse Haven to Willard Richards, 21 August 1855, *Millenial Star*, 17:781–82.

August 28 [1855]

Started about 7 in the morning in the company of Bro. Wesley for Bedford, distance about 65 miles. Arrived at Bedford between 11:00 and 12:00 at night. Stayed at Bro. [George] Prince's.

August 29

Spent the day at Bro. Prince's. In the evening went on to Mr. Smith's. His wife would be baptized if he would let her. Slept there that night.

August 30

Spent the day in Bedford at Bro. Prince. Called in the afternoon at Mr. Campbell's to see about having a meeting there next sabbath. He was not at home. His wife was friendly and said she would speak to him about it.

August 31

Spent the day at Bro. Prince. Not a very pleasant place to stay at. He had a large family but little room. They appear kind and friendly in their way. Bro. Wesley says they were brought up in the country where they had not much opportunity to learn manners.

September 1, 1855

Spent the day in Bedford. Not a very agreeable place to stay at. I am anxious to get away.[55]

Though anxious to leave, Haven spent four more days in Bedford. Finally, on 6 September, he departed for Grahamstown, though not by the most direct route. "Bro. Francis Prince came with me 14 miles," Haven wrote in his journal.[56] Due to rumors of a gathering mob and potential harm to the missionary, the young teenager was sent along to guide him over a mountainous trail. Haven proceeded safely, though it wasn't until the evening of the next day that Francis was able to reach his home.[57]

Persecution continued to hound the missionaries in the Eastern Cape until the time of their departure. On 3 October, as William Walker was returning to Port Elizabeth from Fort Beaufort, he came within sight of a place where he had been burned in effigy a short time before. Fearing for his safety, he hid until dark in order to pass through undiscovered:

I concluded that I was safer among wild beasts than to stop in town. About the time I got into the edge of town it clouded up very thick

---

[55]Haven, op. cit., 28 August–1 September 1855.   [56]Ibid.
[57]Kossen, op. cit.

and black, every appearance of a heavy storm. I could hardly see my hand before me. . . . I travelled on twelve miles through a country inhabited by wild beasts, and over a crooked road with a forest of Mimossee [mimosa] thorn trees on each side. . . . Arrived at the Inn at twelve o'clock. In calling the Landlord, when I told him, he said he would not have undertaken it for $1,000.[58]

By this time most church members had moved to Port Elizabeth in anticipation of emigrating to Zion, though the Prince family remained at Mancazana.[59] A ship, the *Unity*, was purchased by three South African members—Charles Roper, Thomas Parker, and John Stock—for twenty-five hundred pounds sterling, but when it departed from Port Elizabeth on 28 November 1855, only eighteen Mormon passengers, including Leonard Smith and William Walker, were on board. Seventeen days later, on December 15, Jesse Haven boarded the *Cleopatra* in Cape Town to sail to Liverpool. And with that the South African Mission was effectively closed, as most of the new members remained, waiting and wondering when their day to emigrate would come.

A total of 176 people had been baptized in the Cape Colony, of which 121 remained in good fellowship awaiting emigration (thirty-six had been excommunicated and a few had emigrated elsewhere).[60] In 1857 two missionaries, Ebenezer Richardson and James Brooks, both of whom had served missions in England, were sent to South Africa and continued to labour there for another six months before returning to America. Meanwhile the members, many of whom had made great sacrifices to support the Perpetual Emigrating Fund, were becoming increasingly anxious to emigrate, and yet, with no direction from American missionaries, they languished and remained in Africa, wondering if they would ever make it to Zion.

---

[58]Walker, op. cit., 52, entry of 3 October 1855.

[59]According to LDS Church membership records at the time of her death, George and Sarah Prince's daughter Susannah was born in Bedford on 15 November 1855; a record made by Susannah at the time of her marriage in the Endowment House in Salt Lake City on 2 December 1872, show that she was born at Mankazana on 14 November 1855. From these records it is obvious that the Prince family remained in the Mancazana/Bedford area after the American missionaries departed South Africa.

[60]Wright, op. cit., 143.

Chapter XI

DISHARMONY AND OCCUPATION

BEFORE THE MORMONS began settling there in 1847, the westward-bound pioneers went through the Great Basin rather than to it. Encompassing about 190,000 square miles, the Great Basin is a vast, arid area in which water flows to the interior rather than to the sea. Bounded by the Wasatch Mountains on the east and the Sierra Nevada-Cascade range on the west, nearly all of the land in the basin is either mountainous or desert and therefore unattractive to settlement, which is why the Mormons, in their search for isolation, chose to locate there.

But Brigham Young had a master plan of colonization, and parties were sent in all directions from the Salt Lake Valley to scout the basin and beyond for places amenable to settlement. In November 1849, Parley P. Pratt was commissioned to take a company of about fifty persons to explore the "southern country." The purpose of the expedition was to pass over the southern "rim of the Great Basin," to become acquainted with the character of the country beyond and ascertain its suitability as a place for settlement.[1]

Pratt returned with encouraging information, believing the area to be semitropical with sufficient land to support several communities. Of particular interest to Brigham Young were reports of rich deposits of iron ore, for while Young feared that gold fever would weaken the devotion of the Saints, he also was

---

[1]Parley P. Pratt, *Autobiography*, 338.

fully aware that iron was a necessary element in the building up of the kingdom. In the autumn of 1850 a small company, including John D. Lee, was sent south to colonize newly-formed Iron County, both to produce agricultural products to support an iron industry and to provide a halfway station between southern California and the Salt Lake Valley.

Lee returned to Salt Lake City in June 1851 to settle his affairs and to move the remainder of his family to southern Utah. At the October General Conference a resolution was offered that a company led by Lee should be authorized to establish a settlement at the junction of the Rio Virgin and Santa Clara rivers. Lee left soon after the resolution was presented and, upon his arrival in Parowan, wrote to President Young that they had "reached this city in good health and spirits with a company of nineteen waggons without the loss of a single animal on the way."[2] A few months later, upon returning to Parowan after exploring the Virgin Valley, he wrote with great enthusiasm:

> We can raise cotton, flax, hemp, grapes, figs, sweet potatoes, and fruits of almost every kind, be independent of our kind Christian friends who drove us from their midst. When I stood in the midst of one of these valleys and contemplated on the glory of the latter-day work, it was like a fire shut up in my bones. . . . I could scarcely content myself to stay . . . 'till another fall.[3]

Late in the summer of 1852 Lee moved his family to a place on Ash Creek at the base of the Pine Valley Mountains, about twenty-five miles south of Cedar City. Elder George A. Smith, in a letter to the *Deseret News* that was published on 8 December 1852, described the settlement:

> Six miles south of Cedar is a Fort called Walker, containing three families with nine men capable of bearing arms. . . . About 19 miles south of this, on the first water, south of the rim, of the Basin in Washington County, attached to Iron Co. John D. Lee and Elisha H. Groves and Company are building a Fort on Ash Creek, called Harmony. Fifteen men are capable of bearing arms; 51 loads of lumber have been taken there from Parowan, and 6 teams are constantly

---

[2]John D. Lee, *On the Mormon Frontier*, I:133.
[3]*Journal History of the Church*, 7 March 1852.

employed building the fort. One of the first rooms erected is intended for a school house. The point is well selected for military purposes and commands the Springs and about 160 acres of farm land on the Creek. It is about 20 miles north of the Rio Virgin, which is inaccessible to teams until a road is worked at considerable expense, but when done, will no doubt probably shorten the distance to California about 35 miles.[4]

From its appearance, Harmony seemed to be a promising site for settlement: grass was plentiful and the fertile land itself was relatively level, sloping gently towards the south and well suited for farming. Thomas Brown, an English convert to Mormonism who had journeyed from New York across the plains to Utah, wrote in May 1854,

> We left Cedar City & nooned at Peter Shirts' Creek, and rolling till near Sundown passing through some of the best grazing land I have seen in America and apparently the best of arable land arrived at Bror. Jno. D. Lee's old settlement.[5]

The location of the settlement was spectacular, lying in the midst of geologic wonder. Immediately to the west was a volcanic laccolith that, uncovered by millennia of erosion, became the Pine Valley Mountains, whose highest peak rises to 10,324 feet above sea level; to the north lay the south rim of the Great Basin; to the east, about five miles distant, was the northwestern extreme of the Colorado Plateau, with striking red sandstone finger canyons and cliffs that were described by Wilford Woodruff as "red rocks standing like pyramids 1,000 feet high;"[6] and to the south was a lava-covered Black Ridge that for many years was impenetrable to pioneer wagons. "This is a good grazing Country & a splendid mountain scenery," wrote Woodruff.[7]

Fifty missionaries were called at General Conference in October 1853 to settle in this spectacular area and labor among the Indians. Thomas Brown, one of the missionaries, was awestruck by the magnificence of the setting:

> What abrupt terminations are these to the two chains of mountains

---

[4]*Deseret News*, 8 December 1852.
[5]Thomas D. Brown, Juanita Brooks, ed., *Journal of the Southern Indian Mission*, 18.
[6]Woodruff Journals, 4:276, 19 May 1854.   [7]Ibid.

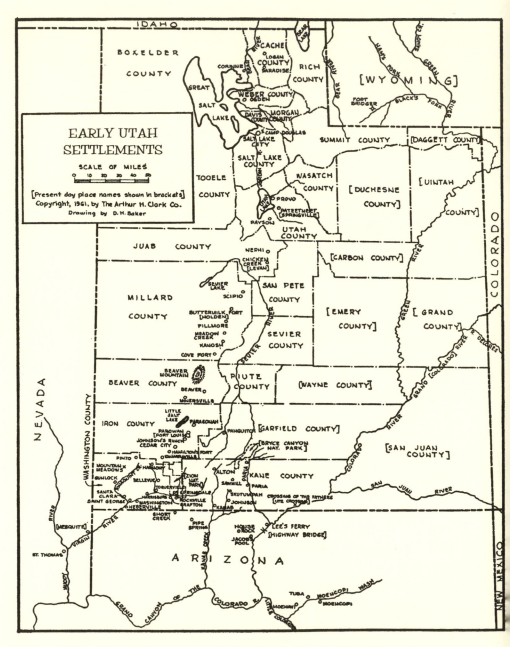

EARLY UTAH
SETTLEMENTS

SCALE OF MILES
0 10 20 30 40 50

[Present day place names shown in brackets]
Copyright, 1961, by The Arthur H. Clark Co.
Drawing by D. H. Baker

From Juanita Brooks, *John D. Lee*, The Arthur H. Clark Company, 1962.

east, and west, like leaping off places at the world's end? But see over Ash Creek to the east, what table lands are these broken off so abruptly? by some floods of water? what lofty spires! what turrets! what walls! what bastions! what outworks to some elevated Forts! what battlements are these? what inaccessible ramparts? From these no doubt are often heard Heaven's artillery cannonading.[8]

The first group of missionaries left Salt Lake City on 14 April 1854. Resourceful and fearless, they were well fitted for their assignment and had the deep faith that was necessary to carry out the task to which they had been called. Upon their arrival at Harmony on 2 May they found twelve to fifteen families living in tents, wagons, adobe houses, and dugouts. Unfortunately, as Thomas Brown described, it was "evident at a glance" that the site selected by Lee was "too small for more than one man and his family."[9] Shortly thereafter, Brigham Young visited the settlement:

> In April we arrived at Fort Harmony, put in a small crop, made a water ditch about four miles long, when here came President Brigham Young and a party of friends from Salt Lake. We held meetings at Fort Harmony. President Young told us to travel among the Indians, learn their language, teach them to work, and if possible teach them the gospel. He also advised us to build the fort in a different place.[10]

The new fort was about four miles north of Lee's camp, "a good location a great quantity of Grass & good soil."[11] Two hundred feet square with adobe walls two feet thick and ten to sixteen feet high, the new Fort Harmony was designated as the headquarters of the Southern Indian Mission.[12] According to Young, it was the best of its kind in the territory.[13] In the center a well was dug one hundred feet deep to supply culinary water; at the same time, a canal was constructed to carry irrigation water to the new development.

---

[8]Brown, op. cit., 46.   [9]Brown, ibid.

[10]Thales Hasting Haskell, *An Enduring Legacy*, 2:328. According to Thomas Brown, the clerk of the mission, the missionaries actually arrived on 2 May 1854, not in April.

[11]Woodruff, op. cit., 4:278, 20 May 1854.

[12]Brown, op. cit., 31.   [13]Andrew Karl Larson, *I Was Called to Dixie*, 26.

The ditch, however, was as porous as a sieve, and the settlers soon discovered that the watershed in this place, so close to the rim of the Great Basin, was insufficient to sustain much of a settlement, so some of the missionaries settled on the Santa Clara. For the next two years both groups labored among the Indians, struggling at times to overcome discord that was related to the strong personality of John D. Lee:

> *Sunday 18th March* [1855]. Brors Savage & Hopkins & Leigh from Cedar City spoke to us this day. After they had spoken of the good spirit they felt in our midst, & the great work we had accomplished in the building of our fort, J.D. Lee arose and spoke of the evils resulting from disunion, one asp in our midst did or would destroy all! (?) Tho' unpleasant, I here deem it necessary to record a few facts, which I think under his presidency militate against the harmony of Harmony—[14]

But whatever disunity may have been present during this time disappeared in late 1856 as a "reformation" movement swept among the Mormons throughout the Utah Territory. Jedediah M. Grant, the fiery and fervent second counselor to President Brigham Young, manifested in Provo on 13 July 1855, an early hint of what was to come:

> I wish to see those who profess to be saints act as saints ought to act. . . . The church needs trimming up, and if you will search you will find in your wards certain branches which had better be cut off. The kingdom would progress much faster, and so will you individually, than it will with those branches on, for they are only dead weights to the great wheel. . . . I would like to see the works of reformation commence, and continue until every man had to walk to the line, then we would have something like union. . . .[15]

As new communities were settled, many Saints had become preoccupied with the struggle to survive on the frontier and had often neglected individual spiritual matters, including attendance at church. Drought and a grasshopper plague in 1855, along with rapid immigration into Utah, combined to threaten economic

---

[14]Brown, op. cit., 117.
[15]Jedediah M. Grant, 13 July 1855, Provo Conference; *Deseret News*, 24 October 1855.

stability. Church leaders, convinced that the problems they faced were divine reminders that all was not well in Zion, preached reform with vigor.

At a prayer circle meeting on 7 September 1856, Brigham Young announced that he wanted his counselors, Heber C. Kimball and Jedediah Grant, as well as the Twelve, to go among the people and preach the gospel. The "Reformation" was launched six days later in a conference at the Kaysville Ward, where Allen Taylor was serving as bishop. Jedediah Grant had been sent to preach repentance and reform, but "when he got there he felt like baptizing and confirming them anew into the church."[16] And that is precisely what he did:

> Prest. Grant enjoined upon the Saints to observe the utmost decorum and reverence while the sacred ordinance of baptism was being attended to. After prayer, he proceded to baptize Bishop Allen Taylor and his counselors, Reddick N. Allred and Dorr P. Curtis. Nearly 500 Saints were immersed under the direction of Prest. Grant, aided by Bishop Taylor. . . . After baptism the Saints repaired to the bowery, where the ordinance of confirmation was attended to. . . . The Spirit of God was poured out to a great degree, and peace and happiness characterised the whole assembly.[17]

At the close of the four-day conference, Bishop Taylor and his counselors addressed the congregation, followed by Isaac Allred and, finally, Jedediah Grant, who adjourned the conference, "blessing the people in the name of the Lord."[18] At the same time Grant was in Kaysville, Brigham Young was rebuking the Saints in Salt Lake City for lying, stealing, swearing, committing adultery, and quarreling among husbands, wives, and children. While Grant then took his thunderous rhetoric to from Kaysville to Farmington, Centerville, and Bountiful, John Young began preaching at settlements south of Salt Lake City, starting in Spanish Fork where four hundred people—presumably including John H. Redd and his family—were rebaptized.[19] Speaking in Salt Lake City of the Reformation, Wilford Woodruff said:

---

[16]*Deseret News*, 1 October 1856.   [17]Ibid., 24 September 1856.   [18]Ibid.
[19]Ibid., 22 October 1856. The Redds were members of Spanish Fork Ward.

The spirit of God is like a flame among the Leaders of this people
& they are throwing the arrows of the Almighty among the people.
J. M. Grant is pruning with a sharp two edged sword & calling
loudly upon the people to wake up & repent of their sins.[20]

The Reformation spread rapidly throughout Utah and
seemed to be fostering a renewed dedication to the church, just
as the First Presidency had desired. By the end of October it had
reached Harmony and many of the leaders in the south had been
rebaptized including John D. Lee. One of Lee's wives, Rachel,
wrote:

> ... never Since Harmony has been Settled has thare been such feel-
> ings of penitence and contrition and joy and thankfullness to God
> for his mercies and loving Kindness toward us through all our
> wickedness, and hardness of heart that have existed in this place one
> toward another.[21]

The Reformation was the continual center of attention in Harmony week after week, and yet a visit by three elders from Cedar
City in December 1856, according to Rachel Lee, "showed clearly
that that Reformation had scarsly [*sic*] commenced in our midst
yet."[22] Moreover, the Harmony Saints seemed to feel sufficiently
unworthy, in the context of the movement, that the important
Sacrament of the Lord's Supper, of which only the worthy are to
partake, was not administered at Harmony until 17 May 1857—
more than eight months after the start of the Reformation.[23]

On July Fourth the Saints in Harmony took some time out
from the frenzy of the Reformation to celebrate the nation's
birthday along with many people visiting from Cedar City,
including a brass band and choir.[24] Though the Fourth was "a Day
of joy and gladness," the real celebration in Utah was on 24 July,
the tenth anniversary of the entrance of the Saints into the Salt
Lake Valley.[25] Ironically, on the evening of the 24th, news reached
Salt Lake City that the United States Army was on route to put
down the "rebellion" in Utah.

---

[20]Woodruff, *Journal*, 4:440, 9 October 1856.
[21]Rachel Andora Woolsey Lee, "Journal," 11, entry from May 1856.
[22]Ibid., 19, entry of 14 December 1856.   [23]Ibid., 41, entry of 17 May 1857.
[24]Ibid., 44, entry of 4 July 1857.   [25]Ibid.

There had been an increasing outcry in the United States Congress regarding polygamy, which at that time was practiced openly in Utah, and there was great criticism of the church's control of the Utah territorial government. Many politicians of both parties spoke out against the Saints, including Stephen A. Douglas, whom the Mormons previously had counted as a loyal friend. As early as 28 June the *Deseret News* had reported debates in the East as to whether there was any "necessity of sending troops and officers to establish peace in Utah." One week later, Brigham Young spoke in the tabernacle regarding the rumor that troops might be sent to Utah.[26] And yet the Saints still were somewhat perplexed by the events, since they considered themselves to be loyal American citizens.

Nevertheless, the Mormons wasted no time in making preparations to defend Zion. The Nauvoo Legion was already in place, having been organized on 15 January 1857 into thirteen military districts (with the Davis County military district organized by Allen Taylor).[27] On 1 August, Lieutenant General Daniel H. Wells informed his legion of two thousand men that Utah was about to be "invaded by a hostile force."[28] Three days later, Apostle George A. Smith left Provo to deliver military orders to the commander of each of the southern Utah towns. At Harmony, Rachel Lee recorded Smith's visit in her journal:

> 16th [August 1857] there was no meeting held this day but preparing to receive G.A. Smith.
>
> 17th George A. Smith and company having arrived last evening and this morning the brethren paraded in order to show the officers of this place how to discipline their men aright.... At seven o'clock met in the meeting house.... President G.A. Smith delivered a discourse on the spirit that actuated the United States towards this people—full of hostility and virulence, and all felt to rejoice in the Lord God of our fathers.[29]

It was the profound misfortune of the California-bound Fancher Train, a group of families from Arkansas, to enter Utah

---

[26]Eugene E. Campbell, *Establishing Zion*, 237.

[27]*The Contributor*, vol. 9, no. 6, April 1888, 203.

[28]Anderson, *Desert Saints*, 170.   [29]Rachel Lee, "Journal," 46–47.

at this time. The fiery preaching of George A. Smith and others, coming on the heels of the Reformation, had already created a war-like hysteria among the Mormons, and boastful anti-Mormon statements reportedly made by the party as they traveled through central Utah on their way south further antagonized the Saints. And then, as they camped on the western side of the Pine Valley Mountains at a place called Mountain Meadows, they encountered the ultimate tragedy.

Indians, who generally liked the Mormons but distrusted the "Mericats" (as they called all non-Mormon whites), attacked the Fancher Train at Mountain Meadows on about 7 September. The siege failed and the Indians returned to their camp where John D. Lee, who had crossed the mountains from his home in Harmony, met them. Lee managed to calm the Indians temporarily, but in a subsequent meeting of the Indians with some Mormons from Cedar City, plans were hatched to exterminate the Fancher group.

Lee claimed that the instructions for the attack came directly from Isaac Haight, the president of the Cedar City Stake and the presiding church authority in southern Utah.[30] Whether or not that was true, it is undeniable that on Thursday, 10 September, Lee was joined by a group of men from Cedar City and other southern Utah settlements and on the next morning entered the Fancher camp at Mountain Meadows under a flag of truce. Lee convinced the immigrants to lay down their arms, after which, upon the order, "Do your duty," the 120 men, women, and older children of the train were executed.[31]

Two weeks later, Lee arrived in Salt Lake City "from Harmony with . . . an awful tale of Blood."[32] The awful tale was, of course, the massacre, the blame for which Lee placed on the Indians. That, at the time, was good enough for Brigham Young, who had more important things to worry about with the United States Army steadily approaching.

With winter close at hand, in order to delay the army from making it to the Salt Lake Valley, the Nauvoo Legion resorted to

---

[30]John D. Lee, *Mormonism Unveiled*, 218–220.
[31]Campbell, op. cit., 250–51.   [32]Woodruff, *Journal*, 29 September 1857.

a sort of guerilla warfare. General Daniel Wells, in a letter to Major Joseph Taylor (Allen Taylor's brother and one of the highest-ranking officers in the Legion), instructed that the advancing army be delayed by every means possible:

> On ascertaining the locality or route of the troops, proceed at once to annoy them in every possible way. Use every exertion to stampede their animals and set fire to their trains. Burn the whole country before them, and on their flanks. Keep them from sleeping by night surprises; blockade the road by felling trees or destroying river fords, where you can. Watch for opportunities to set fire to the grass on their windward, so as if possible to envelope their trains. Leave no grass before them that can be burned. Keep your men concealed as much as possible, and guard against surprise. . . . Take no life, but destroy their trains, and stampede or drive away their animals at every opportunity.[33]

A few days later Major Taylor rode into an enemy camp, supposing it to be friendly, and was captured. In his possession were the incriminating orders whereupon, as Taylor soon learned, his captors planned to put him on trial for treason. Whether he would have been found guilty of the offense and hanged, as he had heard rumored, became moot when his captors were distracted one evening while building a campfire in the midst of a furious storm and Taylor was able to escape, running barefoot after losing his stockings, more than three miles with his boots in his hands.[34]

Through the captured orders the army knew exactly what to expect from the Mormons, but the scorched earth policy was effective nevertheless. In addition to burning grass both in front of and behind the approaching army, the Mormon raiders destroyed several hundred thousand pounds of army supplies, much of it on the night of 4 October, under the direction of Major Lot Smith.[35] That, along with other similar raids, was sufficient to stall the army's movement long enough to force it to spend the winter in a makeshift city of tents and improvised shelters at a place in western Wyoming that was called Camp Scott.

---

[33] *The Contributor*, vol. 3, September 1882, 380. The letter was dated 4 October 1857.
[34] Ibid., 381–383.
[35] Ibid., 286

Remarkably, no life was lost on either side in any of the engagements. But Brigham Young knew that the Saints could not afford to fight the United States Army and decided to pursue a "Sebastopol policy," patterned after the 1855 Crimean War episode in which the Russians, in a hopeless situation, burned the city of Sebastopol and left the ruins for the British and French forces.[36] As early as 13 September 1857, Young preached from the Tabernacle pulpit,

> Before I will suffer what I have in times gone by, there shall not be one building, nor one foot of lumber, nor a stick, nor a tree, nor a particle of grass and hay, that will burn, left in reach of our enemies. I am sworn, if driven to extremity, to utterly lay waste, in the name of Israel's God.[37]

By March 1858, Brigham Young had completed plans to move the Saints in the northern settlements to the White Mountain country—an uncharted desert region to the west of Utah's southern settlements that straddles the present Utah-Nevada border. It was an area of good grass and water rumored to be able to support a population of five hundred thousand. "I am going there where we should have gone six or seven years ago," proclaimed Young at a special council on 21 March in the tabernacle.[38] This came even as Colonel Thomas Kane, the old and valued friend of the Mormons, was undertaking a special mission of peace.

In the early winter Kane, hoping to help avoid an armed conflict between the army and the Mormons, had visited President Buchanan in an attempt to persuade him to send an investigation commission to Utah. Buchanan was in no mood to compromise but did give the colonel his unofficial blessing to go to Utah to try to achieve a peaceful solution. In January 1858 Kane, at his own expense, went to Salt Lake City by way of Panama, San Francisco, Los Angeles, San Bernardino, and southern Utah—by far the fastest route available, particularly in the middle of winter.

---

[36]Richard D. Poll, "The Move South," *BYU Studies*, vol. 29, no. 4, p. 65.

[37]*Journal of Discourses*, 5:231.

[38]Clifford L. Stott, *Search for Sanctuary: Brigham Young and the White Mountain Expedition*, 57.

Though Kane was warmly greeted in Salt Lake City when he arrived on 25 February, church leaders were skeptical of his ability to bring the conflict to a peaceful conclusion. And so, while Kane was meeting in Wyoming with military leaders and Alfred Cumming, who had been designated by the federal government as Brigham Young's successor as governor of Utah, a great "move south" was initiated.

More than thirty thousand residents of Salt Lake City and settlements north of the Salt Lake Valley were instructed to leave their homes and go south. Only a few of the younger and stronger Saints were to remain to take care of property and, if necessary, set fire to the straw-filled homes. Those in Harmony and other southern Utah settlements were not to move but were instructed to send wagons and provisions to northern Utah to assist the exodus.[39]

The bishops organized their wards in the familiar military fashion of tens, fifties, and hundreds. The move south began just as governor-designate Cumming arrived at Salt Lake City in the company of Thomas Kane, who had been successful in his negotiations. Cumming turned out to be amiable and treated Brigham Young with respect, but his pleas to the Mormons to remain in their homes fell on deaf ears, probably due to their great distrust of the army and of the government. Each of the wards was assigned a provisional destination in Utah, Juab, Millard, or Iron counties, but few went farther than the Utah Valley. Most of the Kaysville Saints went to the town of Lehi, while others settled in Provo, Spanish Fork, American Fork, and other small towns. Reddick Allred sent his family to Nephi while he remained behind with the rear guard.[40]

The dispossessed northern Saints remained in the south for about two months. Some relocation in Utah Valley took place as the great influx of humans and animals overloaded the camps and pasturelands that had been allocated by the local wards. The population of Provo, for example, had swelled from about four

---

[39] *Church History in the Fulness of Times*, 375.
[40] Reddick Allred, op. cit., 5:347. As leader of the Davis County Military District, it seems
  likely that Allen Taylor also remained behind.

thousand to as much as fifteen thousand. Accommodations were crude, varying from covered wagons and canvas tents to dugouts and temporary board shanties.

But life went on despite the hardships as births, deaths, marriages, and divorces took place as before the exodus. On the way south, on 22 April just outside of Salt Lake City, Elizabeth Taylor, the third of Allen Taylor's four wives, gave birth to Annie Taylor. In Spanish Fork, John H. Redd, one of the earliest settlers of Utah Valley, succumbed on 15 June from complications of having been kicked in the head by a horse.[41]

President Buchanan had issued a "full and free" pardon on 6 April, but the Mormon leaders did not accept it until 12 June. By the time the army passed through Salt Lake City on 26 June the city was deserted and ready for burning. It was a disappointment for the soldiers, who had desired a military victory. A week later a military reservation called Camp Floyd was established in the Cedar Valley, approximately forty miles west of Salt Lake City.

On 30 June, after the army had established their headquarters, Brigham Young authorized the return of the destitute and tattered Saints to their homes. Allen Taylor's family returned to Kaysville, but Reddick Allred joined his family at Nephi and, like several hundred other people, decided to make a new home in central Utah. Allred sold his home, worth five hundred dollars, for one yoke of oxen worth one hundred dollars, and moved to Spring City in the Sanpete Valley, along with his father Isaac and several other members of the Allred family.[42] James H. Imlay, who had been a resident of Salt Lake City, relocated to Kaysville, perhaps taking advantage of land that had been vacated by those such as Reddick Allred, who did not return. The Redd family remained at Spanish Fork, with the oldest son Lemuel Redd assuming leadership of the family in his father's absence.

Despite the presence of an occupying army in the Utah Territory, the Mormons held their heads high, convinced that they had not been defeated. The settlement between the Mormons

[41]Lura Redd, *The Utah Redds and Their Progenitors*, 228.
[42]Reddick Allred, op. cit., 5:348.

and the government, however, was a truce rather than a solution, as the Saints and soldiers remained "enemies," but at least the threat of war was over.

In the relative calm that prevailed, John Cradlebaugh, associate justice in charge of the southern district of the territory, set about to discover the truth about the affair at Mountain Meadows. As the investigation into the massacre progressed, the finger of accusation was pointed squarely at John D. Lee, though others who participated in the atrocity also were sought. In April 1859 Judge Cradlebaugh and his military escort headed south with the intent of capturing and bringing to justice those responsible for the massacre. As the two hundred U.S. troops reached Beaver, advance notice of their approach reached Lee and his cohorts, who then went into hiding. Lee fled into the mountains east of Harmony, whence he could watch activities on his own farm. From his lookout perch he wrote:

> Sat. May 14th [1859]. Pleasant. I stood on the summit of the mountain east of Harmony about 12 noon and with my spy-glass looked over the whole valley. Saw some of my family; from this point I could overlook the whole country, from the tops of the mountains down to the base, and a more lovely and beautiful landscape I never saw before; the snow caped mountain on the south with the lofty pines on its summit clothed in their green foliage, gently sloping to the North and North East, tinged with red and blue down to the slopes of the mountain; the vale covered with green vegetation intermingled with shady groves of cedar, presented a romantic though majestic scenery. My residence and farm appeared more dear and lovely to me than ever.[43]

For the time being Lee was safe. Judge Cradlebaugh and the troops, resigned to the fact that they could do nothing, returned to Salt Lake City, whereupon Lee went home. His life became as normal as could be expected, but though he would experience a few peaceful years there, John D. Lee was on the road to infamy and, because of him, Harmony was on the map.

---

[43]John D. Lee, Charles Kelly, ed., *Journals of John D. Lee, 1846–47 and 1859*, 205–6.

Chapter XII

MOVING SOUTH

AFTER THREE FRUITLESS YEARS of waiting to go to Zion, the first South African Saints sailed for America in early 1859, five aboard the *James Buck* and another twenty-eight aboard the barque *Alacrity*. One year later the *Mary Pearce* sailed from Port Elizabeth with eleven church members; shortly thereafter, on 5 April 1860, the *Alacrity*, on which George Prince, his wife, and their eight children were sailing, departed from Port Elizabeth.[1]

The *Alacrity* anchored briefly in Cape Town, where another company of Saints boarded, bringing their total to seventy—the largest Mormon group to emigrate from South Africa.[2] From Cape Town the five-masted ship sailed to the Isle of St. Helena, where Napoleon had been banished in 1815 and lived until his death in 1821.[3] After St. Helena it was onward to Boston, where they arrived on 18 June, seventy-three days after their departure from Port Elizabeth. Rumors had preceded the arrival of the ship in Boston harbor, and the docks were crowded with the curious who expected to see a shipload of black Africans.[4]

The immigrants went by train from Boston through Chicago to St. Joseph, Missouri—the end of the line of the Hannibal and St. Joseph Railroad—from which they traveled by boat to Florence, Nebraska, near the site of the old Winter Quarters.[5] After

---

[1]The *Alacrity* was a sailing ship built in 1856 at Sunderland, England. It was 111 feet long, had five masts, and was built of white oak with copper and iron fastenings. See Conway B. Sonne, *Ships, Saints and Mariners—A Maritime Encyclopedia of Mormon Migration, 1839–1890.*

[2]Ibid., 264.

[3]Robert Bodily, "Journal of Robert Bodily," 7.

[4]Wright, op.cit., 154.

[5]Bodily, op. cit., 9.

resting for a few days in Omaha, they bought provisions, made necessary preparations for the trip across the plains and, on 20 July, commenced the final leg of the trip, departing Florence in the William Budge Company.

Typically frail, Sarah Prince was not only in poor health as the journey began, but also was pregnant and had to ride while all but the youngest children walked. Through the sale of his land and possessions in South Africa, George Prince had enough money to provide adequately for his family during the trek, but the trip still was too rigorous for Sarah who, about halfway across the plains, gave birth to premature twins who died and were buried beside the trail.[6]

The expectations of the South African Saints had spiraled steadily upwards in the years of waiting to emigrate. After six arduous months of travel by sea, rail, and wagon train, they finally arrived, on 5 October 1860, in the Valley of the Great Salt Lake. On first glance, however, this was not the paradise that George and Sarah Prince had anticipated, and George could not refrain from telling his wife, "Sarah, I wish we were back in Africa!"[7] But his disappointment was as transitory, as was his stay in Salt Lake City, and after a few weeks his family, along with several of his South African compatriots, moved to Kaysville— where Allen Taylor still served as bishop—and became neighbors and close friends with the family of James H. Imlay.[8]

When the South African Saints arrived, Utah was still an occupied territory, though the end of the U.S. Army occupation was in sight. In March 1860, orders were sent to General John-

[6]"Story of Sarah Ann Prince."

[7]Manetta Prince Henrie and Anna Prince Redd, *Life history of William and Louisa E. Lee Prince*, 60.

[8]Robert Bodily, who accompanied the George Prince family from South Africa to Utah, also settled in Kaysville and wrote: "In the spring of 1861 my Father bought a farm in Kaysville on the state road leading to Ogden. The Bishop of the ward was Allen Taylor, a very pleasant, easy going man. The young people seemed to do about as they pleased. I have seen young men come into meeting with spurs and leggins on and seemed to think it was all right and in dances act in a very disorderly way, but after a while the ward was reorganized with Christopher Layton Snr. as Bishop and conditions changed immediately. The meeting house that had been started years before was completed and the young people respected him and were more orderly." *Journal of Robert Bodily*, 12.

ston to reduce his command. The *Deseret News* reported on May 23, after the departure of some of the troops, that the "blacklegs, thieves and murderers are not so plenty hereabouts by half as they were two weeks ago, with a fair and increasing prospect that their numbers will grow less. . . ."[9] Moreover, there were growing signs that the remaining troops would be needed elsewhere for a greater conflict; on 28 September, a week before George Prince and his fellow countrymen arrived in Utah, Salt Lake City resident Charles Walker recorded in his diary, "I see by the Paper that South Carolina is ripe for dissolveing the union."[10]

There was a growing feeling of confidence and, perhaps, a little smugness among the Saints as news of the 20 December 1860 vote of the South Carolina legislature to secede from the Union reached Salt Lake City. The Saints remembered clearly that Joseph Smith had received a revelation twenty-eight years earlier, on 25 December 1832, that "wars will shortly come to pass, beginning at the rebellion of South Carolina. . . ."[11] The revelation accurately prophesied that "the Southern States shall be divided against the Northern States, and the Southern States will call on other nations, even the nation of Great Britain . . . and then war shall be poured out upon all nations."[12] This was, by itself, a clear validation of their faith in their Prophet. Far removed from worldwide turmoil and strife, the Saints began to feel again as though they were living in Zion. Charles Walker wrote on New Year's Eve 1860:

> The United States are on the Brink of Destruction and Civil War. Italy is fighting with in herself. The English and French are at war with China. France is making heavy preparations for War. England is fortifying Herself and all the Nations of the Earth seem to be getting ready for Destruction. In fact all the world seems in comotion while the Saints here in the vallies of the Mountains are enjoying Peace and Plenty.[13]

When fighting broke out at Fort Sumter on 12 April 1861,

---

[9]*Deseret News*, 23 May 1860.
[10]Charles Lowell Walker, *Diary of Charles Lowell Walker*, 29 September 1860, 140.
[11]*D&C*, 86:1.   [12]Ibid., 86:3.
[13]Walker, 31 December 1860, p.155.

marking the beginning of the Civil War, the remaining forces at
Camp Floyd prepared to return to the states, leaving Utah in
peace. For about a year it looked as if Utah would have no military participation in the war until, on 28 April 1862, Brigham
Young received a message by order of President Lincoln to "raise,
arm and equip one company of cavalry for ninety day's service."
The company was to have officers and from fifty-six to seventy-
two privates and was "to protect the property of the telegraph
and overland mail companies in or about Independence Rock
(Wyoming) . . . till the U.S. troops can reach the point where
they are so much needed."[14]

It is noteworthy that the request from the President bypassed
territorial officials and went directly to the head of the church.
The strategy worked, for whereas it normally took weeks to field
a mounted company, the Mormon outfit, formed under the
command of Lot Smith—the same officer who led Mormon
forces that burned U.S. Army supply wagons in 1857—was ready
to ride in just two days.[15] Among the seventy-two privates who
enlisted were Francis Prince and James Imlay, the eldest sons of
George Prince and James H. Imlay.

The day after their start, the troops were met by Brigham
Young at the mouth of Emigration Canyon east of Salt Lake
City and were promised that, if they would live their religion and
obey their commanding officers, not one should "fall by the hand
of the enemy."[16] The non-believer would have wondered how
Young could make such rash assurances, but it was a company of
believers—the only body of troops during the Civil War that was
sponsored by a religious faith—and they trusted their leader
implicitly.[17]

Young's promise, however, did not extend to hardships, of
which there were many. The late spring weather was terrible, with
ten feet of snow, impassable roads, rains, floods, and washed-out
bridges. Provisions were sparse, as the men had to equip and arm

[14]"Utah and the Civil War," *Heart Throbs of the West*, 2:427.
[15]*Deseret News*, 30 April 1862.
[16]Margaret M. Fisher, *Utah and the Civil War*, 25–26.
[17]E. B. Long, *The Saints and the Union: Utah Territory During the Civil War*, 88.

themselves, since they were far away from an established military post. In mid-July about two-thirds of the company, including Prince and Imlay, followed a group of Indians, who had stolen more than three hundred head of horoses and mules from near Fort Bridger, northward to the head of the Snake River Valley.[18] At one stretch, the company was without food for eight days and was glad to eat wild roots, onions, and the dry caked flour that had stuck to the inside of wet sacks. So touched was Francis Prince by the experience that he could never recount it without shedding tears.[19]

The company returned to Salt Lake City on 9 August and was mustered out by 14 August. One man had drowned in the Snake River but, true to Brigham Young's promise, no man had been lost to the enemy; nevertheless, the expedition was one of the most hazardous in the annals of Indian warfare in Utah.[20] The conclusion of the mission marked the end of direct involvement of Utah in the Civil War, though Utah was not unaffected by the war. To the contrary, the war made goods much more difficult to obtain from the states, and church leaders recognized more than ever before the wisdom of being self-sufficient. In 1860 President Young again began to expand the frontier of his commonwealth. Ironically, the expansion was aided to a large extent by an economic windfall resulting from the 1858–61 U.S. Army occupation.

As the last troops left Camp Floyd (renamed Fort Crittenden because former Secretary of War John Floyd had joined the Confederacy) in July 1861, the task was left to Colonel Philip St. George Cooke to close the post and dispose of all properties that could not be hauled away.[21] In a fire sale of major proportions, four million dollars' worth of goods was sold for one hundred thousand dollars. William Clayton wrote on July 16, 1861 to George Q. Cannon:

[18]Seymour B. Young, "The Snake River Expedition," *Improvement Era*, vol. XXV, no.7.
[19]Juanita Williams Kossen, "History of Francis Prince, Pioneer."
[20]Orson Whitney, *History of Utah*, 2:47.
[21]Cooke had replaced General Albert Sidney Johnston in 1860; Johnston, who left the U.S. Army a year later and joined the Confederacy, died at the Battle of Shiloh on the thirty-second anniversary of the Mormon Church, 6 April 1862. Cooke was, coincidentally, the final commander of the Mormon Battalion in 1847, leading that company from Santa Fe to Los Angeles, where it was disbanded.

Dear Brother—Today commences the sale of all the Government property at Camp Floyd, by auction-buildings, grain, hay, and everything except arms and ammunition, soldiers clothing and wagons and teams. They will move away to the States within two weeks and thus end the great Buchanan Utah Expedition, costing the Government millions and accomplishing nothing except making many of the Saints comparatively rich, and improving the circumstances of most of the people of Utah.[22]

The newfound prosperity enabled Brigham Young to enlarge the scope of colonization, but whereas most of the earlier expansion had been to the north, this time he looked south with an eye on cotton. As early as 1851 it was proposed at the general conference in Salt Lake City that "John D. Lee form a settlement at the junction of the Rio Virgin and the Santa Clara Creek, where grapes, cotton, figs, raisins, etc. can be raised."[23] Lee was eager for this mission and went south in 1852 but stopped at Harmony, where the climate was unsuitable for growing cotton.

The first attempt to grow cotton in the Great Basin, however, had not been in southern Utah but in Kaysville (then known as Kay's Ward). In a letter to the editor of the *Deseret News* dated 16 October 1852, Reddin Allred wrote:

Editor of the News:—Last season I came to the Valley, and brought with me two or three dozen cotton seeds, which I planted on the 15th of May, and to my satisfaction, it grew and matured before the frost interfered. . . .

Allen Taylor would plant five acres, if he had the seed. I will have a pint or more of seed, which will be planted next season. I would be glad when I return from my mission (to Hawaii), to see the high lands covered with cotton, resembling the snowy mountains for whiteness. . . . I believe from what I have seen, that it can be made a profitable crop.[24]

Allred, it turned out, misjudged the potential for growing cotton in Kaysville, whose climate was not conducive to the crop. It was no secret that a far more suitable climate was found in southern Utah—where John D. Lee was called to go in 1852—but the

[22]William Clayton, LDS *Millennial Star*, No. 35, 31 August 1861
[23]Campbell, *Establishing Zion*, 253.
[24]Reddin Allred, *Deseret News*, 6 November 1852.

first crop was not grown there until 1855, when Jacob Hamblin planted a small piece of virgin land in Santa Clara. Various attempts were made over the next several years to find suitable land for cultivation, but by 1860 there were only eight small settlements in Washington County, though the crops throughout the area were "reasonably good."[25]

The outbreak of the Civil War had cut off the supply of cotton cloth from the South, and thus it became imperative that Zion produce its own. Brigham Young's visit to southern Utah in May 1861 convinced him of the possibilities for growing cotton there. Young decided to devote the October General Conference to promoting immigration, but when he called for volunteers, only one man raised his hand.[26] A call was then issued to 309 families to go St. George on a "Cotton Mission."[27] This was not a mission in the traditional sense of proselytizing, but rather one in which the family was expected to move south and remain there in order to help in the production of cotton.

The new "missionaries" began arriving in November and December and were greeted by weather of biblical proportions— rain that started on Christmas Day and continued intermittently for forty days everywhere but in Harmony, where a liberal amount of snow was thrown into the mixture. John D. Lee, who on 22 December had been chosen President of the Harmony Branch, recorded on 4 January, "Fort Harmony is almost decomposed and returned back to its native element."[28] William and Harvey Pace and George Washington Sevy, all of whom had recently arrived from Spanish Fork, helped Lee move five of his wives and their families to safer abodes.[29] Left behind was his wife Sarah Caroline, who was thought to be living in the strongest area of the fort. The day before Sarah Caroline was ready to move, however, the walls of the fort caved in, killing two of her children.[30]

---

[25]James G. Bleak, "Annals of the Southern Utah Mission," 1:58.
[26]Campbell, op.cit., 254.
[27]Twenty-three Swiss families also were called to go to Santa Clara, but they were to grow fruit and grapes rather than cotton.
[28]"Harmony Ward Record," 4 January 1862.
[29]Ibid., 19 January 1862.   [30]Ibid., 6 February 1862.

BENJAMIN J. REDD

After Fort Harmony was abandoned in spring 1862, some of the residents went north and founded a settlement called Kanarra, while others went four miles west and established the town of New Harmony, which remained very small despite the arrival of new settlers from the north. George W. Sevy and brothers James and William Pace were among the first three hundred missionaries to be called officially to go south, but there were also volunteers who swelled the numbers. For example, when William Pace was called to leave Spanish Fork to assist in the settlement, he persuaded his sons Wilson Daniel, Harvey Alexander, and John Alma to go with him. Per advice of Erastus Snow, president of the Cotton Mission, after arriving at Harmony in mid-December 1861 they located themselves upon Ash Creek near their friend John D. Lee, who had baptized several members of the Pace family in Tennessee in 1843.[31]

The circle of volunteers to settle in New Harmony expanded a short time later when, in Spanish Fork, Lemuel Redd (John H.

[31]"A Biographical Sketch of the Life of James Pace."

LEMUEL REDD
Courtesy of the Church Archives,
The Church of Jesus Christ
of Latter-day Saints.

Redd's eldest surviving son) answered the call.[32] The decision to go undoubtedly was a family matter: Redd's sisters Ann Mariah and Ann Elizabeth were married to brothers Wilson and Harvey Pace, who, along with Redd's brother-in-law, George W. Sevy, already had settled in New Harmony.[33]

In spring 1862 Lemuel Redd packed his family, nineteen-year-old Benjamin, and Luke—a thirty-four-year-old son of a former slave—for the move to New Harmony.[34] Lemuel was already

[32]That Redd was a volunteer is made clear by the fact that he wasn't among the first missionaries called in October 1861 and was in New Harmony at least by June 1862, nearly four months before the second group of missionaries were called in the general conference in October 1862. Even if they volunteered, however, it is clear from many family histories that those who went south considered it a calling.

[33]Sevy was married to Phoebe Malinda Butler, the sister of Lemuel Redd's wife Keziah Jane.

[34]Nelle Spilsbury Hatch, *Mother Jane's Story*, 7, 17. Luke was the son of Venus who, along other slaves, were set free in Tennessee by John H. Redd in Tennessee in 1844 after he embraced the Mormon religion. Venus and another former slave named Chaney chose to remain with the family and moved with them to Spanish Fork; though invited to move with the family to New Harmony, they chose to remain in Spanish Fork. Luke appeared on the 1870 New Harmony Census as a black, forty-two-year-old carpenter and used the surname Redd.

somewhat familiar with the road, having traveled it in 1856 when he was called to go on a mission to Las Vegas; information gleaned from that journey as well as from those who were called in 1861 to settle St. George made the route seem familiar and friendly.[35] With a heavy wagon drawn by oxen and a lighter one drawn by mules, and with Ben and Luke following on foot to watch after trailing livestock, the family said goodbye to Spanish Fork.

After a tiring three-week journey, Lemuel Redd and his family arrived in New Harmony and quickly determined that there was no reason to travel further. Harmony had lost half of its inhabitants following the winter deluge, as eleven families went to Kanarra. Even with the addition of George Sevy, Lemuel Redd, and five Pace families, by June 1862 there were only seventeen taxpayers in New Harmony, indicating about that many families.[36] The new families worked hard to build new homes at the new town site, sometimes even forsaking Sunday meetings in the process:

Sunday May 24th, 1862
This morning Bishop H. Lunt (from Cedar City) and J. D. Lee visited the Bretheren Paces and Sevy and requested them to come to meeting and stop their working on the Sabbath. At 11 o'clk Public meeting. The brotheren attended meeting for the first time. . . .
The new Settlers are not much inclined to attend meetings.

Sunday June 1st, 1862
This morning some of the Bro. Paces called upon Prest. Lee to accompany them to explore the canyons in search of timber. He told them to come to meeting and I would go with them on Monday, to this they declined. Said they had too much to do.

---

[35]Ibid., 18. Lemuel and his father were called to go on a mission to Las Vegas to establish a settlement and to open up lead mines for the purpose of making bullets. Lemuel went to Las Vegas in February 1856; his father was to follow in the autumn, but no lead was found in the mines (silver was discovered but was unsuitable for bullets) and Lemuel returned to Spanish Fork in September before his father had departed.

[36]Bleak, op. cit., 103. Only males were considered taxpayers, so plural wives living in separate abodes were not counted. By way of contrast, Virgin City had 215 and St. George 130 taxpayers. The five Pace families were those of brothers James and William, and William's sons Wilson D., Harvey Alexander, and John Alma.

NORTHEAST CORNER OF OLD FORT HARMONY
The Kolob Fingers of Zion National Park are in the background.
Photo by William R. Palmer, about 1936.
Courtesy of Special Collections, Sherratt Library, Southern Utah University.

Sunday June 15, 1862
At the usual hour of meeting Bro. Sevy, Redd and families, the
sequel was the administration of Prest. Lee, found place in their
hearts. They repented and came to meeting and confessed and
talked good.[37]

Having "repented" and decided to attend Sunday meetings,
Lemuel Redd still found sufficient time to build a log house for
his family. For a chimney he used rocks and adobe bricks from the
crumbling fort. "You want to remember this spot, honey," Redd
told his daughter Jane as they gathered rubble from the old fort.
"From here, the first missionaries to the Indians were sent."[38]

[37]"Harmony Ward Record," 24 May 1862, p.11. The record for the first several years was
kept by John D. Lee.   [38]Hatch, op. cit., 21.

Those first missionaries made little headway in either converting or "civilizing" the Indians of southern Utah as the natives kept
many of the customs that seemed barbarous to the Mormons. A
discouraged Jacob Hamblin wrote to George A. Smith in September 1858, asking to be allowed to work among the "nobler races"
of Indians, specifically the peaceful Moqui (later called Hopi) who
lived across the Colorado River.[39] Hamblin made several visits to
the Moquis and on each occasion he tried, without success, to get
a few of the Indian leaders to accompany him back to Utah, with
the idea of further cementing their friendship and impressing
them with the advantages of cooperation with the Mormons.[40]

On 26 October 1862, at the St. George Bowery a conference
was held, at which Hamblin told of the virtues of the Moquis.
Apostle Orson Pratt spoke next of predictions of the *Book of
Mormon* relative to missionary work among the Lamanites and
stated that he wanted "20 or 25 men to accompany Brother Hamblin to the Moqui villages." At the afternoon conference meeting
a list of twenty-one Indian Missionaries was read, beginning
with "Jacob Hamblin of Santa Clara" and ending with "Benjamin
Redd of Harmony."[41]

The missionaries were ready within a month and departed
from St. George in late November, equipped with supplies prescribed at the conference, including a rifle or revolver (or both)
and "Tea, Sugar, Coffee, Molasses, and as many comforts as each
person may deem necessary to make himself comfortable."[42]
Heading south from St. George, the missionaries crossed the
rugged area later known as the "Arizona Strip" and came to the
Colorado River, where the drop-off from the tableland above to
the river below was precipitous, making the descent to the river
slow and difficult. Once across the river the company trudged
onward, pioneering a new route to the Indian villages.

---

[39]Juanita Brooks, "The Southern Indian Mission and its Effect Upon The Settlement of
    Washington County," 15.
[40]Juanita Brooks, "Indian Relations on the Mormon Frontier," *Utah Historical Quarterly*,
    vol. 12, no. 1–2, (January–April 1944), 24.
[41]Bleak, op. cit., 107–108. Four names subsequently were added to the list and twenty-five
    missionaries were sustained by the conference. See Bleak, 112.
[42]Ibid.

Jacob Hamblin was no stranger to the Moquis, having visited three previous times, and the Indians received him and the other missionaries in "a very friendly manner." This was not a proselytizing mission, but one of exploring of a new route and promoting friendship with the Moquis. The new route—which crossed the Colorado River west of the Grand Canyon—was much slower than had been expected and therefore was not acceptable. But Hamblin still hoped to be successful in teaching the Moquis a new way of life and once again invited the Moqui people to send some of their "chief men" to visit Utah and talk with Mormon leaders. The invitation initially was rebuffed on account of a tradition forbidding the Moquis to cross the Colorado River but, after further consultation, the Indians decided to send three of their men to Utah with the Mormons.[43]

The return trip to St. George was via a route east of the Grand Canyon established on previous trips to the Moquis. Fording the Colorado on New Year's Day 1863 was difficult and dangerous due to deep water and flowing ice. Hamblin, anticipating that his three Moqui guests would balk at crossing the river, shrewdly forwarded their blankets and provisions with the first group to cross, whereupon the Indians concluded that they must follow.[44]

After returning to St. George on 10 January 1863, Jacob Hamblin and William B. Maxwell took their three guests to Salt Lake City to talk to Brigham Young and other Mormon leaders, where the Indians "were greatly interested in what they saw and in the way they were treated."[45] Meanwhile, Benjamin Redd, having completed his mission, rejoined his brother's family in New Harmony. His stay would be short, however, as an even greater assignment than his missionary expedition loomed.

The prelude to the new task occurred in the spring of 1860 when Joseph W. Young, a nephew of Brigham, departed from Salt Lake City with an ox-train of twenty-nine wagons. The company traveled to the Missouri River, where they picked up supplies, merchandise, and machinery, and then returned to

---

[43]James A. Little, *Jacob Hamblin*, 280.   [44]Ibid., 281
[45]Bleak, op. cit., 121.

Utah in the fall, proving that it was possible to make a roundtrip in the same season. After Joseph Young delivered a sermon at the October 1860 general conference on "the science of Ox-teamology," the handcart system that had been used since 1856 was abandoned and preparations were made to send teams from Utah to the Missouri River the following season to bring back immigrants and merchandise.[46]

There was great merit to the plan. The handcart system, under which those lacking the wherewithal to procure teams were advised to cross the plains by handcart, had fallen into disfavor before the 1860 immigration season. Even before the Civil War, it was estimated that the Saints paid between ten and thirty thousand dollars each year in the Missouri Valley for cattle wagons, and the war decreased the supply and increased the cost of all items.[47] In sending wagons east from Utah this money was kept within the church, but Utah products were taken and sold in the Midwest and needed machinery and merchandise were purchased and transported back to Utah.

Two hundred wagons were sent in 1861 and two hundred sixty-two the following year on "down and back" trips, as they were called, but none of those were from southern Utah. That all changed in 1863 when, on 15 March, a letter was read to the Saints in St. George calling for fifty-five ox or mule teams from Washington County "to assist the poor from the Old and from the New Worlds."[48] The town of New Harmony, with fewer than a hundred people, was asked to furnish three teamsters and three outfits of wagons, with four yoke of cattle and one thousand pounds of flour for each wagon—a heavy assignment compared with what was requested of other settlements.

John D. Lee, who had attended the conference at St. George, brought back word of the call to New Harmony on 25 March and the outfits were raised immediately—one by Lemuel Redd and George Sevy, another by George Hill, and the third by William,

[46]Arrington, *Great Basin Kingdom*, 206–7.   [47]Ibid.
[48]Bleak, op. cit., 124. The letter, from Edward Hunter, S. W. Hardy and J. C. Little in Salt Lake City was dated 25 February 1863.

James, Harvey and Wilson Pace.[49] On the following day Lee recorded:

> Thursday March 26th, 1863
> It being fast day meeting was held at 9 o'clk A.M. during which Prest. Lee laid on hands, blessed and set apart M. H. Darrow, Geo. Woolsey and Benjamin J. Redd for the 3 teamsters from Harmony according to the vote of the Conference.
> Benjamin J. Redd requested a dance previous to leaving, which was accompanied with a good spirit.[50]

All of the requested men, teams, and supplies were to be in Salt Lake City on a specified date in April, ready for the trip east. Redd, Woolsey, and Darrow, having an additional three hundred miles to travel before reaching Salt Lake City to join the other teams, "rolled out in good spirits" from New Harmony on Sunday, 29 March.[51] Once in Salt Lake City, they and the other teamsters were formed into ten companies, consisting of 384 wagons, 3,604 oxen, and 488 men, which transported 236,000 pounds of flour to the Missouri River.[52]

Whereas in 1861 and 1862 most of the immigrant wagon trains were independent of the teamsters from Utah, in 1863 only two of the twelve companies to cross the plains were not "down and back" units. For the teamsters the trip was long and arduous, especially for those from southern Utah who had to travel a roundtrip distance of over twenty-eight hundred miles—roughly the distance from New York to San Francisco. There was time for fun as well as for work, but in the end the ordeal of being on the trail for nearly eight months created friction amongst the trio from New Harmony:

> Sunday Nov. 22, 1863
> Prest. Lee proceeded to settle some difficulties arising among M H Darrow, Geo. Woolsey and Benj. J. Redd, teamsters who crossed the plains the fall season to aid the immigration. Satisfactory confessions were made and all difficulties settled.[53]

---

[49]"Harmony Ward Record," 25 March 1863, 18–19.
[50]Ibid., 26 March 1863, p. 20.   [51]Ibid., 29 March 1863.
[52]William W. Slaughter and Michael Landon, *Trail of Hope*, 139.

New Harmony enjoyed a modest growth in population with the addition of five families from Kaysville while the teamsters were on the trail. Allen Taylor, his son William Riley, and his brother William W. responded to a call to go south and relocated in Harrisburg, about twenty miles south of New Harmony on the Rio Virgin, in July 1862, to join their brothers-in-law, Allen and Hosea Stout.[54] They remained in Harrisburg for about a year before moving to New Harmony.

Then, in early 1863, thinking that the warm climate of southern Utah would be beneficial for his wife's health, George Prince packed his family and joined a company of Saints going to St. George. James H. Imlay also decided to go south at the same time, and together they were among a handful of settlers in spring 1863 to start a settlement halfway between St. George and Washington, called Middleton.[55] This was true desert country, not only dry with limited access to water, but also very hot, where summer temperatures well above one hundred degrees Fahrenheit are the rule.

As was often the case in new settlements, the first homes in Middleton were dugouts built into the red dirt of a hillside, at the base of vermilion sandstone cliffs, which provided a picturesque if inhospitable backdrop. Sarah Prince had no need for curtains in her dugout, for there was but one door and no windows. The single opening, however, provided sufficient access for a wide variety of insects to enter and take up residence, including flies, mosquitoes, fleas, and, of course, the pesky and ubiquitous bed bug, the pioneer's most bothersome hindrance to a good night's sleep.

The 1863 pioneers had the misfortune of moving to Middleton in a year of drought in the south. A general lack of grass, grain, and hay due to the dry conditions led many to unload draft animals to the northern settlements in exchange for breadstuffs. Paradoxically, in the midst of a drought, springs and seeps provided abundant breeding grounds for mosquitoes that inflicted

[53]"Harmony Ward Record," 22 November 1863, p. 24–25.
[54]Bleak, op. cit., 102.   [55]Ibid., 126.

many with malaria.[56] With the extreme desert heat thrown into the mixture, it was not surprising that James H. Imlay soon moved his family to New Harmony, where the climate was cooler, water more plentiful, malaria not a problem, good grazing lands, and an inexhaustible supply of logs for houses on the nearby mountainside.

Francis Prince, who had been courting Mary Elizabeth Ann Imlay and evidently found life in Middleton unpleasant without sixteen-year-old Elizabeth at his side, subsequently followed the Imlays to New Harmony.[57] The move paid off for Francis (who preferred to be called Frank), as the courtship progressed to marriage on 26 December 1864. Their first home was made of split logs in which the only dry refuge during a storm was under a rawhide stretched over the bed. A trench in the dirt floor through the house served as a drain.[58] Benjamin Redd also benefited from the arrival of new settlers in New Harmony, specifically Allen Taylor's daughter Clarissa, who was born in 1849 while her father's wagon train company took shelter from the snow at Fort Bridger. Clarissa caught Benjamin's eye and they were married on his twenty-third birthday, June 20, 1865, though she was not yet sixteen years old.

The addition of new residents at New Harmony—and elsewhere in southern Utah—also had a pronounced effect on Harmony's original settler, John D. Lee. Most of the new colonists were not familiar with the fervor that had characterized the period of Mountain Meadows Massacre and looked upon the murder of the emigrants with great horror. Those from Spanish Fork who settled in New Harmony were a largely sympathetic lot who had known Lee since his missionary days in Tennessee, but those from Kaysville and elsewhere had no such connection with Lee and were unhappy that he remained president of the Harmony branch. Lee himself recorded on February 18, 1864,

[56] Andrew Karl Larson, *The Red Hills of November: A Pioneer Biography of Utah's Cotton Town*, 57–61.

[57] Luella Adams Dalton, "History of New Harmony."

[58] Sheldon Grant, "Harmony, Fort Harmony, New Harmony and Surrounding Area," 65.

"Inasmuch as considerable dissatisfaction has been for some time previous with Bro. Lee as President in Harmony he manifested a willingness to resign his office."[59] Two weeks later, on March 5, the situation came to a head:

> The people of the Branch were called together by Bishop Lunt [of Cedar City Ward, of which Harmony Branch was a part] for the purpose of settling their difficulties resulting in a better state of feeling.
>
> Prest. Lee tendered his resignation as President of the Branch which was accepted.
>
> On motion made by Thos. A. Woolsey, it was seconded and unanimously carried that James H. Imlay be our President; whereupon Bishop Lunt proceeded to set him apart by the laying on of hands, to discharge the duties of that office.[60]

Lee accepted the change in seemingly good spirit. On the day he was replaced a call was issued for two more "down and back" teams, and Lee recorded that "Prest. Imlay attended to the requisition with becoming spirit and energy." But something was different, as his frequent entries in the Harmony branch record, which previously had been made almost weekly, trickled virtually to a halt. In fact, the only entry for the rest of the year 1864 was in September, and that to record that Brigham Young, accompanied by seven of the twelve apostles, had preached to the people of New Harmony.[61] The candle that had burned so brightly in John D. Lee was flickering, and life for him in New Harmony would never again be the same.

---

[59]"Harmony Ward Record," 18 February 1864, 25.

[60]Ibid., 5 March 1864, 25–26.

[61]Ibid., September 1864, 26. The apostles were accompanying President Young were: Orson Hyde, Amasa Lyman, Ezra T. Benson, Lorenzo Snow, George A. Smith, Wilford Woodruff, and George Q. Cannon.

Chapter XIII

INDIANS IN CONFLICT

A SITE FOR THE TOWN of New Harmony was chosen after Old Fort Harmony was destroyed in February 1862, but somehow the message wasn't received that the people actually were supposed to reside there. Brigham Young, visiting New Harmony with seven of the Twelve Apostles in September 1864, "advised the people to survey a town site and live in it instead of upon their farms."[1] Though not residing in a town proper, a total of twenty-five families and 225 inhabitants were counted at the time of Young's visit.[2]

The early Mormon missionaries in southern Utah had the good fortune of choosing Piede territory in which to settle. The Piedes—who were closely related to and thought by some to be branch of the Paiutes—were a particularly docile and peaceful band of Indians. The newly arrived missionaries at Harmony in 1854 found the Indians to be "very friendly" and "very timid." The timidity, James Bleak surmised, "arose from the fact that bands of Utes and Mexicans had repeatedly made raids upon them and had taken their children" and had "sold them as slaves."[3] Former U.S. Indian Agent Dr. Garland Hurt generally agreed, writing in 1860, "The Py-eeds [Piedes] are perhaps the most timid and dejected of all the tribes west of the Rocky Mountains, being regarded by the Utahs [Utes] as their slaves." So pervasive was the

---

[1]Bleak, 169.
[2]"Harmony Ward Manuscript History," 20 September 1865.
[3]Bleak, op. cit., 17.

slavery, Hurt reported, that scarcely one-half of the Piede children were raised in their own band.[4]

The Piedes, as well as the Paiutes, greeted the Mormons warmly. The missionaries desired to convert rather than to subjugate the Indians and were allowed to settle peacefully at Harmony. Moreover, the Piedes had few skills for self-protection, as evidenced by the slavery imposed by the Utes on their children, and expected that the Mormons would provide a protective buffer against their enemies.

Things didn't work out as the Indians had expected. The settlers—not just at Harmony but also throughout Utah—took the choice land along the creeks. Their livestock devoured most of the vegetation that produced the nutritious seeds on which the natives subsisted. The Indians had accepted the Mormons in good faith, not realizing that the white man's custom was permanent occupation of the land. In their frustration, dispossessed Indians began to raid cattle herds for food, particularly in remote areas away from large settlements. In response to the rebellion, the Mormon policy became, "Feed the Indians. It is cheaper to feed them than to fight them."[5]

Indian resentment of the Mormons gradually increased, especially after the arrival in 1861 of the "cotton missionaries." The Piedes and Paiutes were less aggressive, but the Navajos had been resentful from the earliest contact with the cotton colony. At various intervals, the raiding Navajos would cross the Colorado River on missions of plunder and revenge.[6] As early as March 1864, Erastus Snow sent a message to warn "the Navajos not to let their thieves visit us again unless they make satisfaction for the horses they have stolen from our people, lest some of our angry men slay them."[7]

During the early months of 1865 Indian raids became somewhat common throughout the Rio Virgin region. The Utes, spurred on by drought conditions that greatly affected their food

[4]Captain J. H. Simpson, *Report of Explorations Across the Great Basin of the Territory of Utah for a Direct Wagon-Route from Camp Floyd to Genoa, in Carson Valley, in 1859*, 462.
[5]H. Lorenzo Reid, *Dixie of the Desert*, 153.
[6]Ibid., 155.   [7]Bleak, op. cit., 146, letter of March 8, 1864.

supply, made raids in the valleys to the north. Then, in the midst of a summit on 9 April in the Sanpete Valley concerning cattle killed and consumed by the starving Indians, an intoxicated Mormon named John Lowry violently jerked a young chieftain from his horse and began to fight him. The enraged Indians, under the leadership of a dynamic young Ute named Black Hawk, returned the next day and killed two white settlers.[8]

Colonel Reddick Allred, commanding eighty-four members of the Nauvoo Legion, followed the Indian raiders up Salina Canyon. A careful ambush had been laid, however, and Black Hawk's men poured down murderous fire while the militiamen searched in vain for cover. Allred had no choice but to order a retreat; the situation appeared to be hopeless, but miraculously only two of his men and several horses were lost.[9] Within days three more Mormons were killed and substantial numbers of cattle and horses were stolen in the Sanpete Valley. Soon much of Utah was engulfed in the "Black Hawk War."

Frightened Piedes told Erastus Snow of Black Hawk's threats to come south to attack the Mormons and to "capture Piede women and children."[10] On 5 January 1866, a Piede runner arrived in St. George with news of another attack by the combined force of Utes, Paiutes, Navajos, and Apaches, this time at Pipe Spring, just south of the present-day Utah-Arizona border.[11] Responding to word of the raids, an expedition of forty-four men under Captain James Andrus, including Frank Prince's brother Richard, left St. George on 12 January for Pipe Spring. Less than a week out, a dozen of the men happened upon two Paiutes who were skinning beef.

The Indians initially denied any knowledge of the raid but had their memories jogged by some heavy-handed prodding and led a group of the soldiers to the bodies of rancher James Whitmore and his ranch hand, Robert McIntyre. Another group of soldiers was led to a Paiute camp where fresh rawhide and sev-

[8]Roberts, *Comprehensive History*, vol. 5, p. 149–150.
[9]Reddick Allred, "Diary."
[10]Letter of Erastus Snow to Brigham Young, 4 November 1865.
[11]Bleak, op. cit., 209–210.

eral sheepskins were found. In a scuffle, two Indians were shot dead and a third wounded. The wounded brave and four others were marched off as prisoners.[12]

When the two groups of soldiers reunited, the second group lost their composure upon seeing the bodies of the slain white men and shot the Paiute prisoners on the spot. "Thus did retribution overtake them on the scene of their crime," reported James Bleak.[13] The Paiutes, maintaining that the Najavos were guilty of the raid, were incensed that seven of their Paiute brethren were killed and became bolder in their attacks. Throughout the region the Paiutes and the Navajos seemed to be working hand-in-hand, apparently united in the common cause of retaliation.[14]

The Mormon leaders worried that the smaller southern Utah colonies were too weak to resist attack and ordered that settlements with "less than 150 well armed men" should be abandoned. New Harmony fell well short of that requirement but Brigham Young informed Erastus Snow that Harmony and Kanarra (also known as Kannaraville) were to be sustained.[15] As was the case with other settlements, they were to construct "good and substantial forts, with high walls and strong gates."[16]

The need for fortifications was real. When the first missionaries settled at Harmony, Indian depredations were few, though the natives far outnumbered the white settlers. By June 1866, however, depredations were being committed almost daily throughout southern Utah. "There is certainly a cause for all this," wrote John D. Lee. "Every thinking, candid & reflecting mind will acknowledge it. Bro. E[rastus] Snow said that in almost every Instance our troubles with the Natives were brought on by imprudent & rash conduct on the part of some of our brethern."[17]

The subject of "forting" for protection from Indian raids suddenly was foremost on the minds of the southern Utah Saints. Erastus Snow met the citizens of Harmony at noon on Saturday, 16 June 1866, and "instructed them about forting." At the Sunday

---

[12]John Alton Peterson, *Utah's Black Hawk War*, 220–222.
[13]Bleak, op. cit., 205.   [14]Reid, op. cit., 158–159.
[15]Cleland and Brooks, *A Mormon Chronicle*, entry of 11 June 1866, vol. 2, p. 19.
[16]Bleak, op. cit., 2 May 1866 letter from Brigham Young to Erastus Snow, 215.
[17]Cleland and Brooks, op. cit., entry of 9 June 1866, 19.

meeting the next day, William Pace, George Sevy, and John D. Lee addressed the congregation "on the subject of Forting &c."[18] James Bleak summarized the activities of the Southern Utah Mission at midyear:

> July, 1866, was a very busy month. Of course Independence Day and Pioneer Day were celebrated.
>
> Pres. Erastus Snow and company called to accompany him, did much traveling so as to advise and instruct the people to guard themselves from Indian depredations. Forts and other defenses are progressing in most of the settlements. There is much moving from settlements to settlements.
>
> Military Muster and drills necessarily occupy their part of the time.[19]

Despite military preparations, the July holidays were celebrated in New Harmony as elsewhere in southern Utah. Horse races were held to celebrate the Fourth of July, followed by a dance at the schoolhouse.[20] The celebration of Pioneer Day, commemorating the arrival of the 1847 pioneers in the Salt Lake Valley, was even larger and much more raucous:

> *Harmony, Teus., July 24th, 1866.* About 10 Morning it was anounced that there would be some Horses racing & foot racing for Beer. I had the fastest stalion or Horse on the ground & my son by Aggathean, J. Williard, was the fleetest on foot. About 3 Evening the Juvenile crowd gathered arround the Beer Barrel, more like Pigs arround a Swill tub, & Frank Prince stood by with a stick to wrapp the youngsters off. Unluckily he hit little Wilford Pace on the mouth causing the Blood to run freely. Soon Jas. Pace, the Father of the Boy, came to punish the Beer Keeper & a fight took place. Scratched & choked each other a litle. When they were parted by Allen Taylor, J. Imlay & myself [John D. Lee], it was with much ado that I could quell the riot & make Peace as the crowd was taken sides. Finally the two combatants made friends. The next was a dance & the drinking of two Barrels of Beer, got up by a Jentile, John Sevy, who payed the Fiddler. I was requested to take charge & Preside over the Dance, which I endeavored to do till about Midnight, when they became so unruly through the influence of Beer that I dismissed the Dance & tried to get them home. During the dance, Richardson & Lemons

---

[18]Ibid., entries of 22–24 June 1866, 20–21.   [19]Bleak, op. cit., 231.
[20]Ibid., entry of 4 July 1866, 22.

were about to take a knockdown. Harmony is certainly runing down below the lowest genteel vulgarity. A change must soon take place or the Name of Harmony Must be changed.[21]

Five days later, on Sunday, 29 July, the heavens opened with a vengeance. A party of church leaders, including Erastus Snow and James Bleak, encountered hail at Pinto—about fourteen miles northwest of New Harmony—that measured more than an inch in diameter.[22] Unlike the protracted forty-day storm of 1861–62, this was a sudden, violent cloud burst in Comanche Canyon that John D. Lee called "a desperrate rainstorm in the west mountains."[23]

Ann Eliza Imlay heard a great roar and told her seven-year-old daughter Sarah to run to the church house and tell her father, James H. Imlay, that a flood was coming. On her way back she encountered rising water that already was up to her knees. Frank Prince grabbed Sarah, put her on top of a chicken coop and told her to stay there while he ran back and rescued his wife Elizabeth (Sarah's older sister), their seven-month-old baby James Franklin, and Elizabeth's two-year-old sister Keziah Jane Imlay. After the floodwaters receded, a search found Sarah asleep on top of the chicken coop, exactly where Frank had left her.[24]

Striking the first field on the north side of town, the flood damaged nearly every farm for a distance of about three miles on Ash Creek. A small piece of rich bottomland belonging to James H. Imlay was nearly ruined. William W. Taylor, who suffered more than most, measured hail washed against his field to the depth of two feet. Many acres of wheat and corn were leveled to the ground.[25] The little log house that Benjamin Redd had built for his wife Clarissa and their two-month-old daughter, Sarah

---

[21]Ibid., entry of 24 July 1866. Aggathean, who died on 3 June 1866, was John D. Lee's first wife. Her actual name was Agatha Ann. J. Imlay was either James H. Imlay or his son John. John Sevy was the son of George W. Sevy. Richardson was Robert Richardson, who was married to Allen Taylor's daughter Sara Jane. Lemons cannot be identified.

[22]Bleak, op. cit., 232.

[23]Cleland and Brooks, op. cit., entry of 29 July 1866, 24. The "west mountains" were the Pine Valley Mountains.

[24]Sarah Engle Imlay Evans, "The First Big Flood of New Harmony."

[25]*Journal History of the Church*, 30 July 1866, letter of Joseph L. Heywood to the *Deseret News*.

Elizabeth, was nearly destroyed and subsequently was abandoned.[26]

The flood caused considerable damage to houses in low-lying areas of the town, and John D. Lee may not have been exaggerating when he wrote that the flood was accompanied by "Hail Stone the sise of hen's Eggs."[27] From a safe distance, Wilson D. Pace surveyed the flood damage with his brother Harvey and Lemuel Redd and noted "even Jim Pace's pigs were washed away." Harvey Pace asked rhetorically, "Will the town and our people be safe?"[28]

The question was posed regarding the flood but was equally relevant concerning the Indian conflict. In the few weeks since Erastus Snow counseled the people of New Harmony "in relation to forting against Indian depredations," reported Joseph Heywood in a letter to the *Deseret News*, "commendable efforts have been made in that direction." New Harmony seemed to be safe, but the Indian threat in southern Utah still was pervasive.

Erastus Snow visited New Harmony on 7 August and, after "a drill & inspection of arms," informed the residents that a company of sixty-five mounted and well-armed soldiers would leave the following Thursday (16 August) to reconnoiter the country in search of "Hostile Indians."[29] A volunteer cavalry corps, actually numbering sixty-one soldiers—including New Harmony volunteers Frank Prince, Lemuel Redd, Robert Richardson, and Eli N. Pace—was mustered under the command of Captain James Andrus. The company left St. George on 18 August, riding an estimated 440 miles "through an exceedingly rough, broken country" to an unexplored region at the confluence of the Green and Colorado rivers.[30]

After five days a detachment of six soldiers was chosen to return to St. George to give details of the company's movement. They had only gone a few miles, however, when they were ambushed. One of the soldiers, Hiram Pollack, lay hidden and saw four Indians shoot Elijah Averett full of arrows, killing him

---

[26]Juanita Williams Kossen, "Benjamin Jones Redd."
[27]Cleland and Brooks, op. cit., 24.
[28]Evans, ibid.
[29]Cleland and Brooks, op. cit., entry of 7 August 1866, 25.
[30]Bleak, op. cit., 246–48.

FRANCIS AND MARY ELIZABETH ANN PRINCE
In front of their New Harmony home, about 1920.

instantly. According to Frank Prince, Pollack heard somebody say
in perfect English, as another arrow was pumped into Averett's
body, "There, take that, God damn you," and suspected that the
Indians were led by a white man.[31] The soldiers pursued the Indians but were successful only in recovering some stolen horses;
they subsequently found a deserted fortified hideout but had no
further contact with the Indians, and after twenty-six days the
expedition was completed.[32]

[31]Juanita Williams Kossen, "History of Francis Prince." The Indians may well have been
   led by a white man. The Shoshoni head chief Washakie acknowledged to Indian Super-
   intendant F. H. Head, "Great numbers of white men, thieves and murderers, who were
   outlaws because of their crimes had taken up their residences among the Indians, and
   were always inciting them to outrages; often leading in their stealing raids." See Peterson, op. cit., 336.   [32]Bleak, op. cit., 235–236.

After the New Harmony volunteers returned to their homes in late September 1866, only 140 inhabitants were counted, a significant decrease from the 225 who lived there in 1864.[33] A probable reason for the decline was the constant threat of Indian attacks, for hysteria still was present even though New Harmony had not been touched directly by the Black Hawk War. Elizabeth Prince, for example, reported that Black Hawk himself came to her door one day while her husband Frank was away and demanded food. The Indian became enraged when she replied that she had no food and threatened her with a knife. In a bluff, Elizabeth grabbed an empty shotgun and leveled it at the intruder, who backed out of the door and ran.[34] It is doubtful that Elizabeth Prince could have been sure that the aggressor was Black Hawk, but there was no doubt concerning the fear that existed in New Harmony due to the Indian conflict.

There also was tension resulting from the enlarging gulf between John D. Lee and many if not most of the townsfolk, among whom he was in general disrepute. Whisperings about Lee's role at the massacre at Mountain Meadows not only continued, but the stories became more numerous and sensational. To make matters worse, the flood had swept away the fencing that kept livestock out of Lee's corn and wheat fields. "The majority of the inhabitants of this Place have turned their Stock into the Field to destroy the grain," asserted Lee. "No other man except J. H. Imlay has even made a rod [of fencing]. . . . I had come to the conclusion that men considered it no crime to destroy my crops," he continued with the clear implication that the intrusion was intentional.[35]

Allen Taylor and George Bennett offered to compensate Lee for damage caused by their horses; Lee forgave them, but there were conspicuous signs of contention in the community. At the conclusion of a meeting on 12 November to settle the damage to Lee's fields, branch president James H. Imlay said that Sabbath

---

[33]Ibid., 238. Among the 140 were only 23 men. An agricultural report also stated that thirty four acres were planted in wheat, ninety-eight acres in corn, twenty-two in potatoes, and eight in cane (for molasses).

[34]Williams, op. cit.   [35]Cleland and Brooks, op. cit., entry of 12 November 1866, 32–34.

meetings—none had been held for nearly three months—would resume "if the People would attend." When Lee went to the meeting house on the following Sunday, however, the door was closed:

> I sent for the Key. Prest. Imlay came but refused to have meeting, said the hour was Past. I replied that there had been no meetings for near 3 months & I did not think it best to be too particuelar as several attemps had been made to get the people togeather, but in vain . . . I said, In as much as he required such prompness of the People, why did he not open meeting at the apointed hour himself & thereby Set the example?[36]

Backed into a corner, Imlay at first resisted but finally consented to opening the doors of the small (twenty-four by twenty-two feet) building "if the People could be got togeather."[37] The meeting was held but Imlay's tenor was, at least in Lee's eyes, still rather hostile:

> We had quite a good meeting. Still saw that the Prest. [Imlay] was envious rather then thankful & his remarks were rather wounding to me & others & more calculatd to brake up a meeting then increase it.[38]

Through the strife, as Lee increasingly became a pariah in many New Harmony circles, one constant in his life was the unconditional friendship of the Redd family. "Because of his missionary efforts in behalf of my family, we were never allowed to speak ill of John D. Lee, and I taught my own children to have respect for his name," wrote Lemuel's daughter Maria Luella.[39] Maria's older sister Mary Jane echoed the sentiment, noting, "His name had ever been a familiar one in our home, and one ever spoken of with great respect."[40] Given the close ties between the two families as well as the increasing friction between Lee and James Imlay, the story of Lemuel Redd's quest to obtain the necessary recommend to marry a second wife—Sarah Louisa Chamberlain—is not surprising:

---

[36]Ibid., entries of 12 and 18 November 1866, 34.
[37]Ibid., entries of 18 and 25 November 1866, 34–35. Lee stated that he would enlarge his own family hall, "making it 25 by 22, feet, one foot larger then presant Public Meeting."
[38]Ibid.   [39]Maria Luella Redd Adams, *Memories*, 14.
[40]Hatch, *Mother Jane's Story*, 24.

When he [Lemuel Redd] started to the city, I [J. D. Lee] had advised him to get an other recomend besides Pres. Imlay's, as Pres. B. Young did not think too well of Imlay. . . . When he Made his buisiness known upon the recomend of Pres. Imlay, Pres. B. Young replied, I don't know any such Man as Prest. Imlay; get some other man to recomend you. Upon which Elder Musser said: Don't you know Bro. Imlay, that we took Brakefast with in Harmony? Certainly, I do, replied Pres. B. Y. Then turning to Bro. Redd, Who are you, Bro. Redd? Are you a son of John Redd that lived at the Spanish Fork? Yes, was the reply. Well, he was a pretty good man, but would do as he pleased; this partly recomend you.[41]

Greater harmony existed in the small town in the ensuing months. The Imlays and the Lees found it in their disposition to dine together on several occasions and in the early spring Ann Eliza Imlay, the town midwife, delivered John D. Lee's latest son, Samuel James.[42] For the most part it was life as usual, seemingly free of the Indian raids that plagued other regions. In late November 1866, however, fear of more Navajo incursions induced authorities in St. George to build outposts to guard mountain passes against the Indians.[43]

Before the garrisons were completed, on December 28, Frank Prince's younger brother, William, and Mendis Cooper, who later married Frank's sister Sophie, rode into St. George from Harrisburg and reported that forty or fifty Navajos were headed for the Harrisburg fields.[44] On the same day, fourteen Navajos stole thirty horses and thirteen head of cattle from settlers at Pine Valley, directly on the other side of Pine Valley Mountain from New Harmony. A Nauvoo Legion force led by James Andrus chased and overtook the raiders, recapturing most of the animals and killing seven of the Indians.[45]

It is not certain whether the Navajo raids were associated with Black Hawk, who was tiring and soon withdrew from the conflict. In any case, reports of the incursions unnerved Mormons all over southern Utah. Fortunately, their defense preparations proved to be more than adequate: A telegram sent by Brigham

[41]Cleland and Brooks, op. cit., entry of 20 January 1867, 46.
[42]Ibid., entry of 14 March 1867, 57.   [43]Walker, op. cit., entry of 25 November 1866, 273.
[44]Bleak, 243.   [45]Ibid., 247.

Young on 18 May warned bishops and leading men of the north-ern settlements that Black Hawk and his braves were on their way north to make raids, "the Settlements South being too well prepared for them to attack."[46]

In addition to consolidating smaller settlements and building forts, in 1867 the Saints in the south raised a rather formidable militia. Known as the Iron County Division, it consisted of about five hundred men from as far north as Fillmore. Under the command of Brigadier General Erastus Snow and Captain James Andrus, the company trained first at St. George but then moved to New Harmony in order to escape the summer heat.[47]

The Harmony Flat was covered with tents as the men took part in spirited sham battles, accompanied by lively tunes played by a military band from St. George. What began as a military exercise became a major event as three thousand people from throughout southern Utah attended a three-day celebration honoring the troops. "Apostle [Erastus] Snow was there all dressed up in a uniform and made a fine speech," recalled Moroni Spillsbury, one of two-dozen members of a band from Toquerville. "People camped in tents and wagons all over the flat. . . . We had horse races and a big time. We had a big parade and we played in the parade."[48] Though it was short lived, Fort Harmony Camp provided a perfect defense for New Harmony throughout the months of its existence.

While at New Harmony presiding over the military drills, on 20 August 1867, Erastus Snow asked the local church members if they desired to become a separate ward rather than remain a branch of the Cedar City Ward. The entire meeting was surpris-ingly parliamentary in nature. After they voted to establish a new ward, Snow asked the congregation for suggestions for a new bishop, whereupon Samuel Worthen, George W. Sevy, and Wil-son D. Pace were nominated. President Snow then inquired of presiding elder James H. Imlay regarding the character of the

[46]Peterson, op. cit., 338.

[47]Henrie and Redd, *Life history of William and Louisa E. Lee Prince*, 87; a monument was erected on the site by the Daughters of the Utah Pioneers to commemorate Fort Har-mony Camp.   [48]Moroni Spillsbury, "Utah Pioneer Biographies," 27:40.

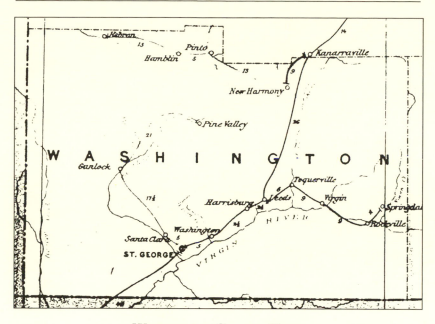

WASHINGTON COUNTY, UTAH
From "Post Route Map of the State of Utah,
showing post offices in operation on the 1st of March 1899."

three nominees; Imlay favored Wilson Pace, Snow concurred, and the congregation voted unanimously to sustain him as the first bishop of Harmony Ward.[49]

The establishment of a new ward may have given an emotional boost to the Harmony Saints, but it had little effect on daily life, sometimes to the chagrin of church leaders. John D. Lee recorded, after attending a Sunday meeting in Cedar City in January 1868:

> At the close of the meeting a Letter was read from Pres. E. Snow instructing the Bishops to sever every Person from the Church who will not keep the word of wisdom, Pay their Tithing & donate of their substance to help bring the Poor Saints from the old country. Bishop Lunt asked my opinion of the letter or epistle. I replied that I would Rather have that Epistle start from Brigham the Head. To carry out

---

[49]"Harmony Ward Record," 20 August 1867, 30–31.

the Letter & spirit of that Epistle would cause ¾ of this community to be cut off from this church. He certainly is ahead of the Times.[50]

As a matter of fact, the New Harmony Saints were faithful in supporting emigration and seemed to pay tithing (Lee took "a load of Tithing" to St. George in February 1868), but the Word of Wisdom was kept no better there than elsewhere in Utah.[51] Though Brigham Young instructed bishops at the April 1867 conference that "every Elder in Israel must know that whiskey, tobacko, tea and coffee are not good for them to take," the Word of Wisdom didn't become a binding law among the Saints until many years later.[52] Pioneer Day, in particular, would not have been complete in New Harmony at that time without a couple barrels of beer.

With a bishop in town rather than one twenty miles away in Cedar City, meetings probably were held with a bit more regularity than when James H. Imlay was presiding elder, but in Utah's first two decades the Saints did not go regularly to any church meetings anyway.[53] The meeting house in New Harmony was much too small to allow all members to attend the same service and was probably like most similar buildings in Utah— uncomfortable to sit in, too hot in the summer, and too cold in the winter.

Moreover, smaller communities such as New Harmony had to call repeatedly on the same people to preach, leading to repetitious and often boring meetings.[54] The Sunday meetings also at times became very contentious. On 13 January 1867, Lee addressed the Saints and recorded, in his self-congratulatory manner, that he "enjoyed goodly Portion of the true spirit while Speaking." And then, according to Lee, sparks flew:

> Jas. Russell was then givd the Floor, & to my surprise he gave vent to vomit of spleen & malice, oppsing everything good that I had said—to the disgust of every Saint presant. I asked the Pres. [Imlay]

---

[50]Cleland and Brooks, op. cit., entry of 25 January 1868, 96.

[51]Ibid., 97.   [52]Hartley, William G., op. cit., 278.

[53]Hartley, William G., "Common People: Church Activity During the Brigham Young Era," in *Nearly Everything Imaginable; The Everyday Life of Utah's Mormon Pioneers*, 249.

[54]Ibid., 255.

if he considered it rite to suffer the Pulpit, where truth should desciminate & the words of Life, Peace & Joy & goodwill to all mankind should be dispnsed, Turned into a Place of venum, ridicule & slander, removing all good impressions made by the Spirit & causing a chill damper over all the assembly. He made no reply & I left the Room.[55]

Occasional contention in meetings should not come as a surprise in a small Mormon settlement like New Harmony, where church and town affairs were so intermingled as to be indistinguishable. Local government was, in essence, church government, and those in authority in the church frequently made decisions for the community. Less than two weeks after the formation of Harmony Ward, for example, recently ordained bishop Wilson Pace discussed in a Sunday meeting the status of New Harmony entries in the first county fair at Washington, clearly a secular matter. Former presiding elder James H. Imlay was dropped as "the chairman of the committee for Harmony" while Frank Prince, Benjamin Redd, George Sevy, John D. Lee, and George Buns were selected to make arrangements to take the town's exhibits to the fair.[56]

The fair at Washington turned out to be a successful affair for Harmony, which garnered thirteen "diplomas." On the trip home, William Prince joined the contingent.[57] While training at Fort Harmony Camp, William had gone to a dance at New Harmony with Maggie (Margaret Nebraska) Imlay, the sister of his pal John, but when he got there he was attracted immediately to Louisa Lee, a daughter of John D. by his first wife, Agatha Ann. It was love at first sight for William, who decided in a moment that he wanted to marry Louisa.[58]

John D. Lee did not take kindly to the prospect of having "that young, unsettled boy" as a son-in-law, having already chosen an older, well-established man for Louisa. That man, however, was married, and Louisa had no desire to be a polygamous wife. She had never before defied her father's wishes, but this time she

[55]Cleland and Brooks, op. cit., entry of 13 January 1867, 42–43.
[56]Ibid., entry of 1 September 1867, 85.   [57]Ibid., entries of 7 and 8 September 1867, 85–86.
[58]Henrie and Redd, op. cit., 87–88.

stood up to her father and said, "I owe you everything, Father, but the right to choose my husband, and I'm going to marry William Prince."[59]

The marriage took place at New Harmony on 23 January 1868, but did not rate an entry in John D. Lee's journal, perhaps due to his initial disapproval of the union, but perhaps also due to the deepening trials that Lee faced. Returning on 9 December 1867 from a trip to Salt Lake City, Lee found that bad management of his farm by his son James had destroyed nearly all his crop and noted, "It was one of the darkest times I had witnessed for some time."[60] But, despite his faith, things managed to get worse: "A darker time I have not seen for many a year to sustain a large family with Bread. About 50 mouths to fill daily—yet my trust is in god. . . . I find that I have too Many Irons in the fire to be proffitable."[61]

To help make ends meet, Lee rented his farmland to Frank Prince, James H. Imlay, and Allen Taylor in exchange for one-half of the crops.[62] For Frank Prince, in particular, it was a great opportunity, since the first years of his marriage had brought hard work but little pay, and he had nary a silver dollar in his possession. Frequently he would shuck corn for Harvey Pace during the day to get enough fodder to feed his horses at night. Once, after selling a cow for eight dollars, he rode all the way to St. George, where he purchased and proudly rode home with a pound of rice, three pounds of white flour, and three pounds of sugar.[63]

In the meantime, things began to go from bad to worse for John D. Lee. Just after he divided his farmland, while he was away in Washington his wife Emma received a "fictitious" letter giving him ten days to escape or he "should be hung up in that old Fort Harmony for being in the Mountain Meadow Massacre."[64] Emma accused George Hicks and John Lawson of writing the letter, but regardless of the authorship the message

[59]Manetta Prince Henrie, *Descendants of John Doyle Lee, 1812–1877*, 351.

[60]Cleland and Brooks, op. cit., entry of 8 December 1867, 93.

[61]Ibid., entry of 1 April 1868, 100.

[62]Ibid. Web Jolly and T. Keele were also listed as renters in this entry, but an entry on 12 April made it clear that the land was "let to Imlay, Prince & Taylor."

[63]Williams, op. cit.   [64]Cleland and Brooks, op. cit., entry of 12 April 1868, 100–101.

was clear that John D. Lee would encounter increasing difficulties as long as he lived at New Harmony.

Toward the end of the year 1868, all of southern Utah began to worry about another difficulty that began to resurface. Black Hawk had made peace with his Mormon neighbors in the fall of 1867 and along with other Indian leaders signed a peace treaty earlier in 1868, ending the war that had taken the lives of about seventy-five settlers in three years. But the Navajos didn't sign on and in November commenced raids in the south, driving away stock.

Typically the Navajos struck swiftly and fled before any expedition arrived. Because the raids were sporadic, the settlers had to be on guard constantly. Frank Prince, though small in stature, had courage that was tempered through his experience in the Frontier Wars in South Africa and the Civil War and Black Hawk War in America; on many nights he served New Harmony as the town sentinel.[65] He also had the advantage of being an expert marksman: When teams were chosen for a wolf hunt, Frank Prince was James Pace's first choice (while Joseph Imlay took John D. Lee).[66] When all else failed, Frank relied on his equine equivalent of a watchdog—a horse that, he was convinced, could "smell an Indian."[67]

But there was no way to stop a massive, well-coordinated surprise attack. The Mormons certainly thought they were well prepared: On 7 September 1869, in the midst of a three-day drill that took place on the Harmony Bench, there was a "Brilliant sham Fight" at which "The soldiers upon the whole Made an imposing appearance."[68] But less than two months later, on 30 October, Navajos made almost simultaneous raids on New Harmony, Kanarra, Cedar City, Hamilton's Fort, Parowan, Beaver, and Paragonah.[69] New Harmony lost sixteen horses and Kanarra fifty-eight in the raid.[70] John D. Lee estimated that he had lost up

---

[65]Williams, Juanita, op. cit.

[66]Cleland and Brooks, op. cit., entry of 22 November 1869, 128.

[67]Williams, Juanita, op. cit.

[68]Cleland and Brooks, op. cit., entry of 27 August 1869, 123.

[69]Cleland and Brooks, op. cit., entry of 2 November 1869, 124.

[70]Bleak, "Annals," Book B, 25–26. Among others, Benjamin Redd lost a two-year-old colt, James H. and Joseph Imlay each lost one horse, and William W. Taylor lost five horses.

to forty horses, including "some valuable horses of fine Blood," in various incursions.[71]

Lee had more to worry about than losing horses, however, namely a trespassing dispute, this time with John Lawson and George Dodds, in which both sides threatened to shoot the other. A shoot-out with Lawson was thwarted when Joseph Wood interceded and grabbed Lee's gun, but Lawson returned the next day with Allen Taylor and three of Taylor's sons. Two of Lee's wives, Emma and Ann, threw hot water in Lawson's face, wrestled an ax from his hands, threw him on the ground, and pounded him in the face. The melee was broken up and Lawson and Taylor departed, but not before Lee "shamed Bro. Taylor to be led into such Meanness."[72]

Lee was confident that he was in the right, but he was clearly in the minority in Harmony in that respect. At a court held in Kanarra—rather than in Harmony—by Bishop L. W. Roundy, Lawson was found to be at fault and was fined twenty-five dollars. Lee's account, however, tacitly admitted his growing unpopularity in New Harmony:

> The Bishop then called on every Man & Boy that had heard the case (which comprised about all the ward) to vote for or against the descission. When every hand was up, not one negitive vote was to be seen. Thus showing a difference of oppinions in 2 setlements, Harmony & Kannarah. Harmony would have Justified an apostate in spreading desolation to a man's door & deprecate the Idea of defending even a Person's private Rights.[73]

John D. Lee's days in New Harmony were numbered, but not for a reason he could have anticipated. In the early spring of 1870, he met Brigham Young at Beaver. In a private conference, Young advised Lee to move from New Harmony—quite possibly due to the controversy that had divided the small town.[74] When the two men met again in September, Young repeated the advice:

> After Prayer Prest. Young gave me some kind Fatherly council. Said to Me that he would like to have Me Gather My wives, sons &

---

[71]Cleland and Brooks, op. cit., entry of 9 November 1869, 125.
[72]Ibid., entry of 29 November 1869, 128–130.
[73]Ibid.   [74]Brooks, *John Doyle Lee*, 288.

Daughters around me & setle in any of the Places we should Select
& start the Family order, stating that I had passed through a great
deal of Hardship in my Life & Now he would like to see me Enjoy
Peace the balance of my days.[75]

Lee took the advice this time and sold his unfinished house
and most of his farm to his good friend, Lemuel Redd, for forty-
five hundred dollars.[76] By mid-November he left New Harmony, traveling first to Kanab and then to Pipe Spring, where he
met some of his family, three loaded wagons, and about thirty-
five head of loose cattle, in the charge of his son-in-law, William
Prince. It was there that he was received a letter notifying him
that he had been excommunicated from the church, a result of
his actions in 1857 at Mountain Meadows.[77]

A heartbroken Lee returned to St. George in December
where he talked briefly with Brigham Young and Erastus Snow
before going to New Harmony. News of the excommunication
seemed to have softened some hearts in Harmony, where Lee
was invited to speak at the Sunday meeting:

> I bore testimony to the onward progress of this Kingdom & of Prest.
> B.Y. The assembly was Meltd down to tears. At the close of Meet-
> ing, Groups stood around telling their feelings. Wm. Taylor Said
> that I had More friends that day then I ever had in Harmony before
> & that they would defend me to the last &c.[78]

The benevolent feelings didn't last long. Lee tried to settle
accounts with those who owed him money but, according to
him, met with resistance from James Imlay and George and John
Sevy, who refused to pay their accounts. Even Frank Prince
refused to pay for some fencing materials, giving as a reason that
somebody had taken about fifty pickets. "Sawyers & others did
likewise," wrote Lee.[79] This was all seen through Lee's eyes, of
course, but it was very clear that, with few exceptions (the Redds,
in particular), it was John D. Lee versus the rest of the town.

---

[75]Cleland and Brooks, op. cit., entry of 5 September 1870, 136.

[76]Ibid., entry of 12 September 1870, 142.

[77]Ibid., entry of 18 November 1870, 144. The letter was from Albert Carrington, who
became an apostle in 1870 and a counselor to Brigham Young in 1873.

[78]Ibid., entry of 23 December 1870, 153.   [79]Ibid., entry of 6 January 1871, 155.

The Indian conflict was waning and, probably as a result, the population of the outer settlements grew: In the 1870 U.S. Census, Harmony numbered 243 and Kanarra 280 souls. During his southern Utah trip in September 1870, Brigham Young noted that the Indian threat had diminished and decided that it was time to reestablish some of the vacated settlements. Subsequently he directed George W. Sevy to take his two families (he had married his second wife, Maggie Imlay, in 1868) and to be in charge of the resettlement of Panguitch, a small town near Bryce Canyon that had been abandoned in 1867 in the Black Hawk War. Sevy answered the call in March 1871 and was joined in the move to Panguitch by James H. Imlay.

In the meantime, John D. Lee's days in the southern Utah settlements were drawing to a close, and he didn't go quietly. A court was held in St. George on 25 July 1871, to settle a dispute over seven head of Lee's cattle that were taken by neighbors but not returned. Lee won the case and was compensated for the livestock but, in the aftermath, couldn't resist taking potshots at his former neighbors:

> There is an other thing here that I Noticed by the Brethren of Harmony.... I have taken Bro. Wm. Pace's testimony, which by the Bye does not amount to a row of Pins.... Is Jas. [James H.] Imlay here? I wish he was. Will some man from [ ] be kind enough to tell him that we would be Glad that he would keep his Nose out of other Men's buisiness & to Mind his own buisiness for he is always Medling with other Men's Matters & Stiring Mischef.[80]

James H. Imlay was already in Panguitch (where he and George Sevy built a sawmill) and had nothing to do with the case, but that mattered little to the embittered Lee. He had been cut off from the church by his friend and adoptive father, Brigham Young, and was alienated from many if not most of his former friends. He not only had left New Harmony but also, in the process, had burned his bridges; without him, for better or for worse, the small town would never be the same.

---

[80]Ibid., entry of 25 July 1871, 168.

Chapter XIV

THE DECLINE
OF NEW HARMONY

"THERE ARE INDIANS LOUNGING about as in the other Mormon settlements," wrote Elizabeth Kane on the day after Christmas in 1872. "Besides the Pi-edes, who belong to this Sta. [Santa] Clara country, there is a party of Navajoes here today, who were brought in from Arizona yesterday, by the interpreter Jacob Hamblin—a cast iron man who knows what he is talking about."[1] Elizabeth and her husband Thomas Kane—the great friend of the Mormons who was instrumental in the peaceful conclusion of the Utah War—arrived on Christmas Day in St. George, and it took but one day in the town for her to appraise the nature and importance of Jacob Hamblin.

The Indians trusted Hamblin implicitly, and for good reason: He had dedicated his life to making peace with native peoples, and in his many dealings with them he had always told the truth. "This man, Hamblin," wrote Major John Wesley Powell, "speaks their language well, and has a great influence over all the Indians in the region about. He is a silent and reserved man, and when he speaks, it is in a slow, quiet way, that inspires great awe."[2]

Hamblin's tireless efforts over several years were rewarded as peace gradually was reached with the Navajos. Despite some

[1] Elizabeth Kane, *A Gentile Account of Life in Utah's Dixie, 1872–73; Elizabeth Kane's St. George Journal*, 5.
[2] Bleak, "Annals," Book B, 54. Major Powell, of the United States Geological Survey, invited Hamblin to join him in 1870 and 1871 in expeditions to the Grand Canyon region.

petty thievery, the Piedes also returned to their peaceful ways, though that was of little consolation to Clarissa Redd. She and her husband Benjamin had purchased a farm north of New Harmony shortly after Benny, their two year-old son, died in September 1870, and away from the safety of town Clarissa lived in constant fear of the Indians. No matter how benign their appearance, the mere sight of an Indian was enough make Clarissa and others apprehensive. Elizabeth Kane, for example, wrote of her family in 1872 as they spent the Sunday before Christmas at nearby Kanarra:

> My husband and children went to the little meeting-house, whence the boys returned awed by their recollections of the hideous painted faces of some Pi-edes, who had flattened their noses against the window-panes of the building, back of where they sat. "Enough," Evy [Evan] declared, "to give him nightmares for a year."[3]

Clarissa Redd's greatest fear, however, stemmed not from the sight of Indians or even the threat of raids but rather from a personal experience in which she nearly lost her daughter. Sarah Redd, born in May 1866, was a sweet, happy child who was said to have the jolliest laugh around. One day an Indian who had become enamored with Sarah entered the Redd house, threw down some money on the table, and grabbed her by the hand. "Me pay for papoose," he exclaimed, "take white papoose to wickiup." The Indian was nearly to the door with Sarah in tow when Benjamin came to the rescue, gave the money back, and pushed the Indian out of the house.[4]

That may have been the last straw for Benjamin, who for the sake of safety consented to buy a house in town. In his haste, Benjamin put the finishing touches on the adobe home and moved his family into it before the plaster was thoroughly dry. Clarissa, always frail, contracted an illness in the damp surroundings and had not regained her strength when, on August 3,

---

[3]Elizabeth Kane, *Twelve Mormon Homes Visited in Succession on a Journey through Utah to Arizona*, 119. Evan and William, young sons of Elizabeth and Thomas Kane, accompanied their parents on the trip to Utah while two older daughters remained in the East at preparatory schools.

[4]Kossen, "Benjamin Jones Redd."

CLARISSA ELVIRA REDD AND
HER SON BENJAMIN
Benny died on September 19, 1870, a
few months after the photo was taken.
Courtesy of Juanita Blackburn.

1873, she gave birth to a baby daughter. Both mother and child
were weak following the childbirth: A neighbor, Ella Sawyer,
nursed the baby until her death at the age of four months; one
month later, on 18 January 1874, Clarissa died, leaving her husband with two small children.[5]

In the midst of tragedy Benjamin Redd at least had the good
fortune to have a mother-in-law who was willing and able to care
for his children. Sarah Lovisa Taylor, Clarissa's mother and first
wife of Allen Taylor, already had raised to maturity most of her
eleven children, but had room in her life for two more, and for
the next two years Sarah and Mary Redd lived with their grand-
mother Taylor.[6]

---

[5]The baby, Anna Maria Vilate, died on 12 December 1873, the second of four children
(along with Benny) to die young. A third child, Mary Catherine, was born on 22 July
1871.

[6]The 1870 U.S. Census listed Allen Taylor and Elizabeth and Phoebe as residents of Washington, a small town east of St. George, not New Harmony.

Freed from the burden of running his farm while raising his daughters, Benjamin Redd was able to devote himself to a new movement called the United Order that began in St. George in 1874 and quickly spread northward. Total economic unity had been Brigham Young's goal since he assumed control of the church. To this end, beginning in 1868, cooperative institutions were established throughout Utah; in New Harmony the Harmony Co-operative Mercantile Institution was established on 15 May 1869, with Bishop Wilson D. Pace as the president and John D. Lee the largest individual stockholder.[7]

The general success of the cooperative movement in the territory persuaded Brigham Young that the Saints were now ready to live an even higher law of economic unity, the United Order of Enoch, named after Enoch of the Old Testament, who established such a perfect society that the whole city he led was "translated" into heaven.[8] Young foresaw an order in which there would be neither rich nor poor and where wealth would not be a temptation.[9] All members were to contribute their economic property, as with the cooperative mercantile institutions, but the surplus would go to build the kingdom rather than reward shareholders in the form of bonuses or dividends. In addition, all members were to be rebaptized to emphasize the spiritual aspect of their life.[10]

The first United Order was established at St. George in February 1874, after which similar orders were established throughout southern Utah. On 7 April Erastus Snow organized a United Order at New Harmony, while on the same day Brigham Young organized one five miles away at Kanarra. Despite the lofty goals that had been set (or, perhaps, because of them), however, the people of New Harmony worked in the United Order only through the summer before it was disbanded.[11] Although no

---

[7]Cleland and Brooks, *A Mormon Chronicle*, 2:120, entry of 15 May 1869.
[8]Genesis 5:24; Book of Moses (from *Pearl of Great Price*) 7:69.
[9]*Journal of Discourses*, 15:207, 209.
[10]"Harmony Ward General Minutes." Benjamin Redd preceded some of the other New Harmony residents, having been rebaptized by his brother Lemuel on 11 June 1873.
[11]"Harmony Ward Manuscript History," entry for 7 April 1874.

specific reason was given for the failure of the order, there is no question that it was unduly confining and restrictive of economic freedom—a principle that the people were not ready to live.

At about the same time the United Order came to an end in New Harmony, so did John D. Lee's freedom. In 1872, church leaders decided to colonize Arizona and asked the excommunicated Lee to operate a ferry across the Colorado. Lee complied and the ferry was operational by January 1873; within six months, however, he was warned that six hundred soldiers were on their way to arrest him for his complicity in the Mountain Meadows Massacre and he went into hiding.[12]

Several times during his years in exile Lee visited one or another of his wives who had remained true to him, and on occasion returned to New Harmony to visit his friend Lemuel Redd. Even after going into hiding he made at least one trip to the area, in April 1874, to meet Brigham Young at Kanarra.[13] He felt quite secure in the visits, but that changed with the passage of the Poland Bill in 1874, which dismantled Utah's judicial system by giving exclusive civil and criminal jurisdiction to federal courts. Suddenly, Lee was a marked man.

As he visited his wife Caroline and his daughters Louisa Prince and Mary Darrow in Panguitch in November 1874, word somehow got out that Lee was in the area and a posse captured him and took him to jail in Beaver.[14] A first trial resulted in a hung jury, with eight Mormons voting to acquit and four non-Mormons voting to convict. A second trial, however, resulted in a conviction by an all-Mormon jury that seemed to have been willing to bring a guilty verdict on the condition that names of other Mormon participants at Mountain Meadows were left out of the trial.[15]

---

[12]Cleland and Brooks, op. cit., entry of 25 June 1873, 163.

[13]Ibid., entries of 7 and 8 April 1874, 338.

[14]William and Louisa Prince moved from New Harmony to Middleton shortly after their marriage in 1868. To escape the heat they moved to Kanarra, but were forced to leave in May 1871, along with many other families, due to drought, and settled in Panguitch, where they built the first brick home. Mary Darrow was the wife of Marcus Henry Darrow.

[15]Juanita Brooks, *The Mountain Meadows Massacre*, 194–95.

Attitudes in New Harmony and throughout southern Utah toward John D. Lee varied greatly, with more recent arrivals much less forgiving than older settlers. On the one hand, the only thing Marion Prince could remember his grandfather Frank Prince say about John D. Lee was that "he was a dirty old son-of-a-bitch."[16] On the other hand, Allen Taylor's son Independence (Penn) recalled that Lee was "a helpful neighbor, an eloquent speaker, and a graceful dancer." Penn's cousin James E. Taylor said: "I knew John D. Lee well; he was often in our home, and I have been in his. He was a man who had the Spirit of the Lord and lived his religion."[17] But nobody in New Harmony felt more for the man than Lemuel Redd, whose son Amasa Jay wrote:

> Frequently in the years after John D. Lee had gone into hiding, he came back cautiously on business, visiting with and enjoying the hospitality of the people who lived in the home he had begun. He visited them often enough to keep the old friendship alive, and to sanctify it with the finer sensibilities born of his great tribulations. His preservation from the misguided wrath of the law was a matter of deep concern to all members of the Redd household. They heard with alarm of his narrow escapes from his pursuers. It was a day of sorrow to them when he was surprised and arrested, and they suffered in suspense through the long months while he languished in prison awaiting the delayed action of the court. But it was a day of unforgettable anguish when he was brought back to Mountain Meadows over the mountain behind them, and placed before a firing squad.[18]

On 23 March 1877, following his conviction in his second trial, Lee was taken to the scene of the massacre at Mountain Meadows. A photograph was taken of him as he sat on the edge of his coffin. After standing to deliver a final message, he shook the hands of all those around him and asked only that his executioners shoot through his heart, sparing his limbs. As he sat again on the coffin, waiting for the order, he repeated, "Center my heart, boys. Don't mangle my body!"[19] Lee's final request was honored,

---

[16]Oral interview with Marion Prince, 1995.   [17]Ibid., 203.
[18]Amasa Jay Redd, *Lemuel Hardison Redd Jr., 1856–1923, Pioneer, Leader, Builder*, 6–17.
[19]Brooks, op. cit., 210.

ST. GEORGE TEMPLE, 1876
Courtesy of the Church Archives, The Church of Jesus Christ of Latter-day Saints.

and he fell back into the coffin, mortally wounded. The casket was closed and taken to Parowan, from whence it was conveyed by William Prince and Harvey Lee to Panguitch for burial.[20]

For two weeks, Lee's execution was the news of the day throughout southern Utah, until it was overshadowed by the completion and dedication of the St. George Temple. Building temples in the Saints' Rocky Mountain home for years had been a dream of Brigham Young. Frank Prince, who served as a body-guard to Young from Cedar City to St. George in December 1870, said that while in St. George the President surveyed a site outside of the city, put his cane on the ground and said, "We will

---

[20]Edna Lee Brimhall, Gleanings Concerning John D. Lee: A compilation of "gleanings" from the 1930s, 35. From Will Bagley, *Blood of the Prophets: Brigham Young and the Massacre at Mountain Meadows.*

build the Temple right here." After viewing the valley Young continued, "Someday this will be the center of the city."[21]

Concerned about some people leaving the inhospitable environs that characterized most of southern Utah, Young switched into his salesman mode at a November 1871 conference in St. George, prefacing his remarks by saying, "This is a desert country, but it is a splendid place to rear Saints. I regret to hear of any wishing to leave; however there are but few." He then thanked God, in a prayer, "for these barren hills, and for the shelter of these rugged rocks and deserts as peaceful dwelling places for the Saints." Young knew that it was "a hard land in which to get a living," and that the promise of a temple in their midst would be a great psychological boost for the southern Saints.[22]

Lower areas of the temple were dedicated on 1 January 1877, to permit certain ordinance work to be done before the dedication of the building as a whole. Benjamin Redd wasted little time in taking advantage: A widower since his wife Clarissa died three years earlier, Benjamin and Nancy Louella Workman were married in the St. George Temple on February 8 "for time and eternity." Two months later, the April general conference of the church was held in St. George rather than Salt Lake City, for the purpose of dedicating the building as a whole.

The temple had been built from free-will offerings and appropriations from tithing. Despite a great deal of donated labor, the total cost of the building was considerably more than five hundred thousand dollars, but so important was the endeavor that the Saints gave willingly.[23] Benjamin Redd, for one, gave an entire year's work in addition to frequent cash donations to aid in the construction.[24]

It was a matter of great pride to the southern Saints that the St. George Temple was by many years the first to be completed in Utah.[25] The generosity of the Saints in donating to the build-

---

[21]Kossen, "History of Francis Prince."
[22]Larson, "I Was Called to Dixie," 579–80.
[23]James E. Talmage, *The House of the Lord*, 167.   [24]Kossen, "Benjamin Jones Redd."
[25]Temples were completed and dedicated in Logan in 1884, Manti in 1888, and Salt Lake City in 1893.

ing of the temple was all the more remarkable from a people who were little more than self-sufficient and conserved as much as possible to make ends meet. The children of New Harmony and elsewhere, for example, went barefooted in the summer, despite the discomfort, to save their shoes for winter. "I remember how the hot earth burned my feet," recalled Benjamin Redd's daughter Sarah. "I'd run from one sage bush to the next. Then I would sit on the ground and hold my feet in the air to cool off, and it was not comfortable to sit too long."[26] Other children, not so fortunate, had no shoes at all and arrived at school in winter with cold, wet feet.[27]

The weak southern Utah economy was sagging after the completion of the temple—especially under the burden of temple construction debt—when Gentile miners unwittingly came to the rescue. A thriving Nevada mining camp at Pioche offered farmers opportunities to get rid of fresh fruit and vegetables for cash if brought there in good condition, but the town was more than a hundred miles distant from most cotton mission communities. Silver was discovered, however, about halfway between St. George and New Harmony at a location called Silver Reef, and a stampede of miners from Pioche and elsewhere quickly built a thriving mining community.

The population of Silver Reef mushroomed, soon rivaling St. George and probably even larger at its peak.[28] There were banks, boarding houses, hardware, furniture, clothing, and drug stores, a newspaper, barber shops, gambling houses, bakeries, laundries, physicians, dentists, lawyers, etc. However, they had to rely upon their Mormon neighbors for food; the Saints, in return, were very happy to provide—for a good price, of course.

Like others in New Harmony, Lemuel Redd had made a living mainly from the proceeds of his farm and his investment in the New Harmony Cooperative Dairy Herd, but Silver Reef

[26]Juanita Williams Kossen, "History of Sarah Elizabeth Redd Prince Davis."
[27]Redd, *The Utah Redds and Their Progenitors*, 77.
[28]The 1880 U.S. Census gave Silver Reef a population of 1,046; it was most likely larger—perhaps as much as 1,500—in the boom years of 1878–79.

presented an added opportunity, where any surplus could be
sold. "We were growing all the apples and peaches we needed
and much to sell," wrote Lem's daughter Jane, "and all took a turn
with the selling of the sacks and sacks of dried fruit when it was
carried to nearby mining towns. . . ."[29] Proceeds from the sales
were used to buy cotton and bolts of material from the woolen
mills in Washington to make clothing, and leathers, cowhide,
and calf-skins for shoes.[30] William Prince hauled thousands of
shingles from his mill near Panguitch to Silver Reef where he
exchanged them for windows, hinges, nails, and other commodi-
ties.[31]

Over the next few years, however, many people at New Harmony and elsewhere discovered that they had become too
dependent on Silver Reef. Prosperity in the mining town had
been a great boon to the economies of nearby towns, but it was
winding down and left many people in the lurch. "The Silver
Reef mining camp consumed all of the vegetables and hay people had to spare," wrote Allen Taylor's son, Levi Allen.[32] But by
1881, a combination of lower prices for the precious metal and
lower wages led to a strike by the miners and, ultimately, a rapid
decline of prosperity at the Reef, which in turn led to hard economic times for many Mormons:

> When this camp broke up, there was no market for farm produce
> short of Peach [Pioche], a town located about 100 miles distance. It
> was at this time that a number of families left this area for greater
> opportunities, or to further pursue agriculture elsewhere. For this
> reason Father [Allen Taylor] and Mother, with seven children,
> moved to Wayne County, arriving there January 9, 1884.[33]

Most of the residents of neighboring communities remained
after Silver Reef declined, but with changed lifestyles. Gone

[29]Hatch, *Mother Jane's Story*, 27–28.
[30]Redd, *The Utah Redds and Their Progenitors*, 76–77.
[31]Cecil Prince Reid, "Biography of William Prince."
[32]Levi Allen Taylor, "Personal History." Levi was the fifth of twelve children of Allen Taylor and his fourth wife, Phoebe Ann.
[33]Ibid. According to the obituary of Allen Taylor in the *Deseret Evening News*, 29 December 1891, Taylor was released from his calling to the Cotton Mission by Erastus Snow in
the fall of 1883.

NEW HARMONY HARVEST
The Walker brothers of Cedar City brought
their threshing machine to New Harmony about 1885.

were the luxuries from the easy sale of surplus to the mining town, replaced by increased self-sufficiency and spirit of cooperation. Clothing was the work of their own hands, as were carpets, rugs, and bedding.[34] Though every home had an orchard, there was no market for fresh fruit, so great quantities were dried and taken as far as Salt Lake City to be exchanged for essential goods.[35] Nearly every male head of household was a farmer, though typically also raising at least a few cattle or sheep to provide meat. Alfalfa, which was widely grown to provide hay for the cows, was especially valuable since it was easily grown on sandy soil and provided a cure for barren, alkaline lands.[36]

In about 1885, the Walker brothers from Cedar City brought a new farm apparatus to New Harmony that allowed greater efficiency in gathering the crop, but also required cooperation with

[34]Adams, *Memories*, 20–22.   [35]Alice Redd Rich, "Memories of New Harmony," 24.
[36]Hatch, op. cit., 29.

the other farmers.[37] "Every family had its wheat field and at that time, neighbors exchanged work as day after day the horse drawn threshing machine moved from place to place with its crew of workers to do the yearly harvest," wrote Lemuel Redd's daughter Alice.[38] "In the fall when grain was ripe and ready for harvest, an exchange of labor was the usual routine," added Alice's sister Luella. "A farmer whose crops were ready to harvest sent out a call for help. Most all the farmers came, knowing they would soon need assistance. These gatherings were happy times, and the labor did not seem so hard."[39]

The few polygamous families in town, as would be expected, had the greatest number of children to help in the fields. Though only four of approximately twenty-five married men in New Harmony in 1880 had more than one wife (Lemuel Redd, Harvey Pace, Wilson Pace, and William W. Taylor each had two wives), those four households accounted for forty percent of the population.[40] Redd, with the largest family in New Harmony, had the greatest advantage: "The farm," wrote his daughter Jane, "with the older boys working under Pap's management, was soon producing at maximum capacity."[41]

It is clear that Lemuel Redd was the leading citizen of New Harmony in the post-John D. Lee years. Brigham Young recognized this and made Redd the captain of twenty-two men who escorted him on his final trip south.[42] Redd's orchards and melon patches produced far more than his family could consume, so wagon loads of these products were given away to people of surrounding settlements where such things could not be produced.[43] Because there were no dentists, Lemuel had three pair of dental forceps that he used to pull teeth in New Harmony and in neighboring towns, always without a charge. He also on occasion acted as an unofficial paramedic, successfully setting,

[37] *Under Dixie Sun*, 137.   [38] Rich, op. cit., 25.

[39] Adams, op. cit., 25.

[40] 1880 U.S. Census. Lemuel Redd had a total of twenty-seven children; sixteen were living with him in 1880.   [41] Hatch, op. cit., 27.

[42] Jenson, *Latter-day Saint Biographical Encyclopedia*, 2:119.

[43] Rich, op. cit., 25.

for example, the broken leg of Frank Prince's brother George by following directions from a family medicine book by Dr. John C. Gunn.[44]

Everything began to unravel in 1887 for the Redds of New Harmony. The year began with great promise as Benjamin Redd and Frank Prince celebrated the birth of their first grandchild, James Lorenzo Prince, a product of the union in 1885 of Sarah Redd and James Franklin Prince. Benjamin Redd also was busy adding to his own second family, as by mid-summer his wife Nancy was pregnant. But then, on September 16, after fourteen days of "remittent or mountain fever," Benjamin Redd died.[45] "No one knew his heart and inner desires as I did," said his brother Lemuel at the funeral. "He never wronged or hurt anyone intentionally in his life. He was goodness itself. To me who knew him so well, I can truthfully say he was the best man I ever knew."[46]

Even before the death of his brother, life had become very difficult for Lemuel Redd (and the other polygamist men) in New Harmony, due to the passage of the Edmunds-Tucker Act in March 1887. An earlier act of Congress, the Edmunds Act of 1882, prohibited "unlawful cohabitation," but there was little disposition on the part of polygamists in southern Utah to obey the law. To the contrary, codes were created and sent by telegraph to warn communities and polygamists of impending raids by U.S. Marshals.[47] Avoiding capture by the marshals was a cat-and-mouse game that worked in New Harmony, though it was not always successful elsewhere in Utah.

With the Edmunds-Tucker Act, which officially dissolved the Mormon Church as a legal corporation, the government became much more serious in their attempt to stamp out polygamy. Among other things, the act declared that marriages had to be

---

[44]Redd, *The Utah Redds and Their Progenitors*, 91, 93. The book by Dr. John C. Gunn probably was either *Gunn's New Family Physician* (1864) or *Gunn's Newer Family Physician* (1873).

[45]*Journal History of the Church*, 16 September 1877. Family history indicates that the cause of death was typhoid fever.

[46]Redd, op. cit., 271.   [47]Larson, *I Was Called to Dixie*, 628.

FRANCIS PRINCE'S FAMILY
Front: Sarah Redd Prince (wife of James),
Nancy Pace Prince (wife of George)
Middle: sons James, Joseph, George
Back: Etta Deuel (family friend), daughter Eliza, son John

publicly recorded, that wives could be forced to testify against husbands, and that children of plural marriages would be disinherited.[48] Suddenly what had been an enjoyable life was changed into a hectic game of hide-and-seek with the U.S. Marshals in hot pursuit—too hot, in fact, for Wilson and Harvey Pace, who left town in order to avoid arrest.[49]

[48]Richard S. Van Wagoner, *Mormon Polygamy: A History,* 135.
[49]"Harmony Ward Minutes."

Lemuel Redd remained in New Harmony for a period and, in the absence of Bishop Wilson Pace, took charge of local church affairs. With an eye constantly on the lookout for U.S. Marshals, Redd dared not sleep at home, but put up a tent in a remote canyon near Pine Valley Mountain. Each morning, one of his wives put a white flag on the upper pasture gate if it was safe to come home.[50]

As conditions worsened in 1888, Redd moved his second wife Louisa and her family to Bluff, in the remote San Juan country of eastern Utah. Word of his presence gradually leaked out and once again he was on the move—surprisingly, to New Harmony. Along the way, one evening while they were preparing the evening meal, federal officers passed by but were unaware that Lemuel was back in that part of the country and didn't recognize him.[51] Back in New Harmony, fearful that somebody had spotted him during the day, he moved to a new location every night or two, ever careful not to take a misstep in the rattlesnake-infested hills. Though at home, he scarcely could have been farther away.

In a great understatement, the Harmony Ward Record noted, "In 1889 Harmony suffered the same as others under the Anti-Polygamy persecutions, some of the leading men being away from home."[52] With Bishop Wilson Pace and his two counselors, Lemuel Redd and Harvey Pace, on the run, essentially *all* of the leading men were gone, leaving a great spiritual void in the town. In an attempt to fill the void, Lemuel's son William Redd was set apart as the new bishop in February 1890, with Francis Prince and James F. Pace as his counselors.[53]

In October 1890, church president Wilford Woodruff issued a "Manifesto" that declared an end to the practice of plural marriage by the Saints; thereafter federal marshals gradually halted their frenzied polygamist raids, but the damage had been done. The polygamist leaders of the community—Lemuel Redd and Wilson and Harvey Pace—still were absent, and many moved to other settlements, in particular about 150 miles northeast to the

---

[50]Adams, op. cit., 54–55.
[52]"Harmony Ward Record."
[51]Redd, op. cit., 116.
[53]Ibid. James F. Pace was a son of Harvey Pace.

Price River Valley, where the presence of the railroad offered far greater economic possibilities than could be found in their shrinking town.[54] The 1890 U.S. Census showed just how far New Harmony had declined—from a population of 243 in 1870 and 160 in 1880 to a mere 102 souls.[55] Though it was once a growing and relatively prosperous town, fate had conspired to relegate New Harmony to a place that had far greater reason to look to the past than to the future.

[54]Rich, "Memories," 18. At least eight families, including Benjamin Redd's widow Nancy and her three surviving children, moved to Price.

[55]1870, 1880, and 1890 United States Census. The 1880 census showed a population of 150 in New Harmony, but approximately ten residents were on an exploratory mission to the San Juan area of eastern Utah at the time of the census. Individual 1890 census records for most of the nation, including New Harmony, perished in a fire, so only the total population is known.

Chapter XV

ANTONE PRINCE

THE MORNING OF 21 DECEMBER 1890—a Sunday and the first day of winter—Augustus E. Dodge and Levi Savage departed Toquerville for New Harmony. Buffeted by a strong, cold north wind, the thoroughly chilled duo arrived at length at the ranch of Orren Kelsey, a few miles south of their destination, where they gratefully took temporary refuge from the elements. After an hour, warmed by the hospitality of their hosts and a good meal, Dodge and Savage resumed their journey and reached New Harmony just after the noon church meeting had ended.[1]

Dodge presided over the Ninth Quorum of Seventies—which encompassed New Harmony as well as Toquerville—and had received a directive from church leaders in Salt Lake City that he should select four or five of his seventies for missionary labors. The pressure put on the church by the Edmunds-Tucker Act of 1887 outlawing polygamy had caused a slowdown in missionary activity, but after the October 1890 Manifesto by LDS President Wilford Woodruff officially removed church sanction for plural marriage, missionary efforts picked up immediately and continued to accelerate throughout the decade.[2]

After Dodge and Savage arrived in New Harmony, Bishop William Redd appointed a meeting "at early candlelight" to enable them to find "a couple" of New Harmony seventies to

---

[1] Savage, Levi, "Diary of Levi Savage," entry of 21 December 1890.
[2] LDS Church Missionary Department. From 1890–1894, 1,528 missionaries were set apart—a 30 percent increase over the previous five years; 4,128 were set apart from 1895–1899.

serve on a mission. James F. Prince, one of the few seventies to attend the meeting, was interviewed by the leaders and seemed to be willing to go.[3] However, four days later on Christmas Day, Savage returned to New Harmony and was notified in writing that neither Prince nor James Edgar Taylor were prepared to "take a preaching mission" and could not be ready in "less than 6 months or a year."[4]

The decision to go was far easier for the unmarried Taylor than for Prince, who was married, had two children—James Lorenzo and Clara—under the age of four, and had lost an infant child in August of that year. After making necessary preparations, Taylor left for the southern United States in May 1891, where he served for slightly more than two years. On 5 June, one month after Taylor's departure, James and Sarah Prince had another baby boy— George Lawrence; three weeks later James was set apart by George Reynolds for a mission to the northern states, leaving his wife with three small children and the responsibility of running their cattle ranch.[5] His mission was cut short by ill health, however, and he returned after only four months.

Over the next few years he became a well-known cattleman and on 14 November 1896 had another son—Antone Benjamin. Everything seemed to be going well until a fateful day shortly before Antone reached his second birthday. At noon on 4 October 1898, James and his friend Albert Mathis left town to go deer hunting on Pine Valley Mountain. The next morning they set out, without their horses, and agreed to meet at noon at a specified place in the woods. Mathis arrived on schedule but there was no sign of his friend. There were, however, deer tracks and footprints, and Mathis assumed that Prince was stalking his prey.

When Prince didn't show up in camp the following morning, Mathis started out in search of him. A short time later he found his friend lying face down with his gun beside him. Since no wounds were observable, it was assumed that he died from heart failure—perhaps a result of the same ailment that had curtailed his mission seven years previous.

[3]Savage, ibid.   [4]Ibid., entry of 25 December 1890.
[5]"Harmony Ward Record," entry for 1891.

Mathis returned to town to summon help in retrieving the body, which had to be carried three miles since there were no roads through the woods. "The sad affair is a severe shock to his wife, children and relatives," reported the Salt Lake City *Deseret Evening News.*[6] A brief, hastily prepared funeral was held the day after the body was returned.[7]

Prince's death was a major blow to New Harmony, a languishing town that for years had been experiencing loss of leadership as well as of population. The prominent men of early settlement years all were gone: Allen Taylor, wagon train Captain of Hundred for the journey across the plains in 1849 and a man who had capably carried out several important missions at the behest of Brigham Young, died in Loa, Utah, in 1891; James H. Imlay, the first president of the Harmony branch of the church, spent the final twenty years of his life in Panguitch, Utah, where he died in 1890; James Pace, Captain of Hundred in 1850, moved to Thatcher, Arizona, in 1882 and died there six years later; Easton Kelsey, Captain of Hundred in 1851, died in St. George in 1899; Joseph Heywood, an early resident and one of the three Nauvoo Trustees in whose charge church property was disposed of in 1846 to assist the exodus from Nauvoo, had long since moved from New Harmony; and last but certainly not least, John D. Lee, who more than anyone was responsible for founding New Harmony, had been executed at Mountain Meadows in 1877.

More recently, Benjamin Redd, an early missionary to the Indians and a key volunteer in the "down and back" journeys of 1863 to aid the poor in Iowa in their trip to Utah, died in 1887; and Bishop Wilson Pace and his counselors Harvey Pace and Lemuel Redd, the leaders of New Harmony Ward, all left town in the late 1880s with their polygamous families. Most of these men were known far beyond the boundaries of New Harmony; it would take many years for anyone from the town to achieve similar notoriety, but James F. Prince's youngest son, Antone, even-

---

[6]*Deseret Evening News*, Tuesday, 18 October 1898. Several different versions of James F. Prince's death developed through the years, but the newspaper story is the only contemporary account and must be considered to be highly accurate.

[7]"New Harmony Sacrament Meeting Minutes," 7 October 1898.

tually became one of the most notable and well-known men of
the mid-twentieth century to the populace of southern Utah.

As a teenager, Antone Prince already had demonstrated himself worthy of carrying on his grandfather's tradition as a sharp-
shooter. On a rabbit hunt between one team of fourteen men
from Harmony and another from Kanarraville and Cedar City,
Jack Isabell from Cedar said he'd bet a hundred dollars that he
could outshoot any man from the Harmony team. Albert Mathis
grabbed Antone by the arm and said, "Here's a kid who can outshoot you for a thousand dollars." Isabell backed down—fortunately for him—as Antone bagged 148 rabbits, easily outpacing
all others from either team.[8]

After completing his early education at the Harmony school,
Antone attended high school and then Dixie College in St.
George. His second year at Dixie College was cut short when he
met and, on 25 November 1915, married Vilate Cottam, the
eleventh of twelve children of George Thomas Cottam and a
granddaughter of Thomas Cottam, a well-known furniture
maker whose chairs were purchased by Brigham Young for his
Salt Lake Valley homes and also were used in the St. George
Temple after its completion in 1877.[9]

Returning to New Harmony, the couple lived with Antone's
mother Sarah and her second husband, Reese Davis, while their
own home was being built. It wasn't a popular move as far as
Juanita—the eldest of Sarah and Reese's three daughters—was
concerned. Jealousy probably was involved, since Juanita and
Antone had been very close, but a genuine and mutual dislike
existed for many years between Vilate and Juanita: Vilate was
particularly perturbed by twelve-year-old Nita's practice of
climbing on the door and peering through the transit to the bed-
room to spy on newlywed activities.[10]

As soon as possible, Antone and Vilate moved into their new
house and ranch, nearly two miles north of town, which com-

---

[8]Interview with Antone Prince, September 1971.
[9]Marilyn Conover Barker, *The Legacy of Mormon Furniture*, 98.
[10]Interview with Clayton Prince and Virginia Anderson, 27 May 2000.

Antone Prince, his wife Vilate, and his mother, Sarah Prince Davis, in New Harmony, about 1918.

prised a total of about 220 acres on a gentle slope known as the Harmony Bench. A spring that once flowed near their house had dwindled and the house was too far from town to be hooked up to their water supply, so Antone and his brother James Lorenzo (Low) tapped a spring in the foothills of Pine Valley Mountain and ran a one-inch diameter galvanized steel pipeline—buried at least eighteen inches deep to prevent freezing—three and a half miles along the side of the mountain to Antone's ranch. "You might say I'm a pioneer in that respect," Antone recalled modestly of his massive effort.[11]

---

[11]Interview with Antone Prince, 22 April 1975.

After a short stint of raising hogs with Low, Antone decided that there was a greater opportunity to be found in sheep. He bought five hundred head of registered ewes in Parowan and grazed them on Harmony Mountain through the summer. It was a fiasco. "They were just home-raised sheep and they scattered like flies," Antone remembered.[12] That actually turned out for the best, for another type of livestock proved to be far more profitable in New Harmony.

Angora goats evolved on the Anatolian plateau of Turkey near the city of Ankara, from which the name "Angora" is derived. Though the goats were introduced into Spain and France in the sixteenth century, it was not until 1849 that they were introduced to the United States, and sometime between 1910 and 1915 to the Harmony Valley. The value of the goats lay in their lustrous, long coat called mohair, the distinctive properties of which have made it a highly desired and durable fiber for both clothing and home furnishings. Not only was the product valuable, but the goats were also especially well-adapted for the area around New Harmony, due to their dry mountain origin in Turkey where, as in New Harmony, the summers are hot and the winters cold with limited rainfall.

Antone went into the Angora goat business at about the time the United States entered the First World War. After selling the few sheep that hadn't run off, he borrowed the remainder of the needed capital to purchase a herd of goats in Parowan. The agreed-upon selling price of $3.75 a head for the ewes was raised unilaterally by the seller at the last minute to $4.25, but enough money was made in the first year of shearing the mohair to cover the entire debt.

With the Angora goat business beginning to thrive, New Harmony was on the road to prosperity. An enormous market for agricultural goods had been created during the war, helping southern Utah farmers to prosper as never before; as the war ended, however, the market for foodstuffs decreased as quickly as it had ascended, bringing hard times to farmers. The mohair

---

[12]Ibid.

industry, on the other hand, was thriving, making it look even more attractive to those who were struggling working the land.

All fifteen New Harmony men who fought in the war returned safely, but the town was not so fortunate in fighting the great flu epidemic of the same era.[13] On the morning of March 11, 1918—exactly eight months before the armistice was signed to end World War I—an Army private at Fort Riley, Kansas, reported to the camp hospital complaining of fever, sore throat, and headache. By noon, the hospital had dealt with more than one hundred soldiers suffering from a particularly virulent influenza. The disease quickly spread throughout the world, striking early and with such great killing efficiency in Spain that it became known as the Spanish Flu. The worldwide pandemic took the lives of between 30 and 40 million people, including an estimated 675,000 Americans. In New Harmony, Ruth Prince, Antone's sister-in-law, died during the epidemic, as did Andrew Schmutz's wife Cecil, and nearly everyone else in town became violently ill.[14]

Fighting the dual foes of Germany in the war and the flu in the epidemic was a great unifying force for the town, but the unity was shattered and the Prince family divided by events of the next couple of years. Never before—not even at the time of the Mountain Meadows Massacre and the trial of John D. Lee—had such attention been focused on New Harmony.

It all centered around Frank Kelsey, who, like his cousin Antone Prince, was not quite two years old when his father died. Though Frank was three years older than Antone, a bond was forged between the cousins that seemed to be unbreakable. Frank married Lottie Ballard of Grafton in 1913, about two years before Antone married Vilate Cottam, and before long Lottie and Vilate were best friends.

Frank and Lottie Kelsey had two children when their third child, Bevin, died on 21 February 1921, at the age of one month. Nine months later, on or about 1 December, Frank was said to have come home about noon to prepare dinner while Lottie was

---

[13]"Reminiscence of Donald Schmutz," autumn 1982.

[14]Both Cecil and Ruth left infant daughters; Vilate Prince nursed both girls along with her own two month-old son, Clayton, and thereafter referred to herself as "The Jersey Cow."

doing the family washing; he later denied having done so. Shortly thereafter, Lottie suffered from severe cramps, abdominal pains, and vomiting and, after lingering at home without improvement in health for about a week, was taken to the hospital at Cedar City.[15]

Dr. M. J. Macfarlane examined Lottie, who was four months pregnant, and concluded that she suffered from eclampsia, or "toxemia pregnancy." The major sign of eclampsia—convulsive seizures of unknown cause that occur between the twentieth week of pregnancy and the end of the first week postpartum—seemed consistent with Lottie's symptoms, and Dr. Macfarlane deemed it necessary to terminate the pregnancy. The operation was to no avail, however, and on 17 December 1921, Lottie Kelsey died.[16]

That would have been the end of the story—had poison not appeared five months later in the water at the home of his grandfather, Frank Prince, where Frank Kelsey's mother Eliza had lived since becoming a widow in 1895. In a front-page article on 11 May 1922, the *Washington County News* recorded an account of the event under the headline, "Dastardly Poisoning at New Harmony:"

> It appears from what the county officials learned that Mrs. [Eliza] Kelsey was preparing breakfast at the home of her father, Francis [Frank] Prince, one of the best known and most highly respected residents of New Harmony. She made some coffee and on tasting it noticed it was bitter. She threw it out and made some more when Mr. Prince came in; he tasted the freshly made coffee and said at once "strychnine," the poison having apparently been placed in the kettle.
>
> After breakfast they went to the stable to water the horses out of a trough. Twenty minutes after drinking, the horses died, apparently of poisoning.[17]

A water sample was taken from the trough and sent to state chemist Herman Harms in Salt Lake City for analysis. Frank Prince, the tests showed, was correct in his supposition that the water used to make his coffee had been laced with strychnine.

---

[15]"Toxicological Investigation in Respect to the Death of Mrs. Lottie Kelsey," Washington County Court Records.   [16]*Washington County News*, 5 April 1923.

[17]*Washington County News*, 11 May 1922.

Washington County Sheriff Wilford Goff concluded that it was a "premeditated attempt to kill the Prince family," though he had no clues and found it hard to believe that anyone would want to harm Frank Prince, the well-liked patriarch of the community.[18] But suspicions quickly fell upon Frank Kelsey, who within the week was arrested and brought before Justice Ellis Pickett to hear the charges against him:

> That the said Defendant Frank P. Kelsey on the 7th day of May A.D. 1922 at Washington County State of Utah, did willfully, unlawfully and feloniously mingle poison, to-wit, Strychnine with water with the intent then and there that the same should be taken by Eliza Kelsey, Francis Prince and Elizabeth Prince then and there to their injury.[19]

Whatever evidence the authorities may have had was not released to the public, but that mattered little to the New Harmony gossip mill as it shifted immediately into high gear. The case of *The State vs. Frank P. Kelsey* was called in the district court in early September, four months after his arrest, but the state was "unable to furnish much needed evidence and asked for a continuance of the case."[20] Then, in a major surprise, prosecuting attorney W. B. Higgins asked that the body of Lottie Kelsey be exhumed to see if her death resulted from poison.

State Chemist Herman Harms once again was called upon and determined that Lottie Kelsey had enough arsenic in her system at the time of her death to have died from the poison.[21] Within a month, Frank Kelsey, who had been free on bail, was arrested for the murder of his wife. Early on, the *Washington County News* printed that it had intended to give a full account of the preliminary hearing of the case but had decided against doing so because "it appears that there may be difficulty in securing a jury to try the case."[22]

[18]Ibid.
[19]*The State of Utah vs. Frank P. Kelsey,* the Fifth Judicial District Court of Washington County Utah, 15 May 1922.
[20]*Washington County News,* 14 September 1922.
[21]"Toxicological Investigation in Respect to the Death of Mrs. Lottie Kelsey," Washington County Court Records.

All of southern Utah was captivated by the case. The proceedings would take place in the Washington County Court House, a boxy two-story building, completed in 1870, about thirty-six feet wide and forty feet long and adorned by a centrally placed cupola. A large assembly room on the second floor of the courthouse had been used extensively through the years for social parties, but now it was a courtroom, awaiting the commencement of the most spectacular trial St. George had ever seen.[23]

Proceedings in the trial, which began with jury selection on 26 March 1923, were reported extensively not only in the *Washington County News* but also in the two major Salt Lake newspapers, the *Salt Lake Tribune* and the *Deseret News*. From the beginning the trial was a sensation. "The courtroom has been packed at every session, people even kneeling and sitting on the floor, so great has been the interest in the proceedings," the *Tribune* reported.[24] The next day the *Tribune* printed a description that made the trial seem even more dramatic:

> Daily the stream of interested spectators swells. They come from miles around, women with babes in arms and men leaning on the younger for support, housewives with a taste for gossip, farmers who are letting the spring planting wait; an old Indian couple, she in her bright yellow and red clothing and he in his overalls and with evil-smelling pipe. Even the young children race from the schoolhouse to the courthouse when their day's work is done.
> Throughout it all Kelsey remains unperturbed.[25]

Kelsey's calm demeanor must have been wonderment to many of the spectators at the trial. "Stone-like indifference and unconcern have marked the bearing and manner of Kelsey while the trial has been in progress," commented *The Salt Lake Tribune*.[26] The community in general, however, apparently did not share whatever confidence he may have had in his innocence. Maude Schulder, the wife of one of Kelsey's attorneys, was one of several to file affidavits prior to the trial stating "that nearly every person

---

[22] *Washington County News*, 30 November 1922.
[23] Albert E. Miller, *The Immortal Pioneers: Founders of City of St. George, Utah*, 97–102.
[24] *The Salt Lake Tribune*, 5 April 1923.   [25] *The Salt Lake Tribune*, 6 April 1923.
[26] *The Salt Lake Tribune*, 5 April 1923.

to whom she talked or who talked to her about said case expressed the belief and opinion that the said Frank P. Kelsey was guilty of the crime of which he was charged."[27]

Guilt by belief or opinion would not be enough in a court of law, however. After State Chemist Harms confirmed that there was enough arsenic in Lottie Kelsey's stomach at the time of her death to have killed her, the state had to prove a motive. Frank Kelsey, according to testimony, had purchased a nine-thousand-dollar insurance policy on the life of his mother and had "negotiated for an eight-thousand-dollar joint policy for his wife."[28] James Taylor then testified to having heard Kelsey say that he would soon be on "Easy street," a claim that Frank steadfastly denied.[29]

Having tried to show a motive, it was time to establish opportunity to commit the crime. If Frank Kelsey really poisoned his wife, where did he get the arsenic? Fly paper, the prosecution proclaimed. George Prince—Frank's uncle—testified to having kept the product for sale in his small store. And if not fly paper, then perhaps arsenic from Eldon Schmutz, who placed some in a tank to dip about thirty of his Angora bucks as a method of tick control.[30]

Despite their efforts, the prosecution could not establish that Frank Kelsey had ever been in possession of arsenic, so it unleashed a gossip assault in an attempt to establish another motive. Vilate Prince told of affections shown by Frank Kelsey to his wife's sister, Nora Ballard, both at a picnic and after Lottie's funeral. Antone Prince recalled having seen Nora lying with her head on Frank's lap at the picnic and also having seen them together in a car with his arm around her. Antone's mother, Sarah Davis, related how Frank, following his wife's funeral, gave Lottie's wedding ring to Nora.[31]

---

[27]Affidavit by Maude L. Schulder, sworn in Salt Lake City, 23 November 1922, on file at Washington County Courthouse. Others filing similar affidavits included James W. Imlay of Hurricane and John L. Sevy of Salt Lake City, both of whom were descendants of early New Harmony settlers.

[28]*The Salt Lake Tribune*, 3 April 1923.   [29]*Washington County News*, 5 April 1923.
[30]Ibid.   [31]Ibid.

Other witnesses added their juicy morsels about Frank and Nora to the testimonial heap, but none could have been as surprising as the statements given by Antone and Vilate Prince. After all, Antone had been Frank Kelsey's best friend and Vilate was described in testimony as Lottie's "chum," but they broke completely with many others in the family regarding Frank's guilt. Antone's brother Low joined in by claiming that Nora Ballard had posed as Frank's wife while signing a note to Sears, Roebuck & Company, though objection to his testimony was sustained and he was excused without further questioning.[32]

The case presented by the defense was, in actuality, inconsequential. Franks's mother Eliza said that Lottie was despondent over the loss of her baby and suggested that perhaps she took her own life, having said upon the death of her baby that "she would soon die and be with the child."[33] David Ballard, Lottie's father, said that there was no jealousy on the part of Lottie towards her sister Nora.[34] Frank Kelsey, showing emotion for the first time since the opening of the trial, said he never had any arsenic on his farm and tearfully denied making dinner for his wife on the day she became ill.[35] But it was quite apparent, even before the defense presented their witnesses, that Judge William F. Knox already had determined that the prosecution had not proved their case and therefore he would not allow any verdict other than not guilty. "In this case," the judge read in his instructions to the jury, "the evidence produced by the State is what is called and termed in law, circumstantial evidence." Continuing his instructions, Judge Knox slammed the door of decision on the jury:

> No evidence has been offered or received in this case, from which you will be warranted in finding that the defendant ever at any time or place had or possessed arsenic, or that he knew of its use, purpose, or its deadly poisonous effect; and, before you would be warranted in convicting the defendant, the state would have to prove to your satisfaction, beyond all reasonable doubt, that the defendant did pos-

[32] *The Deseret News*, 7 April 1923.   [33] *The Deseret News*, 11 April 1923.
[34] *Washington County News*, 12 April 1923.   [35] *The Deseret News*, 12 April 1923.

sess arsenic, and that he actually caused it to be administered to the deceased Lottie Kelsey, for the purpose of taking her life.[36]

The jury instructions were lifted verbatim from written suggestions to the judge by Kelsey's lead attorney, Samuel A. King, senior partner of a prominent Salt Lake law firm, King and Schulder, who had been hired by Frank Prince to defend his grandson. King seemed to have had a commanding presence in the courtroom and undoubtedly swayed Judge Knox, most of whose key jury instructions actually were written by King, but an impartial observer would have difficulty in disagreeing with the judge's use of King's words based solely on the evidence presented at the trial.[37] The jury, under the circumstances, had no choice but to declare Frank Kelsey not guilty.

Frank Kelsey was, of course, a member of the Prince family, and it was that family that was most divided as a result of the trial. Sarah Davis and her children, in particular, were totally convinced that Frank was guilty, though Frank Prince and many others supported the accused. Even Sarah's family was divided as her husband, Reese Davis, was the first of eleven in New Harmony to sign an affidavit suggesting that the venue for the second trial of Frank Kelsey (for attempting to poison his mother and grandparents) be moved from Washington County due to the "strong feeling of bias and prejudice against the defendant."[38]

The venue was moved, as a matter of fact, to Fillmore, though the change proved to be a mere formality when the charges were dropped by the state, probably realizing that it had even less evidence against Kelsey in the second case than in the first. Left hanging was the mystery of who placed strychnine in the water that killed two horses and somehow ended up in Frank Prince's coffee pot. Equally mysterious was the origin of the arsenic: If Lottie Kelsey self-administered the arsenic due to despondency over her lost child, as was suggested during the trial by her

---

[36]"Instructions of the Court to the Jury," *The State of Utah vs. Frank P. Kelsey,* 13 April 1923.

[37]"Defendant's Requests for Instructions," from Samuel King to Judge William Knox, *The State of Utah vs. Frank P. Kelsey.*

[38]Affidavit, *The State of Utah vs. Frank P. Kelsey,* 5 December 1923.

mother-in-law, where did she obtain the poison? Did she have any greater motive or opportunity than did her husband? And why would she still be despondent over the loss of a previous child while pregnant with another?

The mysteries would remain unsolved, but that mattered not to the exonerated Frank Kelsey. Though a free man, however, his relationship with his cousin and former best friend, Antone Prince, would never be the same. In another affidavit filed to change the venue of the second trial, Kelsey stated:

> Antone and James L. [Low] Prince are two personal enimies [*sic*] of this affiant and have for more than eighteen months past constantly circulated false reports against this affiant and have done all within their power to have this defendant prosecuted not only on the charge of murder but upon the charge now pending against him. . . .[39]

Shortly after the dismissal of all charges against him, Frank Kelsey married his sister-in-law, Nora Ballard, solidifying the suspicions of some of his detractors who believed that they acted too much like a couple even while Lottie was alive. For his part, Frank had one great desire: "Antone," he said longingly to his cousin, "I don't grieve about anyone else in town but you and Vilate, and I can't stand to live without your association and friendship. Can you forgive me and forget and be like we were one time?"[40] It was a noble request but mostly in vain as Antone continued to believe that his cousin was guilty.

For nearly a year, Frank Kelsey had been the center of attention, but now it was time to get back to business, which increasingly was becoming mohair. Antone Prince quietly amassed a herd that eventually numbered four thousand goats, including about one hundred head of bucks for which he paid at least seventy-five dollars and as much as three hundred dollars a piece, a lofty sum in the 1920s. The herd grazed in the Harmony Mountains north of the town in the summertime and was driven about forty miles west to Bull Valley for the winter where it remained through the springtime when the ewes were giving birth to their kids.

---

[39]Ibid.   [40]Interview with Juanita Davis Williams Kossen, 29 June 1994.

One year, after kidding early in Bull Valley, a terrific storm hit and lasted for three days, killing every kid—about eleven hundred—as well as about seven hundred adults. Compounding the misery, some of the goats were inflicted with brucellosis, commonly known as undulant or Malta fever, and in burying the carcasses Antone and his helpers all came down with the disease, which causes weakness and intermittent fever that can persist for months. "It's one of the most damnable things in the world," Antone later recalled.[41]

The loss of the kids hit particularly hard since their softer and more luxuriant hair brought a far better price ($1.25 versus $.75 per pound) than that of the adult goat. Under the best of circumstances the kids had to be tied to a stake exactly where they were born: If the baby goat was not in the location where the mother left it as she went off to feed, she would not search for it upon returning and the kid would be a orphan called a "dogie." The dogies presented a special problem, with no mother to care for them, but they also could be a bit mischievous, as brothers Charles and Frank Petty, each of whom married a sister of Vilate Prince, belatedly discovered:

> One day uncle Charles come down home on the farm and he brought this beautiful new car in, which was black, and dad told him, "You'd better move the car because the kids will get on it." He thought maybe it was [Antone's children] Clayton and me [Virginia]. And so when he went out to go, here were these dogies, and they'd jump up on the running board, up onto the front and slide down the back. And so he went home and he said, "Uncle Frank, now when you go down to Antone's and Vilate's, be sure you leave the car where the kids can't get to it." And uncle Frank thought that it would be Clayton and me and so he left it out over in the field, with a fence around it. Well, somehow the goats got out, and when Frank marched over to the car, here was these kids, jumping up on the thing and sliding down the back.[42]

Along with all of the Angoras, Antone had one large billy goat of a different breed—either an alpine or a Nubian—with large horns. Virginia and Clayton found the billy goat particularly

---

[41]Interview with Antone Prince, September 1971.
[42]Interview with Clayton Prince and Virginia Anderson, 27 May 2000.

useful, hooking it to a wagon to make the four-mile roundtrip into town to pick up the mail. The goat didn't appreciate the conscripted duty, however, and one day sensed the opportunity for revenge:

> Mother sent us with a big pan of fruit, Clayton, [cousin] Avey and I, to go and climb up on this shed and put the fruit out. So we got it all spread out and we got down and all of a sudden we saw this goat come. And the closest place we could get was the outhouse. So we got in there and we braced ourselves and we sat with our feet against the toilet and our backs against the door, and that thing would come BRRRRRRAM and ram it, and mother couldn't find us. . . . We took turns praying.[43]

By 1929, New Harmony had become the goat capital of the state. "Harmony Goat Men Preparing For Record Clip," proclaimed a headline in the *Washington County News*. About thirty-three thousand head of goats were to be "relieved of their winter hair during March;" nearly one hundred thousand pounds of mohair would be shipped in March and April, with a valuation of almost sixty thousand dollars. "Although only in its infancy, this industry promises to be among the leading businesses of southern Utah. New Harmony can boast of owning more goats and producing more mohair than any other town in the state of Utah," exclaimed the newspaper, and Antone Prince had the largest herd of all.[44]

Since the goats spent the summer on Harmony Mountain and the winter in Bull Valley, tended by a herder and a good dog, Antone had discovered that he could quite capably run the goat business without living in New Harmony and decided to move to St. George. The primary motivation for the move remains uncertain. "The drought came and it started drying up, and we got tired and we came down here [St. George]," Antone told Delmar Gott of Dixie College in a 1975 interview.[45] "We lived two and a half miles from town, and there was so much snow," recalled Vilate.[46] "One of the compelling reasons for the folks

[43]Ibid.   [44]*Washington County News*, 28 February 1929.
[45]Interview with Antone Prince, 22 April 1975.
[46]Interview with Vilate Prince, September 1971

moving was that grandpa Cottam started having some major heart problems," said Clayton, intimating that Vilate felt it necessary to move near her parents in St. George to take care of them.[47]

Clouds of trouble began appearing on the horizon just as Antone moved his family to St. George. For eight years, beginning in 1921, the Federal Reserve expanded the money supply by more than 60 percent, and the resultant flood of easy money gave birth to the "Roaring Twenties." But in early 1929 the Federal Reserve reversed course, choking off the money supply and raising interest rates. The resultant deflation that followed the inflation of earlier in the decade wrenched the economy from tremendous boom to colossal bust.

As the country plunged into depression—about six months before the stock market crash on "Black Thursday," 24 October 1929—there was virtually no market for mohair. In an effort to keep the ranchers afloat, the federal government took all of the shearing on consignment at four cents a pound. Sacks filled with mohair weighing two or three hundred pounds filled warehouses. The government's intention was to pay the rancher when the price went back up, but it never happened as the depression lingered.[48]

To feed his family, Antone took any kind of job he could get. He first went to work as an automobile salesman for Lunt Motors but never recorded a sale. He worked in a service station, doing twelve-hour shifts for a dollar a day. Having hit bottom, just when it seemed things couldn't get worse, they did.

In late 1930, Antone's cousin Pratt Prince was visiting St. George with his wife Winnie and infant daughter Daphane and needed to hitch a ride back to their home in New Harmony. Antone volunteered to take them in his truck but became so ill as they were about to leave that Pratt drove the truck while Antone rested. Soon after the trip, Daphane became extremely ill and was rushed to the hospital in Cedar City where she was diagnosed with pneumonia.

---

[47]Interview with Clayton Prince and Virginia Anderson, 27 May 2000.
[48]Interview with Clayton Prince, 29 August 1998.

A few days after he returned to St. George, Antone was still suffering from headache and high fever when a rash appeared, the spots gradually changing to raised, blister-like pustules. The diagnosis was absolutely frightening: Antone had contracted smallpox. Pratt and Winnie realized all too well that Antone may have been contagious and were sick with fear that Daphane had been exposed; as it turned out, she escaped the dreaded disease, but it was only the beginning for Antone.[49]

There is no cure for smallpox. Once infected, absolutely nothing can be done to stop the disease from running its full course and doctors can do little to alleviate the painful symptoms. A minimum of one-third of all people exposed to smallpox die from the disease, and there were times when Antone wished he were dead. As he shaved a week's growth of whiskers, he inadvertently clipped off the pox and his face swelled up like a pumpkin. For at least two weeks he was so ill that the doctors never thought he'd survive. His daughter Virginia, fourteen years old at the time, remembered the scene at their home in St. George, where Antone was quarantined:

> We had a sun porch on that house that was on the southwest corner. That's where the doctor put dad, in there, and mother had a basin of formaldehyde that she would wash her hands and her clothes when she would go in to take care of him. And anyone who wanted to see him would have to climb up a ladder and look in the window. That is the truth.[50]

Antone did recover, but the same could hardly be said of the economy. A major blow to farmers came from the Smoot-Hawley Tariff of June 1930, sponsored by Rep. Willis C. Hawley of Oregon and Utah's own Senator Reed Smoot, who served concurrently as a Mormon apostle, thus earning the nickname of the "Apostle-Senator." The act raised trade barriers in the belief that more Americans would be forced to buy domestic goods, thus helping to solve the nagging unemployment problem. But trade is a two-way street, and foreign governments retaliated with their

---

[49]Letter from Florence Prince Wagner, 25 February 1996.
[50]Interview with Virginia Anderson, 9 August 1998.

own trade barriers, hitting farmers especially hard. Farm prices plummeted and many thousands of farmers went bankrupt.

Goat ranchers were no better off than the farmers, but though the prospect of Antone Prince and the other goat men of southern Utah selling their mohair in the immediate future had been smashed, they thought they saw a glimmer of hope on the horizon. In late June 1931, at a meeting of goat ranchers in New Harmony, it was stressed that a "feeling of optimism is beginning to take the place of the depressed attitude of the people, and that it is the belief of the banking institutions of the country that we are on the upgrade."[51]

They were dead wrong. Not only did was there no improvement, but with another act of Congress things got worse for the goat ranchers—much worse. The Taylor Grazing Act of 1934 ended the open range for grazing. Alarmed by the Dust Bowl and overgrazing, Congress passed the act to regulate all remaining federal rangelands requiring permits issued by a new Grazing Service. Goats, foraging on shrubs and brush in a manner that could leave the land barren, were seen in a most unfavorable light, so the goat ranchers could not secure permits to graze their herds on public lands.

That was the end of the line. With no market for the mohair and no way to feed the goats it was impossible to keep the herd. The government, in their wisdom after passing the act that drove a stake into the ranchers' hearts, made an offer that Antone could scarcely live with but had to accept:

> [The government] said, we'll give you $1.40 a head for your goats. You kill them and produce the hide, we'll give you $1.40 for them. So I had several thousand goats there, and these bucks that I paid $300 apiece for, I had to kill them and skin them for $1.40. We built a corral along Harrisburg trench, right along the edge, and I had half-a-dozen men helping me, and we'd kill the goat in about two minutes and just shove them off this ledge.[52]

Several ravines around New Harmony were filled with the carcasses as other ranchers joined in the slaughter. The goat

---

[51] *Washington County News*, 2 July 1931.   [52] Interview with Antone Prince, 22 April 1975.

industry was dead and Antone was broke. When he borrowed $6,800 in 1929 to buy his house in St. George he was asked if he wanted a long-term loan. "No, I'll pay it off in three years," he replied. Before the crash he said he could have paid it off in one year, but things got so bad that he went to Salt Lake City and told bank officials, "You've got to come and take our home, because I can't pay for it. I haven't got a thing left." The bank had no interest in being saddled with homes that they in turn couldn't unload and politely told him, "You keep on, you're doing okay."[53]

The money received from the government for the goat slaughter helped Antone pay off his loan, but the outlook still was bleak. The depression dragged on with no end in sight, ushering in an occasional sense of desperation. "I'd steal before I'd see them starve," he said in reference to his family, and he most likely was sincere in his statement.[54] Nobody starved, however, for everyone shared what little they had, supplemented greatly by game killed during hunting season.

Not that everyone hunted just in season. During the Thanksgiving holidays in 1935, Antone went to New Harmony to slaughter three pigs and was approached by Frank Kelsey, who wanted to go deer hunting—out of season. After more than a dozen years following the conclusion of the famous trial, Antone's relationship with Frank had thawed enough that Antone agreed to go after taking care of the pigs. "So we went up Kelsey Mare Hollow and," Antone cautioned in an interview with his grandson Greg, "this is off the record now, this is illegal, we went up Kelsey Mare Hollow, we stopped and discussed where we wanted to hunt." Frank went around the hill one way and scared two bucks towards Antone. They were two of the fattest, prettiest deer he had ever seen, and he dispatched them forthwith.

There was just one problem: When he tried to show his booty to Vilate, she burst out in tears for fear that her brother John Cottam, recently elected Washington County Sheriff, would catch them with a deer killed out of season, a serious offence.

[53]Ibid.   [54]Interview with Antone Prince, September 1971.

Frightened when his wife continued to bawl, Antone carried the deer into a field, cut it up, dug a hole and buried it. "Yep, that was the last time I ever killed a deer out of season," he said, but after a very short pause was compelled to add:

> No, I killed one more. I killed one more out of season. You know, when Ed Brooks and Hebe [Cottam] was up there by a stream, Ed Brooks said, "Let's go get a deer." I was quite easily influenced. . . . That was the best deer to eat. Mom pot roasted it right down, she had all these boarders and she had a big black kettle she put full of deer meat, and Ed Brooks, he just eat and eat and eat and eat and picked the bones, that was the best meat he ever ate in his life.[55]

Quite easily influenced, indeed. Also easily rationalized, for at least it put food on the table not only for his family but for the boarders who Antone and Vilate had living in their home to help make ends meet. A confrontation with the sheriff over the poached deer never materialized, but in a twist of irony, as he would soon find out, Antone's destiny was controlled by the fate of Sheriff John Cottam.

---

[55]Ibid.

Chapter XVI

An Unusual Sheriff

"I NEVER HAD A BETTER FRIEND nor knew a better man than John Cottam," wrote Will Brooks, former sheriff of Washington County. "He was my deputy for all the years I was sheriff, and in all that time he did not fail me once. He was so prompt and quick, in fact, that sometimes I would call him in the night, and he'd be at my home before I had my own shoes tied."[1]

Following his return from a church mission in Holland in 1915, Cottam served for twelve years as city marshall and for six years as a deputy sheriff to Will Brooks. Brooks resigned his office on 1 June 1934, to take that of postmaster—a more permanent position with much better pay—and was succeeded as sheriff by Cottam, "a most efficient officer," according to Brooks.[2] He was fearless but also was prone to overestimate his own strength: On more than one occasion his wife told him "that he was liable to break a blood vessel" by his heavy lifting.[3]

An opportunity to test his wife's warning came on the afternoon of 2 June 1936, when a large and very heavy safe at the County Courthouse had to be moved from the Recorder's office into the Clerk's office. Assisted by his son Mason, J. T. Beatty, and Ralph Whipple, Cottam was attempting to lift the safe when he suddenly straightened up, took a couple of steps backward and started to fall. Beatty caught him and eased him to the floor and called for a glass of water, believing that Cottam had

---

[1]Will Brooks, as recorded by his wife Juanita Brooks, *Uncle Will Tells His Story*, 198.
[2]Ibid., 219.
[3]William Howard Thompson, *Thomas Cottam, 1820, and his Wives Ann Howarth, 1820, Caroline Smith, 1820: Descendants*, 296.

fainted. Sensing that the condition was more serious than he had thought at first, Beatty frantically urged that a doctor be called, but it was too late: A blood vessel had burst at the base of his brain, and John Cottam was dead.[4] Informed by his wife Juanita of Cottam's fate, Will Brooks immediately asked, "Who shot him?" for Cottam always carried a gun and took such chances that Brooks figured someday he might meet a bullet.[5]

A good man had been lost, but after a short period of mourning it was time to find a successor. A total of twenty-one men filed applications to serve the remainder of Cottam's elected term, but Antone Prince was not among them. Considering himself unqualified to be sheriff, he was content to work at a variety of jobs, including driving a mail truck from Cedar City to Kanab, working as a fieldman for the State Agricultural Conservation, and serving for the federal government as deputy Indian agent and later as a deputy county agent. While serving in the latter position, about three weeks after Cottam's death, Antone returned home late from a district meeting at Beaver and was told by Vilate that the county commissioners had been trying all day to reach him. He could not imagine what they wanted of him and found it very mysterious that, if he got home by midnight, he was to come immediately to the courthouse. What happened next was beyond belief to him:

> I went to the courthouse and knocked on the door and George H. Lytle, chairman of the county commission, stopped and shook my hand and said, "Congratulations, sheriff," and I said, "What?" He said, "We appointed you sheriff today." I said, "Not me," and he said, "We just appointed you sheriff. We had twenty-one applications filed for the position. We went through them, sifted them out, Rex Gardner mentioned your name. So we appointed you sheriff." I said, "Well, I haven't had any experience, brother Lytle," and he said, "Well, you helped your brother-in-law John Cottam a little." I said, "Yes, I've been out with him a few times. Give me time to talk to my wife." He said, "I'll give you five minutes."
>
> Well, I started to bawl like a baby. I thought a minute and I said, "Well, if you bear with me 'til I learn the game, I'll accept it." He

---

[4]*Washington County News*, 4 June 1936.   [5]Will Brooks, op. cit., 219.

said, "We'll support you 100 percent." I said, "What is the pay?" and he said, "Ninety dollars a month, and you furnish your own car. We'll give you five cents a mile to operate."[6]

Ninety dollars a month was a good but not great wage—he had earned that much driving the mail truck for a year, though he gave up the job because his brother-in-law Charles Petty, who had the mail contract from Cedar City to Kanab, gave him no time off to spend with his family—but at least it gave promise of steady employment. The morning after accepting the job he visited County Attorney Orval Hafen and said, "Orval, they appointed me sheriff last night and I don't know a thing about it." Hafen replied, "Well, I'll be glad to help you in any way I can." District Attorney Ellis Pickett then gave him a copy of the 1933 Utah Statutes and said, "Learn that all by heart and you'll be okay."[7]

Antone memorized the statutes, particularly the section referring to "the duties and responsibilities of the sheriff." Fortunately, he was able to ease into the job as relatively few events during his first year required police action and most of those that did were centered on the possession of wine or liquor.[8] In the most violent case, a "demented Negro," as he was described in the *Washington County News*, stabbed two men on a Union Pacific bus thirty miles west of St. George in December 1936, critically injuring one of them.[9] Three men were arrested and sent to the Utah State Prison for between one and five years for selling liquor to Indians, as were two men convicted of "indecent liberties" with a minor. There were also, of course, the usual intoxication and drunk driving arrests as well as the arrest of a few cattle rustlers, but no case gave any indication that Antone possessed any special law enforcement capability until it was suggested that he look into a crime that actually occurred while John Cottam was sheriff.

---

[6]Interview with Antone Prince, September 1971.   [7]Ibid.
[8]Sheriff Prince kept his arrest records on simple 3 x 4 index cards; for many years the records were in the Washington County Sheriff's office, but they are now in possession of the author.   [9]*Washington County News*, 24 December 1936.

On 18 March 1935, Spencer Malan, a rancher in a small town about fifty miles northwest of St. George called Enterprise, was reported to be missing. John Cottam looked into but couldn't solve the case and Antone had never even heard of it. After being asked by George Hunt, deputy at Enterprise, to investigate the disappearance, Sheriff Prince, dressed in civilian clothes (he almost never wore a uniform), went house to house in Enterprise on 16 November 1937, to gather information.

Hunt, who had a strong suspicion based on the fact that Malan was last seen on St. Patrick's Day in the company of Charles Bosshardt, had been investigating the case for several months.[10] Sheriff Prince and Hunt went to Bosshardt's farm, with Antone pretending to be a soil expert—the experience from his service as deputy county agent had paid off in the guise—while Hunt, who feared Bosshardt, hid out of sight on his hands and knees between the seats of the sheriff's car.[11] Bosshardt became suspicious after being peppered with questions and said, "What's this all about? What are you questioning me like this for?" Antone shook his finger at him and said, "Charlie, I'm charging you with murder in the first degree and you're under arrest right now."[12]

Bosshardt was shocked and said that he first had to finish plowing his soil but was told by the sheriff to forget it. "You go unhitch your horses and go with me to St. George," he declared. Ushering the accused into his car, Antone called Bosshardt's pre-teenage stepson over. The boy was actually the missing man's son; a year after Spencer Malan's disappearance, his wife Eva had divorced him for desertion and married Bosshardt.[13] "You go in and tell your mother that your father has gone to St. George with

[10]The *Salt Lake Tribune* reports that Prince had been working on the case for a year, ever since he had become aware of neighborhood rumors in Enterprise. The *Washington County News*, however, says that credit for solving the case went to Thomas Hunt, who had been keeping a close watch on Bosshardt for a year.

[11]Interview with Antone Prince, 22 April 1975. In the interview, Prince was clear in stating that Hunt remained in the car because he was "scared to death."

[12]Interview with Antone Prince, 21 September 1974.

[13]Before and during the trial, Bosshardt and his wife, the former Mrs. Malan, denied having had an affair prior to the death of Malan. Bosshardt claimed he only married Eva Malan because he felt sorry for her and wanted to help her raise her son. For her part, Eva claimed to have known nothing of the murder—or that her former husband was even dead—until

Sheriff Prince." It was a bold move, since there was no evidence that a crime had been committed, the body of Spencer Malan never having been found. Before the sheriff left with his prisoner, Hunt cautioned, "You be careful, he's a very mean man," but Antone had no fear.

Night was at hand as Antone began the return trip to St. George. After informing Bosshardt that he didn't have to answer any questions, the sheriff began the interrogation. "You might as well go back, because I don't know anything," was Charlie's response. For about ten miles Antone drove along in the dark contemplating his next move when he suddenly whirled at Charlie, pointing at him with his finger while saying, "Charlie Bosshardt, as sure as there is a God in Heaven you are guilty of murder in the first degree, and I can tell you within two places where the body is."

Bosshardt was stunned and asked, incredulously, "Where?"

"Either up in the cedars back of your home or down on the desert in a well," the sheriff replied.

Charlie was dumbfounded. "Down on the desert in a well," he blurted.

Antone couldn't believe his ears: "You mean it is, huh?" It was a bluff, a ruse, a grand deception, but Antone had thrown out the bait and, to his astonishment, Charlie swallowed it whole.

"We had a fight down at the place and George Schaefer and I had to kill him. We took him down on the desert and threw him in this well. Then we shifted a lot of dirt down on him."[14]

It was late at night and Antone had extracted a confession but still had no evidence that a crime had been committed. What if Bosshardt woke up the next morning and decided to recant? What if the body couldn't be found? The quick-thinking sheriff

Bosshardt's arrest. After the arrest, she vowed to stand by her husband; see *Salt Lake Tribune*, 18 and 19 November 1937.

[14]Bosshardt later said that after a dance, while he was mounting his horse at the Malans' corral, Malan had drunkenly approached and attacked him. In self-defense, Bosshardt had hit his friend with an iron bar. Eva Malan's brother, George Schaefer, helped Bosshardt take the body to the well and dispose of it. Schaefer stated that he did not think Bosshardt had been "paying attention" to his sister at the dance and that he did not know how the fight started; see *Salt Lake Tribune*, 18 and 19 November 1937.

concocted another plan. Going to Dick's Café, he told the proprietor, Dick Hammer, to fix up the best meal he could and put a couple of candy bars on the side to sweeten the deal. In the meantime, Antone asked Charlie if he could find the location of the well at nighttime, perhaps fearing that with the new dawn an attorney would appear and tell Bosshardt to keep his mouth shut.[15]

Bosshardt claimed that the killing was not intentional but rather in self-defense, that he and Malan had been best friends since they had known each other, and he was very willing to lead the sheriff—by moonlight—to the well where the body had been deposited.[16] Armed with rope and flashlights and accompanied by City Marshall Paul Seegmiller and Claire Morrow, Antone began almost immediately the arduous task of searching for the body, but the well had partially caved in and was filled with tumbleweed. A crew, spearheaded by the sheriff, worked diligently for two days to remove dirt and impediments from the 110-foot-deep well but still had not found Malan's remains.

The admission to the killing by both Bosshardt and his friend George Schaefer was very big news statewide. On 18 November 1937, the headline of the day in *The Deseret News*, in bold lettering about one inch tall, was: "TWO CHARGED IN SLAYING OF SOUTHERN UTAH RANCHER."[17] After three difficult days of digging, during which time the sheriff openly doubted Bosshardt's veracity concerning the well, Spencer Malan's body finally was recovered, prompting a banner story in *The Salt Lake Tribune*, complete with a large mug shot of Charlie Bosshardt and a diagram of the abandoned desert well in Iron County where the body had been entombed for nearly three years.[18] But, as it turned out, there was one rather significant problem, as Antone explained:

> I tied this rope around his legs and said, "Take him away." He had a blue suit on, and when they started pulling they pulled the right shoulder off and his head. I thought that was all that was necessary.

---

[15]Ibid.
[17]18 November 1937.

[16]*Washington County News*, 18 November 1937.
[18]19 November 1937.

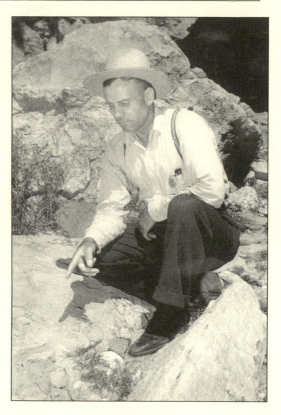

Sheriff Antone B. Prince
served as sheriff for 18½ years,
a Washington County record.

When they started pulling him up the juice from him came down on
me in a stream. Just imagine how I felt.

Well, we took him to St. George and I went to the district attorney and I said, "Ellis [Pickett], we've got this man." He looked at
him and said, "Well, we've got to have the head; without the head we
haven't got any corpus delicti. We need a complete body, a corpus
delicti, so he can be recognized."[19]

So it was back to the well, but it was obvious that locating the
skull would be done at great risk. "Considerable work will have

---

[19]Interview with Antone Prince, 21 September 1974. Pickett's reason for wanting the skull
was to examine it for a fatal blow. Pickett suspected that Malan may have been alive
when he was thrown in the well; if so, the case would not belong in the jurisdiction of
Washington County but of Iron County, where the well was located. When recovered,
the skull did show that death occurred from a blow to the head; the trial was therefore
held in Washington County.

to be done at the well," Sheriff Prince said, "before it will be possible to locate the skull. The well is a death trap as it stands, and another attempt to delve into its secrets would be suicide."[20] Under the direction of E. A. Hodges, state mining engineer, the walls of the well were timbered and, after about five more feet of digging—all by the sheriff since his helpers refused to enter the hole—the badly crushed skull was located.[21]

Following the drama of the original arrest and the search for the body in the well, the trial of Charles Bosshardt and George Schaefer seemed almost an afterthought. Though "the preliminary work by Sheriff Prince, Attorney [Orval] Hafen and Attorney [Ellis] Pickett . . . came in for praise," the prosecution failed to break down the self-defense plea, and the jury came back with a verdict of "Not Guilty."[22] In reality, the prosecution may have made only a half-hearted attempt to assault Bosshardt's self-defense plea, for Orval Hafen recorded in his journal at the time of the arrest, "When I took Bosshardt's confession Wednesday morning I came away feeling that it would be much easier to defend him than it would to demand his life."[23] Antone Prince, predictably, vociferously disagreed: "That was a slap in the face of the law enforcement officer, because even though they killed him in self-defense, they took him down in the desert and threw him in a well and concealed him."[24]

That should have been the end of the story, but about four days after the verdict was read, Antone got a call to go to Bosshardt's farm. Common sense dictated caution, but the sheriff went alone. It was the final surprise of the strange case:

> When I got there they had a big dinner prepared. I'd never seen such a dinner—chicken or turkey, dressing, salads, dressing to go with it. They said, "Sheriff, you were so fair in this trial, you didn't try to do anything but to be fair and just. We wanted to give you a dinner for it."

---

[20] *The Salt Lake Tribune*, 20 November 1937.
[21] *Washington County News*, 25 November 1937.
[22] *Washington County News*, 27 January 1938.
[23] Orval Hafen, "Journal of Orval Hafen," 20 November 1937.
[24] Interview with Antone Prince, 21 September 1974.

Well, naturally, I thought they were going to poison me. They would pass the mashed potatoes, and I'd thank them and let them go all around the table and let everyone take some and when it came back to me I'd take some. My fears were to no avail, because they were just trying to show me consideration because I'd been fair with these men.[25]

Shortly thereafter, Sheriff Prince was called back to Enterprise, where Bosshardt was pointing a gun at Roy Adams. "If you move, I'll kill you right here," Charlie threatened. Antone, typically fearless, took the gun and told him, "I'll take you to jail and lock you up and you'll go forever if I have anything more like this happen." That was the last trouble the sheriff ever had with Charlie Bosshardt.[26]

Unlike John Cottam, who carried a gun with him at all times, Antone was unarmed as he approached Bosshardt. "All the time you were running around without a gun?" he later was asked. "Oh," Antone answered nonchalantly, "I had a gun in my car." In the glove compartment, to be exact, completely out of reach. "That was my philosophy. I never carried a gun."[27]

In retrospect, the wonder is that Antone Prince, not John Cottam, never got shot. The first opportunity for that to happen came on 16 November 1938, a day after Jack Herman Gordon robbed G. W. Simmons of Salt Lake City of his car and money and left him tied in a gulch just west of Santa Clara. Simmons worked himself loose and flagged down an Indian bus driver named Yellow Jacket, who alerted authorities. Notified that a man matching the description of the robber had purchased a ticket for Las Vegas on the Union Pacific Bus line, Antone and G. P. Howell, deputy sheriff, waited for the bus to stop near the Big Hand Café.

The lawmen were too obvious, and a suspicious Gordon escaped through the emergency door of the bus and ran across the street behind the J.C. Penney and O.P. Skaggs stores, where he hid among some packing boxes. Antone went in, unarmed of

[25]Ibid.   [26]Ibid.
[27]Interview with Antone Prince, 22 April 1975.

course, and ordered him to come out with his hands up. As he flashed his light in the direction of the man, however, he saw a gun aimed right at him.[28] "You don't have enough guts to shoot," growled the sheriff in what became a familiar refrain. "Come on out with your hands up."

The next morning at breakfast Antone mused, "I can't figure out why he didn't pull the trigger." A few days later, Clayton and his younger brother Alpine were taking a trailer full of trash out to the city dump and asked their dad for a gun to take with them in case they saw a rabbit. Antone gave them the gun he had just taken from his prisoner, but when they saw a rabbit and Alpine pointed the gun, he was unable to pull the trigger. It finally dawned on Antone that the reason he wasn't shot was the mechanism was jammed.[29]

It was a close encounter, but scarcely the only one he ever had. Henry Ward, the sheriff of Las Vegas, called Antone one night and told him that a man who had just robbed a garage at gunpoint in Las Vegas was headed in the direction of St. George and was armed and dangerous. Sheriff Prince set up a roadblock, which in this case amounted to him standing alone in the middle of the road, armed with a hunting rifle. At two o'clock in the morning, about seven miles west of St. George, he spotted the car:

> I yelled at him to stop and leveled my 30-30 at him but he just kept a coming 'til he got right up to me almost. He plied on his brakes and I had to ask him to come out of the car with his hands in the air. I turned my head just a fraction of a second; I looked back, I looked right down the mouth of his revolver. There we were, out on the desert, just the two of us, and I was looking down his gun. I just stood there, he told me what he was going to do, he was going to kill me and throw me into my own car, haul me so far that I'd never be found.
>
> I let him talk—didn't appear to be frightened, but I was—and finally I said, "You yellow son-of-a-bitch, you haven't got guts enough to shoot—hand me that gun!" His arm dropped and I took

[28] *Washington County News*, 17 November 1938. Gordon admitted his guilt to Judge Will L. Hoyt on the very day he was arrested and was sentenced immediately to five years to life in the Utah State Prison.

[29] Interview with Clayton Prince, 29–30 August 1998.

the gun out of his hand and threw it out in the sand. I left his car right in the middle of the road while I brought him to St. George and locked him up. On the road in he said, "I don't know why I didn't kill you."[30]

Antone knew why. A humbly religious man, each morning he prayed, beginning with the words, "Righteous and Eternal Father in Heaven," and put his complete trust in the Lord. He was not a gospel scholar and never preached to anyone, but he was committed to and had complete confidence in his religion. With very few exceptions (such as staring down the barrel of a revolver) he was never afraid of a man, for through his faith he knew he would be told when it was time to get out; in the meantime, he would be protected. On many occasions he disarmed a man who could just as easily have shot him, but he oozed confidence and always got the gun.

In November 1938, after more than two years in office filling the remainder of John Cottam's term, Antone ran for sheriff for the first time. Following his work in the Charlie Bosshardt case, the returns from Enterprise were predictable: Antone had picked up all but eleven votes, and nobody was quite sure why he didn't get those. He did just about as well in the rest of the county: "Sheriff Antone B. Prince, Democrat, proved to be the best vote-getter," said the *Washington County News*, having more votes and a larger margin of victory than all other candidates in the election.[31]

There was no doubt that Sheriff Prince was widely popular, but it didn't hurt that he ran as a Democrat, a cagey move since heretofore he had been a Republican. "Sweeping seven candidates out of a possible 10 into office, the Democrats in Washington County definitely showed that their candidates were the 'peoples' choice at the polls Tuesday," reported the *Washington County News*.[32]

Ironically, one of the major programs of his new party was indirectly responsible for a significant portion of the crime with

---

[30]Interview with Antone Prince, September 1971.
[31]*Washington County News*, 10 November 1938.   [32]Ibid.

SHERIFF ANTONE PRINCE,
VAE MONROE FENLEY,
DEPUTY ART MITCHELL
Following the arrest of Fenley for the
murder of rancher Royal Hunt.
*Courtesy of Special Collections, Sherratt
Library, Southern Utah University.*

which the sheriff had to deal. The Civilian Conservation Corps,
or CCC, was created by Democratic-controlled Congress in 1933
as an employment measure to provide work for young men in
reforestation, road construction, prevention of soil erosion, and
park and flood control projects. In southern Utah and across the
border on the Arizona Strip there were a total of eleven CCC
camps, with most of the young men hailing from outside Utah,
more than a few of whom got into some sort of trouble while
attached to the corps. In addition to an increase in the crime rate
in Washington County, a CCC boy was responsible for the only

murder that Sheriff Prince knew to be committed in his jurisdiction while he was in office.[33]

Royal Hunt, a rancher who resided at St. George but had a ranch about twenty-eight miles north in the Pine Valley Mountains near Central, met Vae Monroe Fenley, an eighteen-year-old ex-CCC member, on 21 November 1941, and offered him employment at his ranch. Fenley, who had been dishonorably discharged from the CCC for multiple thefts at his camp near Sacramento, worked for two days on the ranch, but on the third shot his boss through a window in the ranch house with a .22-caliber rifle and robbed him. While Fenley saddled a horse with the intention of riding to Nebraska—a trip of over a thousand miles—Hunt revived enough to telephone the operator at Central to report he had been shot. Fenley subsequently reentered the house and shot the wounded rancher three more times, killing him.[34]

Mrs. Mahalia Bracken, the telephone operator, already had called Sheriff Prince, who hurried to Hunt's ranch with his deputy Art Mitchell, Judge George Whitehead, and Royal Hunt's wife. Antone organized a posse that searched all night for the fugitive. Early the next morning a government trapper, known only as Mr. Norman, captured Fenley, who was weakened from his nightlong wanderings in the severe cold. In his possession was Hunt's watch and $21.51 taken from Hunt's wallet. When taken into custody by Sheriff Prince, Fenley initially denied any knowledge of Hunt's death, but with repeated prodding finally admitted that he knew Hunt had $15 in his possession and had killed him to steal the money.[35]

Justice was swift for Fenley. Apprehended on 25 November, he was arraigned on 1 December, with the trial beginning on 6 January 1942, with jury selection; on 12 January, after three hours of deliberation, the jury delivered a verdict of guilty. Offered the

[33]In 1954, former CCC employee Stanley Julius Dzwiacien of Ohio confessed to the murder of a fellow CCC member in 1938 that at the time was ruled a drowning. See *Washington County News*, 14 January 1954.

[34]*Iron County Record*, 4 December 1941.   [35]*The Salt Lake Tribune*, 26 November 1941.

choice of death by firing squad or hanging, Fenley chose the firing squad, and the execution was scheduled for 10 March.[36]

With just fourteen weeks between the time of the arrest and the scheduled date of Fenley's execution, frontier justice obviously still remained to some extent in southern Utah. Fenley, however, was luckier than the previous three men arrested for murder before Antone became sheriff, each of whom was hanged by vigilantes; one of the three, Tom Forrest, who killed a man in Silver Reef in 1881, was taken forcibly from the county jail and was hanged from a large cottonwood tree in front of the home belonging to Vilate Prince's father, George Cottam, leading an onlooker to comment, "I have watched that tree grow nigh onto twenty years, and this is the first time it has borne fruit."[37]

An equally strong confirmation of the frontier justice mentality that existed in southern Utah was the trial that immediately preceded the Fenley case. On 13 October 1941, Sheriff Prince arrested four local men on suspicion of "felonious theft and butchering of a white-faced calf" belonging to Charles Foster near Enterprise.[38] The seriousness of the charge was evidenced by the length of the trial—the transcript, at more than three hundred pages, was far longer than the Fenley trial transcript— but perhaps understandable in an area of the west where the livelihood of many was dependent on their livestock. While the evidence (a couple of gunny sacks filled with calf entrails, hide, and head and ten bottles of calf meat, later donated to charity) did not confirm that the slaughtered calf belonged to Foster, circumstantial evidence was enough to convict one of the men, Alden Pectol, who was sentenced to one to ten years in the penitentiary, though more than twenty local citizens petitioned the court for leniency.[39]

[36]*Washington County News*, 15 January 1942; Antone Prince's arrest records. Fenley's fate thereafter is unknown; the Utah State Prison has no record of him, and the newspapers dropped the story when, two weeks after his arrest, Pearl Harbor was bombed.

[37]Alder and Brooks, *A History of Washington County*, 351; Mark A. Pendleton, "Memories of Silver Reef," *Utah Historical Quarterly*, vol.3, no. 4, October 1930, 117.

[38]Washington County News, 16 October 1941.

[39]Criminal Case #308, *State of Utah vs. Lee Laub, Fred A. Reber, Alden Pectol, and Rex Cannon*.

An area where frontier justice definitely remained well into the twentieth century—if there was any justice at all, that is—was on the Arizona Strip, a vast but sparsely populated area between the Grand Canyon and the Utah-Arizona border. Isolated from the rest of Arizona by the Colorado River and out of the reach of Utah authorities, the Arizona Strip was essentially void of law enforcement, making it an ideal home for a number of polygamists seeking to live without government interference, as well as a variety of thugs, thieves, and cattle rustlers, the most notorious of whom was Bill Shanley.

Born William Franklin Bragg in New Mexico in 1885—he became Shanley after killing a posse member by that name—Bill was a twelve-year-old tending cattle in a remote mountain area of southeastern Utah when he met and for nearly three weeks shared a campsite with four desperados, including Butch Cassidy. The infamous outlaw taught Bill the fine art of his trade and invited him to join his gang; Shanley declined the invitation but did follow Cassidy's direction, eventually becoming one of the great cattle rustlers of all time.[40]

The Arizona Strip, with plenty of cattle, provided a perfect venue for Shanley who, with Honore Cook, rustled and killed cattle and brought the beef across the state line into Utah. In May 1941, Antone got a tip that Shanley and Cook were bringing beef into the cafés in St. George and arrested them; while Cook remained in jail, Shanley was released on one-thousand-dollar-bond but didn't stick around for a trial.[41]

Shanley had made a statement that he would kill the sheriff if he ever came out on the Arizona Strip. Antone most likely had no interest in testing the resolve, and, knowing that he didn't have the authority to go across the state line, he was content to wait until Shanley came to St. George. Months later at the Liberty Hotel, Sheriff Prince spied the fugitive. Going into the hotel, he tapped Shanley on the shoulder and told him he was under arrest. As always, Antone didn't have a gun but said, nev-

---

[40]Grant B. Harris, *Shanley: Pennies Wise—Dollars Foolish.*
[41]*Washington County News*, 8 May 1941.

ertheless, "You'd better hand me that thing under your arm, too, I don't want a scene here." Shanley looked at the sheriff, reached under his arm, and handed over his .45 Colt revolver.[42]

Shanley was given a three hundred dollar fine and six months in the county jail for the "slaughtering of beef without a slaughterer's stamp," the only charge that could be leveled against him in Utah, since the cattle rustling took place in Arizona. For some time Antone carried two or three meals a day from Dick's Café to the prisoner, but after a couple of months said, "Bill, I'm not going to carry another meal to you. If you can't get your own meal, you can starve." Bill looked at Antone and said, "Do you trust me?" "If I didn't think I could, I wouldn't do it," came the response.[43]

Time and again Bill went to Dick's Café, had his meal, and came right back. When his time had been served, Antone took him down to the judge, who said, "The sheriff tells me that you have been a model prisoner, Mr. Shanley. You're a free man." Shanley replied, "Well, I'm not going." Both the sheriff and the judge tried to explain that he was free and had to go, but, turning to Antone, Bill repeated, "I'm not going! You're the only man who's ever treated me like I was a white man, and I'm going to stay."[44]

Bill Shanley was, of course, a white man, but no man had ever treated him with such kindness and trust—perhaps for good reason, not forgetting that he was, after all, a cattle rustler. Many months later, while on business in Kanab, Sheriff Prince heard that Bill was living about seven miles south in the small town of Fredonia and made a special trip to see him. "Come in," Bill said in a gruff voice as Antone knocked on the door. Now in the chicken business, Bill was scalding chickens and looked up and said, "Well, you old son-of-a-bitch, you. Come over here." Shanley threw his arms around Antone and reiterated, "Sheriff, you're the only man who's ever treated me like a white man." Antone couldn't help but respond, "That's quite different from the state-

---

[42]Interview with Antone Prince, 22 April 1975.
[43]Ibid.   [44]Ibid.

Big Hand Café, St. George, about 1955
Courtesy of Nina Atkin

ment that if I ever came on the Arizona Strip you'd kill me."
"Well," said Shanley, "I'll tell you again, if you ever come on the
Arizona Strip, Bill Shanley's home is your home; anything Bill
Shanley's got is yours."[45]

The sheriff continued to trust many prisoners, frequently allow-
ing them to fetch their own meals and then return on their own to
the jail, though one time he got stung. In August 1942, Harold
Messenger, Bill Shanley, and a few other prisoners went to Dick's
Café for breakfast under the charge of Deputy Sheriff Israel Wade.
As they started back after breakfast, Messenger claimed that he
urgently had to go to the rest room and was permitted to go ahead.

[45]Interview with Antone Prince, 21 September 1974.

When Wade arrived at the jail, however, Messenger was nowhere in sight.

Sheriff Prince was notified and found the escapee's tracks in back of the jail and surmised that he had headed north. Driving up to the Sugar Loaf, a boxy, red sandstone formation overlooking the town, he didn't see Messenger and drove towards Washington. When, once again, he couldn't locate the escapee, he came back and drove up the old road toward Enterprise. Getting out of his car, he spotted the man climbing the Black Ridge about a quarter of a mile away. The sheriff ran, out of sight, to a point where he expected the prisoner to come over the ridge; he was in exactly the right location when Messenger cleared the ridge and immediately took him into custody. Held in solitary confinement, Messenger vowed that, when released, he would come back and kill the sheriff.[46]

Undeterred, Antone continued trusting many of his prisoners. A young man from Cedar City named Armstrong was apprehended after breaking into the service station right next to Dick's Café. One night Sheriff Prince got a call from Mesquite, Nevada, warning that a man driving a stolen car was headed for St. George. Antone didn't have a deputy at that time and couldn't find Art Mitchell or Paul Seegmiller to help him. Armstrong said, "Sheriff, if you let me help you, I'll put my life on the line and won't do anything to disgrace you." Antone trusted Armstrong, gave him a gun, and took him to Middleton, where they set up a roadblock and apprehended the fugitive.[47]

Armstrong soon came before Judge George Whitehead, who, on the recommendation of Sheriff Prince, was lenient. After getting out of jail, he joined the army and was sent to Okinawa; while a soldier, Armstrong frequently wrote Antone expressing gratitude for his trust, and sent him a beautiful satin pillow.[48]

At the close of World War II, Antone and Vilate invited their son Clayton and his wife Joy, who were visiting St. George with

---

[46] *Washington County News*, 13 August 1942.
[47] Interview with Virginia Anderson, 7 September 1998.
[48] Interview with Clayton Prince, Wilmer Anderson, and Virginia Anderson by Stephen Prince, April 1999.

their year-old son John, to go to a dance. "I'll get babysitting," said Antone, who soon came back with a young man. "Now you take care of this boy," instructed Antone, "I'll guard him with my life, sheriff," came the response. While at the dance Clayton and Joy asked who the babysitter was. "Oh, one of my prisoners," Antone answered casually.[49]

This was truly a most unusual sheriff. His reputation, already established in the Charlie Bosshardt case, grew to epic proportions in 1940 with his handling of the most famous Dixie College prank of all time. "I'll tell you, *everybody* heard about it," recalled Everard Cox forty-nine years later.[50]

What later became Southern Utah University in Cedar City was called, at the time, Branch Agricultural College (BAC), the archrival of Dixie College. Both schools were rather small, so the teams played football with only six players a side. As the big game approached, Merrill "Bud" Kunz, one of the Dixie players, came up with a brilliant plan. Taking teammate Justin Tolten along to Cedar City, they carefully measured and laid out a large block "D" on an embankment beside the football field.[51] Kunz, who was a skilled carpenter, took great pride in making the letter perfect before pouring gasoline to kill the grass. From top to bottom it measured between twenty and thirty feet, an overwhelming and unwelcome sight for the hometown fans.

It was not well received in Cedar City, and irate officials called Sheriff Prince, who investigated and in short order found the perpetrators. At the behest of leaders at BAC, an assembly was arranged for Kunz and Tolten to meet and apologize to their enemies. "Can you believe this?" said Kunz. "Now I've got to get up in front of the whole school!"

On the appointed day, Sheriff Prince picked up the culpable parties and began to drive them to BAC and their doom. After chastising them, not more than halfway to Cedar City, Antone suddenly put his foot on the brake. "Oh, I can't take you up to

[49]Interview with Clayton Prince, 29–30 August 1998.
[50]Interview with Everard Cox, 10 May 1999.   [51]Ibid.

apologize to those Cedar people," he said as he turned back to St. George. But it was too soon to return—everyone would know they skipped the assembly—so Antone took them to Washington, where they drove through the fields, stopping to get a milkshake, for about as long as it would have taken to go to Cedar City and back before returning to Dixie College.[52]

As word of the escapade made its rounds, Sheriff Prince was elevated to folk hero status among the younger set. Though the Bosshardt case got the most press and the BAC prank story was repeated most frequently, the case that Antone always thought to be his most important was the encounter with Joe Lewis, the FBI's number one most wanted man. So often did he repeat the story in his later years that Vilate, upon hearing just a few words, on one occasion said, "I've got to leave the room, I've heard it so many times!" and on another simply said, "Oh, bull!" Vilate's reaction would seem to indicate that Antone embellished the story each time he retold it, but his account is remarkably consistent not only with the *Washington County News*, but also with the official account in the *FBI Law Enforcement Bulletin*.

On the night of 26 September 1944, Highway Patrolman Loren Squire called Antone to report that he had been shot at twice while attempting to stop a car for speeding. After reaching Toquerville and talking to Squire, Sheriff Prince approached the car and shouted, "If you're in that car, you'd better come out with your hands in the air, because you're surrounded and somebody's going to get hurt." Nothing happened, so he looked in the car and found a box on the front seat that had $364 in silver dollars in it and three brand new guns that had never been fired—a .38 special police revolver, a .32 automatic revolver, and a .22—and well over one hundred rounds of ammunition.[53]

Antone phoned Jay Newman, chief agent for the western district of the FBI, to report the incident. Newman heard enough and interjected, "Do you know who that cookie is?" Antone did-

---

[52]Interview with Lewis Kunz, 8 May 1999. Lewis said that his father got a kick out of two things: that Sheriff Prince didn't make them apologize; and that, through the years, so many others took credit for the prank. Everard Cox, meanwhile, had one regret: "I will have to tell that I'm sorry that I wasn't there."

[53]*Washington County News*, 28 September 1944.

n't, so Newman told him. "Joe Lewis, the number one enemy in America today." Lewis had just robbed the Grant County Bank of John Day at Prairie City, Oregon, and earlier in the year had escaped from the Texas State Penitentiary.[54] "You be careful; by daylight I'll have several agents down there to help you."

"Mr. Antone B. Prince, Sheriff of Washington County, St. George, Utah, who is a fearless police officer took up the search for Lewis immediately after he had fired at the highway patrolman," reported the FBI *Law Enforcement Bulletin*. At daybreak Antone started tracking Lewis. In all his years running livestock, he had become an expert tracker, as recognized by the FBI *Bulletin*: "Sheriff Prince is a tireless worker and has in the past proved himself expert in the art of tracking down fugitives."[55]

After a few days of tracking but not sighting Lewis, the sheriff tried to hand off the case to Newman, who had ten FBI agents with him but declined, saying, "No, it's your baby. You know this terrain of the country; it's up to you. You tell us what to do and we'll do it." While they were talking he received a phone call from Bob Philips who, like all residents of southwestern Utah, had been notified of the search and had spotted Lewis.

Though his tracks were easily identified from the unique rubber heels of his shoes that had a picture of a bell, numerous times Lewis' trail was picked up only to be lost as the outlaw traveled back and forth across the base of the Pine Valley Mountains. On the fifth day, Deputy Sheriff Carl Caldwell and two FBI agents located the tracks and spotted Lewis near a stream. The noise of the running water covered their approach, and when they were close and called for him to surrender, Lewis fired two shots and jumped into the creek. The officers returned fire, fatally striking Lewis in the head.[56]

High praise was given by FBI Special Agent Newman "for the fine cooperation of all branches of law enforcement" and, in particular, for "the trailing ability of Sheriff Prince."[57] The next week, Antone received a personal letter from the famous director of the FBI, J. Edgar Hoover:

[54]FBI *Law Enforcement Bulletin*, 14:6, June 1945, 10.
[56]*Washington County News*, 5 October 1944.

[55]Ibid.
[57]Ibid.

Mr. Antone B. Prince
Sheriff of Washington County
St. George, Utah

My Dear Sheriff,

Mr. Jay C. Newman, Special Agent in Charge of our Salt Lake City Field Office, brought to my attention your splendid work in the case involving Joe Lewis, robber of the Prairie City Branch, Grant County Bank of John Day. I know this case presented unusual difficulties and the outstanding work performed by you is worthy of commendation. Deputy Karl Caldwell of Leeds conducted himself in a most creditable fashion. I do hope you will convey my thoughts to him and to Mr. Robert Phillips of St. George who notified you after he saw the fugitive pass.

All of us in the FBI appreciate your tireless performance of duty, which, coupled with your detailed knowledge of the terrain and your abilities as a tracker, made possible a successful termination of this case.

There is perhaps no way in which I can tell the many other deputies and local citizens who joined hands in a search for this dangerous fugitive just how much we appreciate their assistance.

I hope that I might have the privilege of having a detailed account of this case from you personally at some future date. In the event that you should come to Washington at any time by all means drop in to see me.

With best wishes and kind regards,
Sincerely yours,
[Signed] J. Edgar Hoover

In addition to the Lewis incident, Antone had two cases involving a gun battle. While chasing a stolen car that almost ran down the sheriff—who, once again, thought a roadblock meant standing alone in the middle of the road—Antone and City Marshall Paul Seegmiller fired numerous shots. Though they lost the car after it turned down a dirt road, raising so much dust that they couldn't see where they were going, the FBI later found it just outside of Wendover, Nevada. When the agents came through St. George, they told Prince and Seegmiller that "they had never seen so many well placed shots in a car that didn't stop it," but chided the pair "for not shooting at the men instead of just trying to stop the car."[58]

---

[58]Paul Seegmiller, "History."

The other known case of a gun battle had an almost comical ending. "The tires were shot off Alfred Morris' car by Sheriff Antone B. Prince when the car thieves who were driving it failed to heed the warning to stop," reported the *Washington County News* on 30 September 1943. As Deputy Sheriff Lee Adams drove, Antone peppered the fugitive car with bullets as they raced down Tabernacle Street at a speed of eighty miles an hour. When the sheriff shot out the tires, the car was forced to stop and the two youths jumped out and began running up a hill:

> By the time the officers were stopped the boys were nearly to the top of the hill. Sheriff Prince reports that he called to them and told them to "stop or I'll shoot your legs off." They stopped immediately and were taken into custody.[59]

Antone was no-nonsense in most respects—he may well have shot their legs off if necessary—but he also was compassionate and would try to settle a matter, whenever possible, outside the legal system. "If a juvenile was involved nowadays in some of these offences, they'd have him in court and really make a big deal out of it," said Charlie Pickett, whose father was district attorney for most of the time Antone served as sheriff. "Antone would get these kids who were doing some pilfering—we called it pilfering, it wasn't stealing—he'd get the kids and talk to the parents, and it never got past that. Once Antone would talk to you, you got things straightened out."[60] His sense of fair play could make friends out of enemies, as demonstrated by Bill Shanley and, to an extent, Charlie Bosshardt, but the most unusual example occurred in a totally unexpected location.

After graduating from the Univerity of Southern California School of Dentistry in 1943, Antone's son Clayton took the Utah State Board Examination, the clinical section of which took place at the Utah State Prison, with prisoners as patients. Thirteen graduates lined up to work in somewhat primitive conditions, using an uncomfortable chair that had a board nailed to the back as a head rest and a gallon bucket for the patient to spit in. Seventeen prisoners were brought out, and Les Warburton,

[59] *Washington County News*, 30 September 1943.
[60] Interview with Charlie Pickett, 5 December 1999.

the Chairman of the Board of Dental Examiners, said, "Thirteen of you boys go over there and get in a chair."

Clayton had noticed that one of the convicts, number 17, kept staring at him and, at the first opportunity, made a beeline for his chair. "Is your name Prince?" asked the prisoner. Of course it was. "I thought so. You look just like your dad. He's the one who sent me up here." "Oh, no, there goes my career," thought the young dentist, but the inmate continued: "He treated me more fairly than anyone else in my life." When Clayton finished the dental exam, the prisoner rewarded him with a tooled leather wallet and a braided horsehair belt.[61]

Antone easily won reelection in 1942, and by 1946 had become so popular that nobody bothered to run against him. By 1950, an opponent dared run against him, but Sheriff Prince once again was reelected by a wide margin. Something seemed to be missing, however: The number of arrests had dwindled in the years following 1946. In 1949 there were barely more than a quarter as many arrests as a decade earlier and not many more the following year.[62]

Part of the decrease might be ascribed to the prosperity the country experienced following World War II, and the crime rate seems to have decreased—certainly there were no murders or violent crimes and only a few armed robberies—but the possibility cannot be discounted that Sheriff Prince, after so many years in office, may have started to tire. By 1951, a portion of his attention was drawn elsewhere when he was elected secretary-treasurer of the Utah State Association of County Officials, a situation that became more acute in 1952 and 1953 when he was elected vice-president and then president of the association, but there was one last important case to be handled.

Though the Mormon Church, since the 1890 Manifesto, had disallowed polygamy (though there were still a few church-sanctioned plural marriages in the early twentieth century), the practice of polygamy among some of its members had not entirely disappeared by 1930. The church, in 1933, began putting increased pressure on its members to cease the practice and, in 1935, the Utah

---

[61]Clayton Prince, *Go Stick It in the Ditch: An Autobiography*, 22.
[62]Antone Prince's arrest records.

State Legislature passed an act "Making Unlawful Cohabitation a Felony, and Providing That All Persons Except the Defendant Must Testify in Proceedings Thereof."[63]

Short Creek, a small town of polygamists that in 1935 consisted of twenty houses and a combination store and gas station, had been established on the Utah-Arizona border in Washington County. As the 1935 act elevated "unlawful cohabitation" from a misdemeanor to a felony, the location of Short Creek became very attractive to polygamists, who could cross back and forth over the state line to avoid arrest. In 1939 the state of Utah began cracking down on individual polygamists rather than on the settlement, and on 30 August and 1 September—undoubtedly acting on orders from the state—Sheriff Antone Prince arrested Cleve LeBaron and brothers Richard and Fred Jessop.[64]

LeBaron was a Short Creek fundamentalist, but the Jessops were from New Harmony, living about a quarter of a mile south of town on the old James E. Taylor ranch. The brothers lived in houses about forty yards apart on the property, and two women lived with each brother, according to Vivian Prince, a New Harmony resident who happened to be Antone's nephew.[65]

The trials of the Jessop brothers took place rather quickly. Richard's trial on 19 September, lasted just one day and he was found guilty and sentenced to five years in the state prison.[66] Joseph W. Musser and other fundamentalist leaders were alarmed because Sheriff Prince, District Attorney Orval Hafen, and Judge Will Hoyt all were Mormon and thought they were acting in concert "to stamp out polygamy."[67]

Richard Jessop never served a day in prison, however, for an important point had been made in an appeal to the Utah Supreme Court. The law stated, "If any person cohabits with more than one person of the opposite sex, such person is guilty of a felony." But what, asked Jessop's attorney Claude Barnes, defines cohabitation? The Court agreed with Barnes' argument,

[63]Van Wagoner, *Mormon Polygamy*, 195.   [64]Antone Prince's arrest records.
[65]Interview with Vivian Prince, 29 August 1998.
[66]*State of Utah vs. Richard Jessop*, Criminal 268, 20 September 1939.
[67]Joseph W. Musser, "Journal," September 1939.

stating, "That the parties may have been seen living in the same house does not by itself prove a prima facia case." Ruling that the facts were insufficient to prove cohabitation, the verdict was overturned and Jessop was set free.[68]

It is highly doubtful that Sheriff Prince had any emotional stake in the case. He was a faithful Mormon, to be sure, but the law was his primary concern. Asked if the accused harbored any ill feelings towards the sheriff, Vivian Prince, Antone's nephew and a very close friend of the Jessops' while they lived in New Harmony, said: "No, they didn't, they were friendly to uncle Tone. They never had any ill will. They knew that he was just upholding his job."[69]

A few years passed during which time the polygamists were left in peace, which is all that they wanted, but on 7 March 1944, a massive raid coordinated by the executive branch of the Utah State government, along with FBI agents and U.S. federal marshals, served warrants throughout the region for the arrest of those accused of "unlawful cohabitation."[70] Called into duty once again, Sheriff Prince arrested Fred and Edson Jessop of Short Creek.[71] Though many of the arrested were found guilty in verdicts that were upheld by the United States Supreme Court, the cases against Fred and Edson Jessop were dismissed by Judge Will Hoyt of the Fifth District Court in St. George—the same judge who five years earlier had found Richard Jessop guilty of the same charge.[72]

Sheriff Prince, beyond doubt, would have been happy never to be involved in another polygamist raid, but, unfortunately, the 1944 Boyden Raid (named after one of its architects, U.S. Attorney John S. Boyden) was a mere hint of what was to come. Arizona Governor Howard Pyle, elected in 1950, became concerned that the community of Short Creek had welfare demands on Mohave County, yet its citizens were paying no taxes. Alarmed by an apparent misuse of tax funds for private purposes as well as

[68] *The State of Utah vs. Richard Jessop,* No. 6193, 6 May 1940.
[69] Interview with Vivian Prince, 29 August 1998.
[70] Martha Sonntag Bradley, *Kidnapped From That Land: The Government Raids on the Short Creek Polygamists,* 68.   [71] Antone Prince's arrest records.
[72] Bradley, *op. cit.,* 81.

by the burgeoning population that was doubling each decade and by 1953 included 39 men, 86 women, and 263 children, Pyle orchestrated a surprise assault on the town.[73]

The massive raid took place on 26 July 1953, and involved two hundred law officers, mostly from Arizona, though Pyle managed to secure the participation of Utah officers lest polygamists simply walk across the border to avoid arrest. In defending the raid, Pyle stated that an investigation "had proved that every maturing girl child was forced into the bondage of multiple wifehood" and recalled that the population, just sixteen years before, was two men and a half-dozen wives. "It is easy to see," he said, "that in another 10 years the population of Short Creek would be in the thousands, and an army would not be sufficient to end the greater insurrection and defiance of all that is right."[74]

The invasion from both sides of the state line was set to coincide with an eclipse of the moon at 4:30 A.M. The Arizona force was accompanied by national guardsmen, the Arizona attorney general, judges, policewomen, nurses, twenty-five carloads of newspapermen, and twelve liquor control agents, while the much smaller Utah faction consisted mainly of Sheriff Antone Prince, his deputy, Israel Wade, a few men deputized for the mission, Judge Will Hoyt, district attorney Pat Fenton, and county attorney Pershing Nelson.[75] What was supposed to be a secret raid turned out to be no surprise at all, however, for the polygamists had been tipped off the day before. Instead of being asleep in their beds, most of the populace stood around the city flagpole singing "America" while hoisting the American flag.

It is impossible to tell where the sheriff's sympathies lay, but he was all business. On 29 July, he arrested five women on Arizona warrants, though he released them the next day to return to care for their children.[76] No sooner were the women returned than 125 married women and children attempted a mass escape, only to be turned back by Washington County deputy sheriffs while Sheriff Prince and Israel Wade searched the steep cliffs for any stragglers.[77]

[73]Ibid., 112–123.
[75]*Washington County News*, 13 August 1953.
[77]*The Salt Lake Tribune*, 31 July 1953.

[74]*Washington County News*, 30 July 1953.
[76]*The Salt Lake Tribune*, 30 July 1953.

The raid turned out to be a dismal failure and was certainly the low point of Antone's illustrious career. Though all 263 children were seized, within three years all had been returned to their families in what had become an expensive and unpopular public embarrassment and a public relations nightmare. It was a fiasco to forget, but the polygamists had long memories. Years later, when Antone's grandson Robert Prince began his practice of orthodontics in St. George, he immediately began seeing a number of patients from Hilldale and Colorado City—the name Short Creek had been changed following the 1953 raid. One day, in about 1990, a young polygamist bride casually asked if he was related to Sheriff Prince. Being very proud of his heritage he beamed and said, "Yes, he was my grandfather." All of his patients from the two polygamist towns immediately had their records transferred to another orthodontist.[78]

The luster was gone from being sheriff, and Antone was getting tired. As the 1954 election approached, he told Democratic officials that he wouldn't run, but they put him on the ticket despite his objection. "I never campaigned a bit," he recalled, "only wherever I went I told them what a good man Roy Renouf was and to elect him."[79] Antone's memory may have been a bit selective, since the *Washington County News* reported that "Both candidates had conducted vigorous campaigns," but there is no doubt that he was tired of the office.[80]

Renouf won the election, but out of nearly thirty-five hundred ballots his margin of victory was only sixty votes, an extremely close race considering that Antone ran as a Democrat when the Republicans, led by President Eisenhower, had taken control. His reign was over, and Antone was openly relieved. Now fifty-eight years old, he had served for eighteen years and six months at a time when he was the law. Never before or since did Washington County—or southern Utah, for that matter—have such a memorable sheriff.

---

[78]E-mail of Robert Prince, 20 July 1998.
[79]Interview with Antone Prince, September 1971.
[80]*Washington County News*, 3 November 1954.

EPILOGUE

ON HIS POPULAR 1950s daily CBS television show "House Party," host Art Linkletter regularly had elementary student guests from Los Angeles area public schools. Among the questions he would ask occasionally was, "Do you have anything you'd like to tell the world?" Six-year-old Greg Prince didn't hesitate for a second in answering:

"If anybody's in trouble anywhere in the world, call my grandpa in St. George, Utah."

"Who's your grandpa?"

"He's the sheriff."[1]

Linkletter was tickled enough by the exchange to include it in his 1957 bestseller, *Kids Say the Darndest Things!* Greg's response wasn't meant to be funny, but was merely an honest answer to a simple question. Any of Antone's grandchildren may have said basically the same thing, for he was our hero, he was *The Sheriff*.

Antone, of course, was not going to be sheriff forever, but at least he seemed to be prepared for retired life following his defeat in the 1954 election. His first order of business was to accept an offer from Philips Petroleum to lease the prime piece of property where his house stood on St. George Boulevard to erect a service station. Philips got the better end of the deal, but $50,000 up front plus $175 a month for twenty years proved to be enough for a man whose top salary as sheriff was $210 a month.

Philips bulldozed the house but allowed Antone to take what-

---

[1] Art Linkletter, *Kids Say the Darndest Things!*, 33.

ever materials he wished, which he did liberally, taking the house apart brick by brick. Doors, windows, studding, rafters, everything that was useable was taken to be used in the construction of his new house on the red hill overlooking St. George. The new site provided a wonderful view of the town and surrounding mesas, but more importantly it was immediately above his son Alpine's house, with the two properties connected by a wooden stairway.

He had a hobby that was well suited for retirement. During the years he was sheriff there were two things that Antone loved to do: visit with and help people, and prospect. In his early years of prospecting he looked for gold and silver, but with the coming of the Atomic Age in the late '40s and early '50s, a new craze swept across the Colorado Plateau.

Following the conclusion of World War II, the United States embarked on a massive bomb-building program, and the newly formed Atomic Energy Commission was paying top dollar for uranium, the key component of the bomb. An estimated two thousand prospectors, including Antone, fanned out in search of prehistoric trees that had petrified and soaked up radioactive gases coming up from inside the earth, creating uranium. Armed with a pick, a pair of binoculars, a hand-held Geiger counter, and a few other accessories, the miners staked claims measuring six hundred by fifteen hundred feet on public lands under the Mining Act of 1872.[2]

Antone did his share of prospecting while serving as sheriff, but retirement meant extra time for his avocation. Most of his claims were in Bull Valley, where he had wintered his goats many years before, but he also ventured into Goldstrike and Mineral Mountain in the western section of Washington County. He certainly was not alone, and the haphazard method of marking claims led to confusion and frequent claim jumping, an activity to which Antone evidently was no stranger. "Hell, some of those claims were ten deep," recalled Charlie Pickett. "I saw a sign

[2]Tom Zoellner, "The Uranium Rush," *American Heritage of Invention & Technology*, Summer 2000, vol. 16/no. 1, 56–57.

once in the early '50s on a road in Goldstrike: 'Prospectors Welcome—ex-sheriffs will be gut shot!'"[3]

The search for mineral riches was not always in vain: Charlie Pickett managed to secure a lease for Art Crosby and Earl Cox on state land northwest of Kanarra where uranium was found; they later sold the lease for two hundred thousand dollars.[4] Antone, however, succeeded only in finding thorium, a soft, silver-white radioactive material that is three times as abundant as uranium but virtually worthless. Returning with backpack after backpack, Antone accumulated tons of the rocks that eventually filled an old cesspool on the corner by his house, crammed his garage, and lined the embankment between his house and Alpine's.[5]

Antone had a special relationship with Alpine, due in great part to the fact that the other children moved away from St. George while Alpine stayed home, lived next door, and visited his parents every day. He meant the world to Antone, but on 19 December 1960, that world came crashing down.

Antone and Vilate had just returned from a Monday night dance when she heard a knock on the door. "Where's Antone?" one of the three men on the doorstep asked frantically. They had bad news about Alpine. "Is he killed?" asked Vilate. "We don't know," they responded as they took Antone to the scene of the accident.

It was the night before the Dixie Medical Plaza was to open. St. George had never had a building with office space dedicated solely to the practice of medicine and dentistry, but Alpine, an orthodontist, had spearheaded the drive that resulted in the organization of the Dixie Medical Plaza Corporation. Having noticed a piece of floor molding was loose, Alpine nailed it down but in the process punctured a small copper tubing.

Descending through an access opening, Alpine crawled under the floor to turn off the water. When he did not return in a few

[3]Letter of Charlie Pickett, 11 November 1999.
[4]Interview with Charlie Pickett, 5 December 1999.
[5]Interview with Jim and Marsha Prince, 25 March 2000.

minutes, a dental colleague, Dr. E. L. Cox, went to investigate. Alpine was lying face down on the damp ground near some electrical wires. His head evidently had touched the wiring, which carried 110 volts, and the combination of the leaking water and the electrical shock proved deadly.[6]

A large chunk of Antone's heart was cut out that night. He had lost not only his son but also his best friend. The spirit of the season had been shattered, and the grieving parents immediately took down their Christmas tree; in the years that followed, only once did they have another tree. "They pretty well secluded themselves after that," recalled Maeser Terry, a close neighbor and friend.[7]

Antone was sixty-four years old, but he still had strength and stamina that, particularly on deer hunts, shamed his younger companions. Like a tire with a slow leak, however, he gradually deflated. On his last hunt, with Jim and grandson Greg in 1966, not a shot was fired and, for the first time, Antone complained about his health. "I'm all give-out," he said repeatedly, using a phrase that was part of the local idiom.

Each succeeding year brought further decline for Antone. Eventually he developed extreme difficulty in swallowing. One organ began to fail, then another. On his final trip to Salt Lake City where he was to be examined by medical specialists, Antone was so weak that his son Clayton had to lift him from the plane to the ground. The doctors performed tests but could do nothing. Clayton and his wife Joy took Antone to see his brother Lawrence, but he never got out of the car. Clayton helped Lawrence from the house to the car, and the two brothers sat in the back seat, hugging each other while tears flowed from their eyes, never speaking a word. The end was near, and within a few days after his return to St. George, on 17 April 1977, Antone passed away.

The saga of Antone Prince and his forebears is one of faith— unusually strong faith when measured against today's largely sec-

---

[6]*Deseret News and Telegram*, 20 December 1960.
[7]Interview with Maeser, Marilla, and Fenton Terry, 29 August 1998.

ular standards. George Prince and his family pulled up roots and traveled halfway around the globe to answer the call of their faith and gather to a new land and a new society. Other of Antone's pioneer ancestors, while not traveling as far, were no less responsive, no less courageous, no less sacrificing to the call of faith. They gathered to their Zion, as Jews have to Israel, to affiliate with those of like belief and to build a common homeland.

Unlike the ancestors who gathered to Utah, however, the family after Antone for the most part have scattered across the continent. Antone represented the center of the hourglass, with the gathering sands descending to him and the scattering sands dispersing below him. Only one of his four children settled in St. George, only one other within Utah. The scattering accelerated with the third generation and proceeds yet further with the fourth.

In a similar pattern, all of Antone's children continued to embrace the Mormon faith throughout their lives, while some in the succeeding generations have gone in other directions. Yet all remain heirs to the legacy of their ancestors, most notably an uncommon common man, *The Sheriff.*

Antone Prince lies buried in the St. George Cemetery. The tombstone marking the simple grave bears no epitaph, but perhaps it should, in order to remind future generations that he was an embodiment of his ancestors' faith, courage, and humility and was, above all, a worthy Son of the Utah Pioneers.

Appendix

THE PIONEERS

ALLRED, ISAAC. Born 27 January 1788, Pendleton, Anderson, South Carolina to William Allred and Elizabeth Thrasher. Married Mary Calvert, 14 February 1811, Nashville, Bedford, Tennessee. Died 13 November 1870, Spring City, Sanpete, Utah. Was one of the first in Missouri to be baptized by Mormon elders and was instrumental in organizing the "Salt River Branch of the Church." Was a member of the High Council at Nauvoo. Presided over a branch of the Church at Pottawattamie, Iowa, known as Allred's Branch. His wife Mary died in 1851; on 5 November 1853, he married Matilda Park, a widow with three children. Joined other Allred family members in 1853 to help settle the Sanpete Valley in Utah and found "Allred Town," later known as Spring City. Had twelve children with his wife Mary and one with his wife Matilda.

ALLRED, JAMES. Born 22 January 1784, Randolph County, North Carolina, to William Allred and Elizabeth Thrasher. Married Elizabeth Warren, 14 November 1803, Randolph County, North Carolina. Died 10 January 1876 Spring City, Sanpete, Utah. Was a member of Zion's Camp, which was formed in 1834 on his property at Salt River, Missouri. Was a bodyguard for Joseph Smith at Nauvoo. Was a member of the High Council at Nauvoo. Carried the wounded John Taylor in a sleigh to Nauvoo from Carthage after the murder of Joseph and Hyrum Smith. Became president of the High Council at Pottawattamie, Iowa. His posterity at the time of his death included 12 children, 104 grandchildren, 302 great-grandchildren, and 29 great-great-grand-children.

ALLRED, REDDICK NEWTON. Born 21 February 1822, Bedford County, Tennessee, to Isaac Allred and Mary Calvert. Married Lucy Hoyt, 26

November 1843, Nauvoo, Hancock, Illinois. Died 10 October 1905, Chester, Sanpete, Utah. Served in the Mormon Battalion. Was captain of the second fifty in the 1849 Allen Taylor Company. Served a mission in the Sandwich (Hawaiian) Islands. Married his second wife, Emily Amilla Jane McPherson, 11 January 1856, Salt Lake City, Salt Lake, Utah. Was a major and second in command in the military of Davis County during the "Utah War" in 1857. Married his third wife, Celestia W. Warrick, 5 January 1861. Chosen colonel of the Militia of Sanpete County, and served in that capacity during the Black Hawk War. Served five terms in the Utah Legislature. Had ten children by his first wife and ten by his second.

ALLRED, SARAH LOVISA. Born 14 November 1817, Bedford County, Tennessee, to Isaac Allred and Mary Calvert. Married Allen Taylor, 5 September 1833, Salt River, Monroe County, Missouri. Died 11 March 1879, New Harmony, Washington, Utah. Gave birth to her seventh child, Clarissa Elvira, at Fort Bridger, Wyoming, while crossing the plains to Utah. Had a total of eleven children.

ALLRED, WILLIAM MOORE. Born 24 December 1819, Bedford County, Tennessee, to Isaac Allred and Mary Calvert. Married Orissa Angelia Bates, 9 January 1842, Nauvoo, Hancock, Illinois. Died 8 June 1901, Fairview, Lincoln, Wyoming. Fought with Mormon resistance against mobs on northern Missouri; fled to Quincy, Illinois, to escape recriminations against leaders of the resistance. Was captain in the Nauvoo Legion. Married Martha Jane Martindale in 1857 (probably 6 February). Martha died in 1860. Orissa died in 1878; married Mary Osborne, a widow after Orissa's death. Had twelve children with first wife, two with second wife.

BOWMAN, SARAH. Born 11 January 1819, Exning, Suffolk, England, to Francis Bowman and Sophia Hammond. Married George Prince, 10 October 1837, Exning, Suffolk, England. Died 13 July 1875, Middleton, Washington, Utah. In addition to her ten children (the first of which died before his first birthday), she was pregnant as she crossed the plains in 1860, but twin babies were born prematurely and died along the way.

IMLAY, JAMES HAVENS. Born 6 April 1815, Imlaystown, Monmouth, New Jersey, to John Imlay and Rebecca Havens. Married Sarah Butterfield, who died in 1839. Married 1 February 1842, Bordentown, Burlington, New Jersey. Died 1 February 1890, Panguitch, Garfield, Utah. Went to Utah in 1853 despite being offered a considerable sum of money by his uncle to quit the church and stay in New Jersey. Moved to Middleton, Utah, in 1863, but after a few months moved again to New Harmony. Became president of the New Harmony branch of the Church in 1864 following the resignation of John D. Lee from the post. Moved to Panguitch in 1872.

IMLAY, MARY ELIZABETH ANN. Born 13 February 1847, Bordentown, Burlington, New Jersey, to James Havens Imlay and Ann Eliza Coward. Married Francis Prince, 26 December 1864, New Harmony, Washington, Utah. Died 31 December 1930, New Harmony.

LEE, JOHN DOYLE. Born 6 September 1812, Kaskaskia, Randolph, Illinois, to Ralph Lee and Martha Elizabeth Berry. Married Aggatha Ann Woolsey, 23 July 1833, Vandalia, Randolph, Illinois. Died 23 March 1877, Mountain Meadows, Washington, Utah. Married seventeen other women, including two sisters of his first wife, Aggatha Ann (Rachel Andora Woolsey and Emaline Vaughn Woolsey). From 1839 to 1844 he spent much of his time winning converts in Illinois, Tennessee, and Kentucky. In 1843 he was chosen to guard the home of Joseph Smith in Nauvoo. Served briefly in the Mormon Battalion. Was among the earliest Mormon settlers in southern Utah and a founding father of New Harmony. Exiled from New Harmony and excommunicated from the Church in 1870 as a result of his involvement in the 1857 Mountain Meadows Massacre. Though he continued to the end to profess his innocence, he was convicted for his role in the massacre and was executed at Mountain Meadows; his body was taken to Panguitch, Utah, for burial by William Prince and Harvey Lee.

PATRICK, ELIZABETH. Born 9 December 1793, Mecklenburg County, Virginia, to John Patrick and Sarah Kendrick. Married William Taylor, 22 March 1811, Warren County, Kentucky. Died 27 October 1880, Ogden, Weber, Utah. Her husband William died in 1839, leaving her a widow with fourteen children. Made her home in Kaysville, Utah, until 1771, when she moved in with her son Pleasant Green Taylor in Harrisville. At the time of her death, in addition to her 14 children she had 193 grandchildren, 407 great-grandchildren, and 23 great-great-grand-children.

PRINCE, FRANCIS. Born 31 July 1840, Burwell, Cambridgeshire, England, to George Prince and Sarah Bowman. Married Mary Elizabeth Ann Imlay, 26 December 1864, New Harmony, Washington, Utah. Died 12 August 1929, New Harmony. Reared in South Africa, moved with family to Utah in 1860. Served briefly for the Union Army in 1862 in Lot Smith's company of mounted volunteers during the Civil War in Utah and Wyoming. Served in the Utah Black Hawk War for which he later was awarded an "Indian War Medal."

PRINCE, GEORGE. Born 22 December 1815, Fordham, Cambridgeshire, England, to Richard Prince and Mary Harrold. Married Sarah Bowman 10 October 1837, Exning, Suffolk, England. Died 22 January 1905, Escalante, Garfield, Utah. Went with his wife, one-year-old son Francis, and brother John to South Africa in 1841. Sailed aboard the barque *Alacrity* to Boston in 1860, traveled by train to St. Joseph, Missouri, by boat to Winter Quarters, and by wagon train to Utah in the William Budge company. Had children on three continents (two in Europe, seven in Africa, one in North America). Moved to Middleton near St. George in 1863. His wife Sarah died in 1875. Married Frances Wilkens, 1 February 1877, Salt Lake City. Had two children by second wife and later moved to Escalante.

PRINCE, JAMES FRANKLIN. Born 23 December 1865, New Harmony, Washington, Utah, to Francis Prince and Mary Elizabeth Ann Imlay. Married Sarah Elizabeth Redd, 21 December 1885, St. George, Washington, Utah. Served briefly in the Northern States Mission. Died 5 October 1898, New Harmony. A monument was erected on Pine Valley Mountain at the spot where he suddenly died while on a hunting trip.

REDD, BENJAMIN JONES. Born 20 June 1842, Murfreesboro, Rutherford, Tennessee, to John Hardison Redd and Elizabeth Hancock. Married Clarissa Elvira Taylor, 20 June 1865, New Harmony, Washington, Utah. Died 16 September 1887, New Harmony. Wife Clarissa died 18 January 1874, leaving him a widower with two small children (two others had preceded her in death). Married Nancy Louella Workman, 8 February 1877, St. George, Washington, Utah, with whom he had seven children. Went "down and back" from New Harmony to Iowa in 1863 to assist poor Saints in their move to Utah. Served brief mission to the Indians with a group of missionaries that included Jacob Hamblin.

REDD, JOHN HARDISON. Born 27 December 1799, Stump Sound, Onslow County, North Carolina, to Whitaker Redd and Elizabeth Hardison. Married Elizabeth Hancock, 2 March 1826, Stump Sound. Died 15 June 1858, Spanish Fork, Utah County, Utah. Originally a sea captain; in Tennessee, he purchased several hundred acres of land and had a number of Negro slaves, two of whom—Venus and Chaney—chose to remain with the family and travel across the plains (each with two children) after the other slaves were freed. One of the first residents of Spanish Fork. His wife, Elizabeth Redd, died in 1853. Married Mary Lewis, 2 March 1856. He died from complications arising from being kicked by a horse.

REDD, LEMUEL HARDISON. Born 31 July 1836, Snead's Ferry, Onslow, North Carolina, to John Hardison Redd and Elizabeth Hancock. Married Keziah Jane Butler, 2 January 1856, Spanish Fork, Utah County, Utah. Married Sarah Louisa Chamberlain, 5 November 1866, Salt Lake City, Salt Lake, Utah. Died 10 June 1910, Colonia Juarez, Galeana, Mexico. Father of twenty-seven children. Left New Harmony due to persecution of polygamous families by U.S. government. Eventually settled in Colonia Juarez, Mexico

REDD, SARAH ELIZABETH. Born 12 May 1866, New Harmony, Washington, Utah, to Benjamin Jones Redd and Clarissa Elvira Taylor. Married James Franklin Prince 21 December 1885, St. George, Washington, Utah. Died 21 December 1946, New Harmony. Her husband died in 1898. Married Reese Davis 17 September 1902, St. George. Sarah had five children (one of whom died in infancy) in her first marriage and three in her second. She also reared nine grandchildren who were left motherless.

STOUT, HOSEA. Born 18 September 1810, Pleasant Hill, Mercer County, Kentucky, to Joseph Stout and Anna Smith. Married Samantha Pack, 7 January 1838, Caldwell County, Missouri. Died Holladay, Salt Lake, Utah, 2 March 1889. His wife Samantha died 29 November 1839. Married Louisa Taylor, sister of Allen Taylor, 29 November 1840, Nauvoo, Illinois. Elected captain of a company of Nauvoo Legion in February 1841; promoted to brigadier general in 1845. Married Lucretia Fisher (who left him one year later) and Marinda Bennett (who died in childbirth in 1846) while in Nauvoo. Went to Utah in 1848. Was member of the House of Representatives in Utah in 1849, attorney general in 1850, became one of the first practicing attorneys in the territory in 1851. Went on mission to China in 1853; while he was en route to China, his wife Louisa died. Married Alvira Wilson in 1855, with whom he had eleven children. Called to southern Utah in 1861 to be part of the "Cotton Mission." Was the first city attorney in St. George, Utah. Was made an attorney for the United States for the Territory of Utah in 1862 in an order signed by President Abraham Lincoln. Married Sarah Jones, 1868.

TAYLOR, ALLEN. Born 17 January 1814, Bowling Green, Warren County, Kentucky, to William Taylor and Elizabeth Patrick. Married Sarah Lovisa Allred, 5 September 1833, Salt River, Monroe County, Missouri. Died 5 December 1891, Loa, Utah. Was captain of hundred both in the Brigham Young company in 1848 and in the company that bore his name in 1849. Married Hannah Egbert, 1 January 1858, Salt Lake City. Married Elizabeth Smith 26 November 1856, Salt Lake City. Married Phoebe Ann Roberts 27 March 1857, Salt Lake City. Moved to St. George in 1862, after he was called to the "Cotton Mission." Moved to Loa, Wayne County, Utah with his two younger wives, Elizabeth and Phoebe Ann, after he was honorably released from his mission by Apostle Erastus Snow in 1883 (his first wife, Sarah, died in New Harmony in 1879 and his second wife, Hannah, evidently divorced him, for she married Joseph Brundage in 1874). Had a total of thirty children (eleven with Clarissa Elvira, six with Hannah, one with Elizabeth, and twelve with Phoebe Ann).

TAYLOR, CLARISSA ELVIRA. Born 3 October 1849, Fort Bridger, Uinta, Wyoming, to Allen Taylor and Sarah Lovisa Allred. Married Benjamin Jones Redd, 20 June 1865, New Harmony, Washington, Utah. Died 18 January 1874, New Harmony, one month after the death of her four-month-old infant Anna Maria Vilate.

TAYLOR, JOSEPH. Born 4 June 1825, Bowling Green, Warren County, Kentucky, to William Taylor and Elizabeth Patrick. Married Mary Moore, 24 March 1844, Nauvoo, Hancock, Illinois. Died 11 August 1900, Farr West, Weber, Utah. Served in the Mormon Battalion. After the Battalion was disbanded in San Diego, Taylor served as a bodyguard to Brigadier General Stephen W. Kearney to accompany the general to Missouri; en route they discovered and buried the remains of the Donner party in the High Sierras (most of the bodies had been cannibalized by the survivors of the party). Married Hannah Mariah Harris in 1854. Later married Jane Lake and Caroline Mattson. Served as a major in the Utah militia, still known as the Nauvoo Legion, during the Utah War of 1857. Had twenty-five children from the first three wives (none from the fourth).

TAYLOR, LOUISA. Born 19 October 1819, near Richardsville, Warren, Kentucky, to William Taylor and Elizabeth Patrick. Married Hosea Stout, 29 November 1840, Nauvoo, Hancock, Illinois. Died 11 January 1853, Salt Lake City, Salt Lake, Utah. Her death occurred when she was only thirty-three years old, two days after giving birth to her eighth child, while her husband Hosea was en route to China on a mission for the Church.

TAYLOR, PLEASANT GREEN. Born 8 February 1827, near Richardsville, Warren, Kentucky, to William Taylor and Elizabeth Patrick. Married Clarissa Lake, 2 February 1847, Mount Pisgah, Union, Iowa. Died 16 May 1917, Harrisville, Weber, Utah. Was a member of the Nauvoo Legion and also of the police force in Nauvoo. Served in the Mormon Battalion. Married Mary Eliza Shurtliff, 5 July 1853. Married Jane Narcissus Shurtliff, 6 April 1857. Married Sarah Jane Marler, 20 June 1858. Had a total of thirty-three children from his four wives.

TAYLOR, WILLIAM. Born 21 March 1787, Martin County, North Carolina, to Joseph Taylor Jr. and Sarah Best. Married Elizabeth Patrick, 22 March 1811, Warren County, Kentucky. Died 9 September 1839, near Warsaw, Hancock, Illinois. Was among the earliest Mormon converts in Missouri while living at Salt River, Monroe County. He died during the journey of the Saints from Far West, Missouri, whence they had been expelled, to western Illinois.

BIBLIOGRAPHY

BOOKS

Adams, Maria Luella Redd. *Memories*. S.L.C: Obert C. and Grace A. Tanner Foundation, 1981.

Alder, Douglas D., and Karl F. Brooks. *A History of Washington County*. S.L.C: Utah State Historical Society, 1996.

Allen, James B., and Glen M. Leonard. *The Story of the Latter-day Saints*. S.L.C: Deseret Book Co., 1976.

Allen, James B., Ronald W. Walker, and David J. Whittaker. *Studies in Mormon History, 1830–1997: An Indexed Bibliography*. Urbana and Chicago: Univ. of Illinois Press, 2000.

Anderson, Nels. *Desert Saints*. Chicago: The Univ. of Chicago Press, 1942.

Arrington, Leonard J. and Davis Bitton. *The Mormon Experience*. New York: Alfred Knopf, 1979.

Arrington, Leonard J. *Brigham Young: American Moses*. N.Y: Alfred A. Knopf, 1985.

Arrington, Leonard J. *Great Basin Kingdom*. Cambridge: Harvard University Press, 1958.

Arrington, Leonard J., Feramorz Y. Fox, and Dean L. May. *Building the City of God: Community & Cooperation among the Mormons*. S.L.C: Deseret Book, 1976.

Bagley, Will. *Blood of the Prophets: Brigham Young and the Massacre at Mountain Meadows*. Norman: Univ. of Oklahoma Press, 2002.

Bagley, Will. *Scoundrel's Tale: The Samuel Brannan Story*. Spokane, Wash: The Arthur H. Clark Co., 1999.

Baines, Thomas. *Journal of Residence in Africa, 1842–1849*, 2 vols. Cape Town: Van Riebeeck Society, 1961.

Baldwin, Thomas. *A New and Complete Gazetteer of the United States, 1854*. Philadelphia: Lippincot, Grambo, 1854.

Bancroft, Hubert Howe. *History of California*. San Francisco: History Co., 1884–90.

Bancroft, Hubert Howe. *History of Utah, 1540–1886*. San Francisco: History Co., 1889.

Barker, Marilyn Conover. *The Legacy of Mormon Furniture*. S.L.C: Gibbs-Smith Publisher, 1995.

Barlow, Ora H. *The Israel Barlow Story and Mormon Mores*. S.L.C: Ora H. Barlow, 1968.

Barron, Howard H. *Orson Hyde, Missionary, Apostle, Colonizer*. Bountiful, Utah: Horizon Publishers, 1977.

Beck, Henry Charlton. *More Forgotten Towns of Southern New Jersey*. New Brunswick, N.J: E.P. Dutton, 1937.

Bennett, Richard E. *Mormons at the Missouri, 1846–1852: "And Should We Die. . ."* Norman and London: Univ. of Oklahoma Press,1987.

Bigler, David, ed. *The Gold Discovery Journal of Azariah Smith*. Logan: Utah State Univ. Press, 1990.

Black, Susan Easton and Larry C. Porter, ed. *Lion of the Lord*. S.L.C: Deseret Book Co., 1995.

Black, Susan Easton, comp. *Members of the Church of Jesus Christ of Latter-day Saints 1830–48*. 50 vols. Provo: Brigham Young Univ., Religious Studies Center, 1989.

Book of Mormon. S.L.C: The Church of Jesus Christ of Latter-day Saints, 1987.

Bradley, Martha Sonntag. *Kidnapped From That Land: The Government Raids on the Short Creek Polygamists*. S.L.C: Univ. of Utah Press, 1993.

Brodie, Fawn M. *No Man Knows My History*. N.Y: Alfred A. Knopf, 1945.

Brooks, Juanita, ed. *On the Mormon Frontier: The Diary of Hosea Stout*, 2 vols. S.L.C: Univ. of Utah Press, 1964.

Brooks, Juanita, ed. *Journal of the Southern Indian Mission, Diary of Thomas D. Brown*. Logan: Utah State Univ. Press, 1972.

Brooks, Juanita. *John Doyle Lee, Zealot—Pioneer Builder—Scapegoat*. Glendale, Calif: The Arthur H. Clark Co., 1962.

Brooks, Juanita. *The Mountain Meadows Massacre.* Palo Alto: The Board of Trustees of Leland Stanford Jr. Univ., 1950.

Brooks, Will, as recorded by his wife, Juanita Brooks. *Uncle Will Tells His Story.* S.L.C: Taggart & Co., Inc., 1970.

Brown, Joseph E. *The Mormon Trek West.* Garden City, N.Y: Doubleday & Co., 1980

Brown, S. Kent, Donald Q. Cannon, and Richard H. Jackson. *Historical Atlas of Mormonism.* N.Y: Simon and Schuster, 1994.

Bullock, Thomas, Will Bagley ed. *The Pioneer Camp of the Saints.* Spokane, Wash: The Arthur H. Clark Co., 1997.

Campbell, Eugene E. *Establishing Zion: The Mormon Church in the American West, 1847–1869.* S.L.C: Signature Books, 1988.

Cannon, Donald Q., and Lyndon W. Cook, eds. *Far West Record: Minutes of the Church of Jesus Christ of Latter-day Saints, 1830–44.* Salt Lake City: Deseret Book, 1983.

Cannon, George Q., ed. *Scraps of Biography.* S.L.C: Juvenile Instructor Office, 1883.

Carter, Kate B., ed. *Heart Throbs of the West,* 12 vols. S.L.C: Daughters of Utah Pioneers, 1939–51.

Carter, Kate B., ed. *Treasures of Pioneer History,* 6 vols. S.L.C: Daughters of Utah Pioneers, 1955–60.

Carter, Kate B., ed. *Our Pioneer Heritage,* 20 vols. S.L.C: Daughters of Utah Pioneers, 1961–77.

Clark, James R., ed. *Messages of the First Presidency.* S.L.C: Bookcraft, 1965–1975.

Clayton, William. *The Latter-Day Saints' Emigrants' Guide.* St. Louis: Republican Steam Press-Chambers and Knapp, 1848. Reprinted St. Louis: Patrice Press, 1983.

Clayton, William. *An Intimate Chronicle, The Journals of William Clayton.* S.L.C: Signature Books, 1995.

Cleland, Robert Glass, and Juanita Brooks, eds. *A Mormon Chronicle: The Diaries of John D. Lee, 1846–1876,* 2 vols. San Marino: Henry E. Huntington Library and Art Gallery, 1955. Reprinted S.L.C: Univ. of Utah Press, 1983.

Cole, Alfred. *The Cape and the Kafirs.* London: Richard Bentley, 1852.

Cory, Sir George E. *The Rise of South Africa.* London, N.Y.C., [etc.]: Longmans, Green, and Co., 1926.

Daughters of Utah Pioneers. *An Enduring Legacy,* 12 vols. S.L.C: Daughters of Utah Pioneers, 1978–1989.

DeVoto, Bernard. *The Year of Decision, 1846.* N.Y.C: Houghton-Mifflin Col, 1943.

Doctrine and Covenants of the Church of Jesus Christ of Latter-day Saints. S.L.C: The Church of Jesus Christ of Latter-day Saints, 1981.

Esshom, Frank. *Pioneers and Prominent Men of Utah.* S.L.C: Western Epics, Inc., 1966.

Fisher, Margaret M. *Utah and the Civil War.* S.L.C: Deseret Book, 1929.

Flanders, Robert Bruce. *Nauvoo: Kingdom on the Mississippi.* Urbana and Chicago: Univ. of Ill. Press, 1965.

Ford, Thomas. *A History of Illinois, from Its Commencement as a State in 1818 to 1847.* Chicago: S. C. Griggs, 1854.

Garraty, John A. *The American Nation to 1877.* N.Y.C: Harper and Row, 1966.

Gottfredson, Peter. *History of Indian Depredations in Utah.* S.L.C., 1919.

Grant, Sheldon. *The Harmony Valley and New Harmony, Utah: History and Memories.* New Harmony, Utah, 1999.

Hall, Henry. *Manual of South African Geography.* Cape Town: S. Solomon, 1866.

Harris, Grant B. *Shanley: Pennies Wise—Dollars Foolish.* N.Y.C: Vantage Press, 1980.

Hartley, William G. *My Best for the Kingdom.* S.L.C: Aspen Books, 1993.

Hatch, Nelle Spilsbury. *Mother Jane's Story.* Waco, Calif: Shafer Publishing Co., 1964.

Henrie, Manetta Prince, and Anna Prince Redd. *Life History of William and Louisa E. Lee Prince.* Provo: privately published, 1956.

Henrie, Manetta Prince. *Descendants of John Doyle Lee, 1812–1877.* Provo, 1960.

Hill, Ivy Hooper Blood. *William Blood, His Posterity and Biographies of their Progenitors.* Logan, 1972.

Hill, William E. *The Mormon Trail Yesterday and Today.* Logan: Utah State Univ. Press, 1996.

Hunter, Milton R. *Brigham Young, The Colonizer.* Santa Barbara and S.L.C: Peregrine Smith, 1973.

Illustrated History of South Africa: The Real Story. Cape Town: Reader's Digest Association, South Africa, 1988.

Jenson, Andrew, ed. *Encyclopedic History of The Church of Jesus Christ of Latter-day Saints*. S.L.C: Jenson History Co., 1901.

Johnson, Benjamin. *My Life's Review*. Independence, Mo: Zion's Printing and Publishing Company, 1947.

Johnson, Clark V., ed. *Mormon redress Petitions; Documents of the 1833–1838 Missouri Conflict*. Provo: Religious Studies Center, Brigham Young Univ., 1992,

Kane, Elizabeth. *A Gentile Account of Life in Utah's Dixie, 1872–73: Elizabeth Kane's St. George Journal*. S.L.C: Tanner Trust Fund, Univ. of Utah Library, 1995.

Kane, Elizabeth. *Twelve Mormon Homes Visited in Succession on a Journey through Utah to Arizona*. S.L.C: Tanner Trust Fund, Univ. of Utah Library, 1974.

Kane, Thomas L. *The Mormons: A Discourse delivered before the Historical Society of Pennsylvania, March 26, 1850*. Philadelphia: King & Baird, Printers, 1850.

Kelly, Charles, ed. *Journals of John D. Lee, 1846–1847 and 1859*. S.L.C: Univ. of Utah Press, 1984.

Kirkham, E. Kay, comp. *Daniel Stillwell Thomas, Utah Pioneer of 1849*. S.L.C., 1985.

Knight, Hal and Dr. Stanley B. Kimball. *111 Days to Zion*. S.L.C: Big Moon Traders, 1997.

Korns, J. Roderic, and Dale L. Morgan. *West from Fort Bridger: The Pioneering of the Immigrant Trails across Utah, 1846–1850*. Logan: Utah State Univ. Press, 1994.

Larson, Andrew Karl. *I Was Called to Dixie*. St. George, Utah: Andrew Karl Larson, 1961.

Larson, Andrew Karl. *The Red Hills of November: A Pioneer Biography of Utah's Cotton Town*. S.L.C: The Deseret News Press, 1957.

Lee, John D. *Mormonism Unveiled, or The Life and Confessions of the Late Mormon Bishop, John D. Lee*. St. Louis: Bryan, Brand, 1877.

Leonard, Glen M. *A History of Davis County*. S.L.C: Utah State Hist. Soc., 1998.

LeSueur, Stephen C. *The 1838 War in Missouri*. Columbia: Univ. of Missouri Press, 1987.

Linkletter, Art. *Kids Say the Darndest Things!* Englewood Cliffs, N.J: Prentice-Hall, Inc., 1957.

Little, James A. *From Kirtland to Salt Lake City*. S.L.C: J. A. Little, 1890.

Little, James A. *Jacob Hamblin*. 1881; reprinted in *Three Mormon Classics*, S.L.C: Stevens and Wallis, Inc., 1944.

Long, E.B. *The Saints and the Union: Utah Territory During the Civil War*. Chicago: Univ. of Ill. Press, 1981.

Majors, Alexander. *Seventy Years on the Frontier*. Chicago and N.Y.C: Rand, McNally & Company, 1893.

Mattes, Merrill J. *The Great Platte River Road*. Lincoln: Neb. State Hist. Soc., 1969.

McConkie, Bruce R. *Mormon Doctrine*. 2nd ed. S.L.C: Bookcraft, 1966.

McLellin, William E. *The Journals of William E. McLellin, 1831–1836*. Provo, Urbana and Chicago: Brigham Young Univ. Press and Univ. of Ill. Press, 1994.

Merkley, Christopher. *Biography of Christopher Merkley*. S.L.C: J. H. Parry, 1887.

Merriman, Nathaniel James. *The Cape Journals of Archdeacon N.J. Merriman, 1848–1855*. Cape Town: Van Riebeeck Society, 1957.

Miller, Albert E. *The Immortal Pioneers: Founders of City of St. George, Utah*. St. George, Utah: Albert E. Miller, 1946.

Miller, David E. *Hole-In-The-Rock: An Epic in the Colonization of the Great American West*. S.L.C: Univ. of Utah Press, 1959.

Miller, David E. *Nauvoo: The City of Joseph*. Santa Barbara, Calif: Peregrine Smith, 1974.

Morgan, Dale L. *The Great Salt Lake*. Indianapolis: Bobbs-Merrill, 1947.

Morgan, Martha M. *A Trip Across the Plains in the Year 1849*. San Francisco, 1864.

Mulder, William and Russell A. Mortensen. *Among the Mormons*. N.Y.C: Alfred A. Knopf, 1958.

Nevins, Allan, ed. *Polk: The Diary of a President, 1845–1849*. London, N.Y.C: Longmans, Green, and Company, 1929.

O'Brien, Michael J. *Grassland, Forest, and Historical Settlement—An Analysis of Dynamics in Northeast Missouri*. Lincoln: Univ. of Nebraska Press, 1984.

Peterson, John Alton. *Utah's Black Hawk War*. S.L.C: Univ. of Utah Press, 1998.

Piercy, Frederick H. *The Route from Liverpool to the Great Salt Lake Valley*. Reprint, Cambridge: Harvard Univ. Press, 1962.

Pratt, Parley P. *The Autobiography of Parley P. Pratt*. S.L.C: Deseret Book Co., 1994.

Prince, Clayton. *Go Stick It In the Ditch: An Autobiography*. Privately Published, 1999.

Pringle, Thomas. *Thomas Pringle in South Africa, 1820–1826*. Cape Town: Longman Southern Africa, 1970.

Quincy, Josiah. *Figures of the Past*. Boston: Roberts Brothers, 1883.

Quinn, D. Michael. *The Mormon Hierarchy: Origins of Power*. S.L.C: Signature Books, 1994.

Redd, Amasa Jay. *Lemuel Hardison Redd Jr., 1856–1923, Pioneer, Leader, Builder*. S.L.C: 1967.

Redd, Lura. *The Utah Redds and Their Progenitors*. S.L.C., 1973.

Reid, H. Lorenzo. *Dixie of the Desert*. Zion National Park,Utah: Zion Natural History Association,1964.

Richards, Mary Haskin Parker. *Winter Quarters, The 1846–1848 Life Writings of Mary Haskin Parker Richards*. Logan: Utah State Univ. Press,1996.

Ricketts, Norma Baldwin. *The Mormon Battalion, U.S. Army of the West 1846–1848*. Logan: Utah State Univ. Press, 1996.

Roberts, Brigham H. *The Missouri Persecutions*. S.L.C: George Q. Cannon & Sons, 1900.

Roberts, Brigham H. *The Rise and Fall of Nauvoo*. S.L.C: Deseret News, 1900.

Roberts, Brigham H. *Comprehensive History of the Church of Jesus Christ of Latter-day Saints*. S.L.C: Deseret Book Co., 1930.

Seegmiller, Janet Burton. *A History of Iron County*. S.L.C: Utah State Hist. Soc., 1996.

Sessions, Gene A. *Mormon Thunder: A Documentary History of Jedediah Morgan Grant*. Urbana: University of Ill. Press, 1982.

Simpson, Captain J. H. *Report of Explorations Across the Great Basin of the Territory of Utah for a Direct Wagon-Route from Camp Floyd to Genoa, in Carson Valley, in 1859*. Washington, D.C: G.P.O., 1876.

Slaughter, William W. and Michael Landon. *Trail of Hope*. S.L.C: Shadow Mountain, 1997.

Smith, George D., ed. *An Intimate Chronicle: The Journals of William Clayton*. S.L.C: Signature Books, 1991.

Smith, Joseph, Jr. *History of the Church of Jesus Christ of Latter-day Saints. Period 1. History of Joseph Smith the Prophet, by himself*, 6 vols. S.L.C: Deseret Book, 1902–1912.

Sonne, Conway B. *Ships, Saints and Mariners—A Maritime Encyclopedia of Mormon Migration, 1839–1890*. S.L.C: Univ. of Utah Press, 1987.

Stansbury, Howard. *Exploration and Survey of the Valley of the Great Salt Lake*. Philadelphia: Lippincott, Brambo & Co., 1852.

Stegner, Wallace. *The Gathering of Zion*. New York: McGraw-Hill, 1971.

Stockenström, Sir Andries. *The Autobiography of the Late Sir Andries Stockenström*. Cape Town: C. Struik, 1964.

Stott, Clifford L. *Search for Sanctuary: Brigham Young and the White Mountain Expedition*. S.L.C: Univ. of Utah Press, 1984.

Talmage, James E. *The House of the Lord*. S.L.C: Published by the Church, 1912.

The Essential Joseph Smith. S.L.C: Signature Books, 1995.

Thompson, Leonard. *A History of South Africa*. New Haven, Conn: Yale Univ. Press, 1994.

Thompson, William Howard. *Thomas Cottam, 1820, and his Wives Ann Howarth, 1820, Caroline Smith, 1820: Descendants*. Thomas Cottam Family Organization, 1987.

Thorp, Judge Joseph. *Early Days in the West*. Liberty, Mo: I. Gilmer, 1924.

Tyler, Daniel. *Scraps of Biography*. S.L.C: Juvenile Instructor Office, 1883

Under Dixie Sun. Panguitch: Garfield County News, 1950.

Unruh, John D. *The Plains Across*. Chicago: Univ. of Ill. Press, 1979.

Van Wagoner, Richard S. *Mormon Polygamy: A History*. S.L.C: Signature Books, 1986.

Walker, Charles Lowell, A. Karl Larson and Katherine Miles Larson eds. *Diary of Charles Lowell Walker*. Logan: Utah State Univ. Press, 1980.

Walker, Ronald W. and Doris R. Dant, eds. *Nearly Everything Imaginable: The Everyday Life of Utah's Mormon Pioneers*. Provo: Brigham Young Univ. Press, 1999.

Walker, William Holmes. *The Life Incidents and Travels of Elder William Holmes Walker*. Privately published, 1943.

Watson, Elden J., ed. *Manuscript History of Brigham Young*. S.L.C: E. J. Watson, 1971.

Whitney, Carrie Westlake. *Kansas City, Missouri, Its History and Its People, 1808–1898*. Chicago: The S. J. Clarke Publishing Co., 1908.

Whitney, Orson. *History of Utah*. 4 vols., S.L.C: George Q. Cannon & Sons, 1892–1904.

Woodruff, Wilford. *Leaves from My Journal*. S.L.C: Juvenile Instructor Office, 1882.

INTERVIEWS

Prince, Antone, by Delmar Gott. Special Collections, Dixie College, April 1975.

Schmutz, Donald, by Inez Cooper. Special Collections, Southern Utah University, autumn 1982.

Prince, Antone, by Gregory Prince. September 1971.

Prince, Vilate, by Gregory Prince. September 1971.

Prince, Antone, by Gregory Prince. September 1974.

Kossen, Juanita Davis Williams, by Clayton Prince. 29 June 1994.

Anderson, Virginia, by Stephen Prince. 9 August 1998.

Prince, Clayton, by Stephen Prince. 29 August 1998.

Prince, Vivian, by Stephen Prince. 29 August 1998.

Pickett, Charlie, By Stephen Prince. 5 December 1999.

Prince, Jim and Marsha, by Gregory Prince. 25 March 2000.

Prince, Clayton and Virginia Anderson, by Stephen Prince. 27 May 2000.

MANUSCRIPTS

Allred, Reddick N. Diary. LDS Archives.

Allred, William Moore. Autobiography. LDS Archives.

Appleby, William I. Autobiography. LDS Archives.

Appleby, William I. "Church Emigration of 1849, Fourth Company." LDS Archives.

Bleak, James G. "Annals of the Southern Utah Mission. " Dixie College Library.

Bodily, Robert. "Journal." Utah State Historical Society, S.L.C.

Brooks, Juanita. "The Southern Indian Mission and its Effect Upon The Settlement of Washington County." Washington County Library, St. George, Utah.

Cowdery, Oliver. Letterbook. Henry E. Huntington Library, San Marino, California.

Crosby, Jesse W. "History and Biography of Jesse W. Crosby." Henry E. Huntington Library, San Marino, California.

Dalton, Luella Adams. "History of New Harmony." Typescript in possession of author.

Evans, Sarah Engle Imlay. "The First Big Flood of New Harmony." Harmony Ward Relief Society History, 1992.

Hafen, Orval. Journal. In possession of Jason David Archibald.

Hancock, Levi. Autobiography. Brigham Young Univ. Library.

Harmony Ward Manuscript History. LDS Archives.

Haun, Catherine. "A Woman's Trip Across the Plains in 1849." Henry E. Huntington Library, San Marino, Calif.

Haven, Jesse. Daily journal, 1856. LDS Archives.

Hendricks, Drusilla. Historical sketch. LDS Archives.

Jacob, Norton. Autobiography. Brigham Young Univ. Library.

Judd, Zadoc. Autobiography. LDS Archives.

Kossen, Juanita Williams. "History of Francis Prince and Ann Elizabeth Imlay." Typescript in possession of author.

Kossen, Juanita Williams. "Benjamin Jones Redd." Typescript in possession of author.

Kossen, Juanita Williams. "Sketch of the Life of Captain Allen Taylor." Typescript in possession of author.

Lee, John D. Missionary Journal. LDS Archives.

Lee, Rachel Andora Woolsey. Journal. Brigham Young Univ. Library.

Little, Mary Jane Lyttle. Memories. Copied into the Alfred Douglas Young journal, Brigham Young Univ. Library.

Marshall, James Wilson. "Account of the First Discovery of Gold." James Wilson Marshall Collection, California State Library, Sacramento.

McKean, Theodore. Autobiography. LDS Archives.

Merrill, Clarance. Autobiography. LDS Archives.

Munson, Eliza. Early pioneer history. Brigham Young Univ. Library.

Murdock, John. Journal. LDS Archives.

Musser, Joseph W. Journal. LDS Archives.

Nauvoo Restoration, Inc. Name Index File. LDS Archives.

Nauvoo, Original Property Owners Book. LDS Archives.

Pace, James. A Biographical Sketch of the Life of James Pace. Henry E. Huntington Library, San Marino, Calif.

Pottawattamie High Council Minutes. LDS Archives.

Reid, Cecil Prince Reid. Biography of William Prince. Daughters of
   the Utah Pioneers, S.L.C.

Rich, Alice Redd. "Memories of New Harmony. " Brigham Young
   Univ. Library.

Seegmiller, Paul. "History," in possession of Fayone Whitehead.

Sharp, William, "The Latter-day Saints or 'Mormons' in New Jersey."
   LDS Archives.

Smith, George A. "Minutes of a meeting of The Company of Saints,
   24 June, 1849." LDS Archives.

Smith, George Albert. History. LDS Archives.

Snow, Erastus. Autobiography. Brigham Young Univ. Library.

Spillsbury, Moroni. Personal History. Family History Library, Salt
   Lake City.

Stout, Allen Joseph. Reminiscences and Journal. LDS Archives.

Talbot, Henry James. "The Life of Henry James Talbot in South
   Africa." Family History Library, S.L.C., film #990390, item #1.

Taylor, Joseph Allen. Autobiography. LDS Archives.

Taylor, Pleasant Green. Record of Pleasant Green Taylor. LDS
   Archives.

Terry, James Parshall. Biographical Sketch. Brigham Young Univ.

Watkins, William Lampard. Diary. LDS Archives.

Wright, Evan P. "A History of the South African Mission, Period I,
   1852–1903." Family History Library, S.L.C., Utah.

PERIODICALS

Banks, Loy Otis. *Missouri Historical Review*, XLIII (July 1949).

Brooks, Juanita. "Indian Relations on the Mormon Frontier." *Utah
   Historical Quarterly*, vol. 12, no. 1–2, (Jan.–April 1944).

Clawson, Margaret Judd. "Rambling Reminiscences of Margaret Gay
   Judd Clawson." *New Era*, (May 1974).

FBI Law Enforcement Bulletin. Vol. 14, no. 6, June 1945.

Hartley, William G. "The Pioneer Trek: Nauvoo to Winter Quarters."
   Ensign (June 1997).

Joseph Smith sermon, July 19, 1840. Recorded by Martha Jane Knowlton in *Brigham Young University Studies* 19 (Spring 1979).

Pendleton, Mark A. "Memories of Silver Reef." *Utah Historical Quarterly* (vol. 3, no. 4, October 1930).

Young, Seymour B. "The Snake River Expedition." *Improvement Era*, vol. XXV, no. 7.
Zoellner, Tom. "The Uranium Rush." *American Heritage of Invention & Technology* (Summer 2000, vol. 16/no. 1).

RECORDS

Land records in the Library of the Historical Department of the Church, S.L.C.
Nauvoo Land Records. LDS Church Archives.
South African Mission Historical Report. LDS Church Archives.
The State of Utah vs. Frank P. Kelsey. The Fifth Judicial District Court of Washington County Utah, 15 May 1922.
The State of Utah vs. Richard Jessop, No. 6193, 6 May 1940
Toxicological Investigation in Respect to the Death of Mrs. Lottie Kelsey. Washington County Court Records.

NEWSPAPERS

California Star, Yerba Buena (San Francisco), Calif.
Deseret New, Salt Lake City, Utah.
Latter-day Saints' Millenial Star, Liverpool, England.
Messenger and Advocate, Far West, Mo.
Nauvoo Expositor, Nauvoo, Ill.
Painesville Telegraph, Painsville, Ohio.
Salt Lake Tribune, Salt Lake City, Utah.
Salt River Journal, reprinted in *Missouri Intelligencer*, June 21, 1834. 1833.
Warsaw Signal, Warsaw, Ill.
Washington County News, St. George, Utah.
Western Monitor, Fayette, Mo.

THESIS

Wayne J. Lewis, "Mormon Land Ownership as a Factor in Evaluating the Extent of Mormon Settlements and Influence in Missouri 1831–1841" (Masters Thesis, Brigham Young University, 1981).

DOCUMENTS

Letter from Florence Prince Wagner to Stephen Prince, 25 February 1996.

Letter from Lilburn Boggs to General Clark, 27 October 1838. In *Document containing the Correspondence in relation to Mormon disturbances* (Fayette, Missouri, 1841).

Letter of Charlie Pickett to Stephen Prince, 11 November 1999.

Letter of George M. Hinkle to W. W. Phelps, 14 August 1844. As quoted in Wilcox, Pearl, *The Latter Day Saints on the Missouri Frontier* (Independence, Mo: Herald House, 1972).

Letter of William W. Phelps to *Ontario Phoenix*, 1831, Canandaigua, New York.

INDEX

Pectol, Alden: 276
Perkins, Absalom: 137, 145-146
Perkins, Andrew: 137
Perkins, William: 127
Perpetual Emigrating Fund: 154, 160, 168, 170
Petty, Charles: 255, 264
Petty, Frank: 255
Phelps, William W: 36, 39-40, 43, 52, 56
Philadelphia: 162
Philips Petroleum: 291
Philips, Bob: 283
Pickett, Charlie: 285, 292-293
Pickett, Ellis: 249, 264, 269-270
Piedes: 205-207, 225-226
Pigeon Creek: 116, 120
Pine Valley Mountains: 172-173, 180, 215, 239, 242, 245, 283
Pine Valley: 215
Pinto: 210
Pioche, Nevada: 233-234
Pioneer Day: 209, 218
Pipe Spring: 207, 223
Pitcher, Thomas: 41
Pittsburgh: 162
Platte River: 131, 139, 144, 146-147, 149
Plum Hollow Branch: 117
Plural marriage: 91, 179, 236-237, 239, 286-290
Poland Bill: 229
Polk, James K: 106-107
Pollack, Hiram: 211-212
Polygamy. *See* plural marriage
Port Elizabeth, South Africa: 13-14, 168-170
Pottawattamie County: 132
Pottawattamie High Council: 110-111
Pottawattamie Indians: 115
Pottawattamie, Iowa: 125-126, 297
Powell, John Wesley: 225

Prairie Chicken Branch: 117
Prairie City, Oregon: 283
Pratt, Orson: 122, 131, 157
Pratt, Parley P: 26, 28, 37, 42, 44, 47, 64, 152, 157, 171
Price River Valley: 239
Prince, Alpine: 272, 293-294
Prince, Antone Benjamin: 241-243, 245-247, 251-252, 254, 257, 259-260-261, 272, 274, 280-281, 285-286, 291-295; marries Vilate Cottam, 244; and goat herd, 256; smallpox, 258; appointed sheriff, 264; Spencer Malan murder, 266-271; elected sheriff, 273; Royal Hunt murder, 275-276; and Bill Shanley, 277-279; and Joe Lewis, 282-284; and Short Creek raid, 287-290
Prince, Clara: 242
Prince, Clayton: 247n, 255-257, 272, 280-281, 285-286, 294
Prince, Daphane: 257-258
Prince, Eliza. *See* Kelsey, Eliza Prince
Prince, Francis (Frank): 14, 19, 167, 169, 191, 207, 209-211, 215, 219-220, 223, 230-231, 238-239, 248-249, 253, 300; in Civil War, 190; moves to New Harmony, 203; and Black Hawk War, 221
Prince, George (son of George): 237-238, 251
Prince, George Lawrence: 242
Prince, George: 13, 21, 163, 165, 169, 170n, 188-190, 295, 298, 300; emigrates to South Africa, 14; moves to Oliphant's Hoek, 16; meets missionaries, 167; departs South Africa, 187; moves to Middleton, 202
Prince, Gregory: 260, 291, 294